"Co-Workers, this wouldn't be the very Work of God unless it was being persecuted! Our persecutors themselves, prove this is the very Work of God! We do not invite persecution. We try to avoid it. But the living Christ and your Bible says we will get persecution and false accusation. In this *world, we have to* expect *at the best, careless journalism, and at the worst, irresponsible journalism."*

—Herbert W. Armstrong
Letter to "Dear Family of Co-Workers"
May 25, 1972

"Satan appears as an angel of Light. He palms off enough Truth, along with his errors, that he is able to deceive *the world. It is the Truth which is put forward that deceives people into gullibly accepting the error along with it!"*

The Autobiography of Herbert W. Armstrong
Volume I, p. 338

The Armstrong Empire

A LOOK AT THE
WORLDWIDE CHURCH OF GOD

by Joseph Martin Hopkins

WILLIAM B. EERDMANS PUBLISHING COMPANY

Printed in the United States of America

Library of Congress Cataloging in Publication Data

Hopkins, Joseph Martin, 1919-
The Armstrong empire.

Includes bibliographical references.
1. Worldwide Church of God. 2. Armstrong, Herbert W. 3. Armstrong, Garner Ted. I. Title.
BR1725.A77H66 289.9 74-8255
ISBN 0-8028-1501-1

Chapter 1 is a revised version of "Mr. Jones, Meet Herbert W. Armstrong," which first appeared in Eternity, *October 1972. © 1972 by The Evangelical Foundation, Inc. Used by permission.*

CONTENTS

FOREWORD

Herbert W. Armstrong, an ambitious Iowa youth endowed with remarkable ingenuity, persistence, and salesmanship, overcomes the handicaps of modest circumstances and lack of formal education to achieve success in the advertising world. Reduced to poverty by repeated business disasters, he discovers new meaning for his life through an intensive study of the Bible. He becomes involved in a tiny religious sect, is rebuffed by the sect's hierarchy and decides to launch his own independent ministry. In 1934 he begins weekly broadcasts over a low-power radio station in Oregon. Years of struggle and hardship follow. Then things begin to change. Time is purchased on additional West Coast stations. The broadcasts are extended to the Midwest and Southwest, the East Coast, Europe, the world. The once-local Radio Church of God, soon to blanket the earth with 400 radio and television outlets and a slick magazine circulated free to three million people, is renamed The Worldwide Church of God in 1968. A flourishing college is established on three lovely campuses—two in America and one in England. Its chancellor, a high school dropout, has become an international figure, with access to heads of state and other notables. An unpromising venture begun on a shoestring has evolved into a $56 million per year operation of worldwide scope and influence.

Over against this remarkable success story stand the Armstrong organization's liabilities and dangers. Not least among these is its "one True Church" doctrine, according to which all other religious groups are branded "Satanic" and outsiders attempting to learn something about the Worldwide Church of God are labeled "persecutors."

My interest in the Armstrong movement dates to 1967, when *The Plain Truth* magazine first came to my attention. Two years later, a sabbatical to study indigenous American religions provided an opportunity to visit the Pasadena campus of Ambassador College. The assistant dean of students offered a guided tour of the college's impressive facilities, but he resisted probing questions and denied permission to take interior photographs of the mammoth presses and other equipment. Some time later Harold Lindsell, editor of *Christianity Today*, asked me to write an essay about the beliefs and practices of the Armstrong sect.[1] This led to research so productive that I wrote a subsequent article for *Eternity*,[2] and decided on the more detailed treatment of this book.

At the outset I determined to explore all primary sources available. I did not want to rely exclusively on the writings of others or even on the Armstrong literature. I wanted to investigate the subject with an open mind and produce an objective and unbiased report. Accordingly, I wrote three times directly to Herbert W. Armstrong to acquaint him with my project and solicit his aid. Not a line came back by way of reply.

This silence seems inconsistent with the attitude expressed in the following passage from the Armstrong autobiography:

> Apparently some persecutors think many are interested in hearing about my past life. A number, who do not know me, or the facts, are willing to sell you, for a price, their distorted, deliberately untrue version of it. . . .
>
> I think that if I had lived in the time of Jesus' earthly personal life and mission, and I had wanted to know about Him and what He believed and taught, I should not have gone to His enemies and persecutors, the Pharisees, Sadducees and scribes. I should have gone straight to Him.[3]

Since the doors to the Armstrong offices remained shut, I was compelled to turn to other sources. First-hand observation was afforded by visits to the Big Sandy, Texas, campus of Ambassador College and the Feast of Tabernacles at Mt. Pocono, Pennsylvania. In addition, the Youngstown, Ohio, minister of the Worldwide Church of God was interviewed on three occasions. But it was not until October 1973, after the basic manuscript had been completed, that a meeting with Garner Ted Armstrong was arranged by a former member of the Armstrong organization. (This conversation is reported in a postscript which follows Chapter 12.)

Fortunately, a number of informed, intelligent, and fair-minded resource persons were discovered. A great deal of material was made available when a recently resigned member—a graduate of Ambassador College in Pasadena, who had been personally acquainted with the Armstrongs and other top leaders of the organization—opened his files to me. Others contacted me as a result of the two articles mentioned above. Most of those from whom my information came are former members of the Worldwide Church of God.

It might be charged, then, that most of my sources have an anti-Armstrong bias. But if pro-Armstrongites had been available for research and interview, their judgments would likely have been more biased than at least some of those who have left the movement. For Worldwide Church of God members are taught that Herbert W. Armstrong is God's only true apostle, that his is the only valid work of God today, that his teachings are infallible and nondebatable, that either to criticize or to listen to criticism is a breach of loyalty punishable by excommunication.

Some of the former members with whom I talked were "disfellowshipped" for failure to pay the multiple tithes required by the organization or for daring to raise—or to persist in raising—doctrinal questions or objections. To be sure, a few of them were bitter. But this does not invalidate their testimony. There may have been an occasional tendency to generalize unfairly on the basis of isolated incidents and so to arrive at unwarranted conclusions. But an angry critic is not necessarily dishonest, inaccurate, or unfair. And most of those who provided me first-hand reports were not forced out of the organization at all but left of their own free will, usually because of doctrinal differences.

I have also used extensive quotations from the Armstrong literature, always carefully footnoted. (For ease of reading the publisher has not followed the Armstrong practice of frequent emphasis by capitalizing entire words.) This allows Mr. Armstrong and his writers to present their teachings in their own words, and it also provides some shield against the perennial cries of "persecution" that emanate from Pasadena in response to reporting and assessment of the Worldwide Church of God by "outsiders."

In order to deal with the subject matter as comprehensively as possible, I have related in some detail the story of Mr. Armstrong's life, including the evolution of the Worldwide Church of God from its humble origin in 1934 until the present. Then I have presented in some depth a few of the church's major doctrines. A deliberate omission is the doctrine of man, which is presented piecemeal in the chapters dealing with God, salvation, and eschatology. To deal with it separately would have involved needless duplication of material. In some instances I have merely recorded the Armstrong teachings; in others, I have compared them with the teachings of Scripture and such familiar biblical resources as Strong's *Systematic Theology* and the *International Standard Bible Encyclopedia.*

Every writer brings to his task a theological perspective and presuppositions that are his by consequence of those influences which have combined to shape his thinking—and his response to those influences. No student of the social sciences can begin a research project entirely devoid of preconceived notions, assumptions, and (to be completely candid) prejudices. The reader must make allowances for this when he encounters honest differences of opinion or interpretation. I have tried to refrain from hair-splitting on nonvital subjects of sectarian disagreement. For example, no attempt has been made to vindicate the first-day Sabbath, infant baptism, or any particular view of the millennium. But on theological points which seem to me to be critical, I have made an earnest effort to contend for "the faith once delivered," as I understand it.

I wish to acknowledge with deep gratitude the services of many persons who wrote, telephoned, and sent materials. Most of them wish to remain anonymous. But each one and his contribution is individually recognized and appreciated.

Special recognition and thanks are due John D. Pearson, St. Paul Publishers, Nashville, Tennessee, for preparation of the bibliography; and Mrs. Robert Welch for her indefatigable, competent, and uncomplaining devotion to typing the manuscript.

Appreciation is likewise expressed to the administration and trustees of Westminster College for their generous provision of a sabbatical leave and a grant secured from the Mack Foundation (these made possible the preliminary study begun in 1969) as well as an additional stipend in 1973 to help defray the cost of producing the final typescript.

Also a word of thanks—and an apology—to my wife and children, who were deprived of the companionship of their husband and father for much of the time during the past two years in which the bulk of the work was accomplished.

Last of all, but by no means least, I acknowledge with humble gratitude the stimulation, energy, and guidance of the Holy Spirit, without whom the task could not have been accomplished—and even if accomplished through sheer human effort, will have been in vain.

Biblical quotations are (by permission) from the Revised Standard Version (New York: Thomas Nelson & Sons, 1953) unless otherwise indicated. With rare exceptions, Worldwide Church of God publications quote the King James Version.

—Joseph Martin Hopkins

New Wilmington, Pennsylvania

ONE:

Mr. Jones, Meet Herbert W. Armstrong

One evening as George Smith was idly leafing through *TV Guide* an advertisement caught his eye. "*New* facts about marijuana," exclaimed the caption. He read the smaller print below: "What is marijuana? Could you recognize it? Is it harmful—hallucinogenic? Is it habit-forming, leading to stronger drugs—even heroin? Does it contribute to sexual immorality?" Smith's interest was aroused. "Write for your free copy today. With it you will receive 3 already-paid trial issues of *The Plain Truth*—world's unique news and human-experience magazine. 52 pages, full color. No charge. No obligation."

What was there to lose? Smith filled out the coupon, and not long after a handsome and informative booklet arrived. He found it well researched, convincingly written, and morally sound—"just what the country needs in these days of permissive parents and hippie drug culture," he thought.

Colorful monthly issues of *The Plain Truth* began to arrive. Smith was tremendously impressed by the quality of its paper and printing, its lively and stimulating articles on timely topics of world and national significance. The editorial point of view Smith found most congenial. It was the sort of solid, patriotic, God-fearing conservatism often called middle-American. He was gratified to find articles expressing his own grave concerns about contemporary society: crime, violence, the counter-culture, divorce, pollution, inflation, global hunger, the Indochina War, the Middle East crisis. Booklets dealing with these and similar subjects were offered gratis to those requesting them. Smith sent for several: *Our Polluted Planet*, *Who Will Rule Space?*, *Crime Can be Stopped—Here's How*, *True Womanhood—Is It A Lost Cause?*, *God Speaks Out On "The New Morality."* They all made sense. He shared them with friends and occasionally quoted from them in a Bible class at church. The first Sunday he mentioned *The Plain Truth*, he found that two other members of the class already were subscribers.

From the radio and television log included in each issue, Smith learned about "The World Tomorrow" broadcast, which is carried on more than 300 stations worldwide. The first time Smith tuned in and heard Garner Ted Armstrong (son of the program's founder, Herbert W. Armstrong), he could have sworn he was listening to Paul Harvey. With nearly everything the younger Armstrong said Smith found himself in hearty agreement. He enthusiastically recommended the program to others.

One thing that favorably impressed Smith was that the Armstrongs never, over the air or via the printed page, made a pitch for financial contributions. How can a quality magazine with no advertising be mailed free of charge to more than two million subscribers in a day when periodicals bolstered by several million paid subscriptions plus tens of millions of dollars in advertising revenues are dying? Where does the money come from to send, at no cost to the reader, hundreds of thousands of elaborate booklets? And what of the cost of financing worldwide radio and television broadcasts, three superbly equipped college campuses, and distribution centers strategically situated throughout the world?

Smith did not have far to look for an answer. A box in *The Plain Truth* captioned "How Your Plain Truth Subscription Has Been Paid" carefully spelled it out. Since its inception the Armstrong operation has relied entirely on voluntary, completely unsolicited offerings for its support. Smith began to feel uneasy about freeloading and wondered if he should join the 125,000 "Co-Workers" who undergird "the Work." So he sent in a check. There was a warning that if anyone attempted to pay for any of the free literature, his check would be returned, so Smith explained that this was not his intent.

With the acceptance of his money, Smith found that he was now placed on a special mailing list. But even so, the voluntary nature of his participation was stressed. True, tithing was urged; but there was no *overt* pressure to give. Smith had been increasingly disturbed by the theological liberalism and the social-action orientation of his denomination. He agreed with the Armstrongs' indictment that the historic churches were guilty of apostasy. Gradually he began to switch his tithe dollars from his church to the Armstrong enterprise.

"Enterprise" seemed a vague term for the operation. But Smith could not find an official designation anywhere in the Armstrong literature. The nearest thing to a title he could discover was "Ambassador College," "The Work," or "The true Church of God." He raised the point with a friend who had been involved much longer than he, and was told that the previous name "Radio Church of God" had given way to the "The Worldwide Church of God" in 1968.

Repeatedly the literature emphasized that "the Work" was undenominational, that there was "nothing to join." There seemed to be no overt attempt to proselyte. The rather subtle suggestion was made that the true Church of God went underground after the apostolic age, to reappear only with the establishment of the "World Tomorrow" ministry by Herbert W. Armstrong. Implicit in this allegation was the teaching that the light of divine revelation had been withheld from the historic churches for nineteen centuries, so that all of today's churches except Armstrong's are false and heretical.

As a "co-worker," Smith requested additional booklets and literature covering in fuller detail the actual doctrines of the movement. He enrolled in the *Ambassador College Correspondence Course*, a Bible study course presenting the church's basic teachings. Much of what he now read is not normally covered in publications aimed at the general public, such as the organization's strategy for reaching the unconverted.

> On "The World Tomorrow" and in *The Plain Truth* we do not drive people away by "preaching at" them. We want all people to hear the Good News. So we talk about the things all people want to hear!
>
> But we make these interest-gripping subjects far *more* interesting by injecting *life and spark* and *meaning* into them by use of Biblical material that astonishes—in a nonreligious-sounding manner.
>
> Then there's a lot in how it is done. It is done in the professional manner of a Network news analyst, or a Network documentary.
>
> That's the reason "The World Tomorrow" has either the biggest audience or the second biggest audience on most radio stations.[1]

One of the first things to confront Smith on opening Lesson 1 of the *Ambassador College Correspondence Course* was the statement, "This Course is not denominational .... We are not controlled or subsidized, sponsored or endowed or financed by any sect or denomination."[2] The enrollee was admonished not to "try to *interpret* the Bible. *Don't* take the interpretation of any *man* or *church.* Remember that the Bible interprets itself!" Paradoxically, the pamphlet went on to offer its *own* interpretation as the only true light to be shed upon the Word of God since the first century.

> The Bible has been called "*The Book Nobody Knows.*" This has been mostly true—*until now!* God prophesied of *our time today* when the "true message of the Bible would be understood! ... God said that at *this time* "none of the wicked shall understand; but the *wise* shall understand" (Dan. 12:10) .... through this Course and His inspired Word, God is calling you to understand—to become one of the "wise."[3]

In the printed materials Smith had read, and over the radio programs he had heard, Ambassador College had been repeatedly extolled. Since his son was now a junior in high school, he decided to write for a catalog. It arrived accompanied by an attractive booklet entitled *This Is Ambassador College.* Founded in 1947 with the acquisition of an elegant mansion in Pasadena, Ambassador has annexed additional plush real estate along the city's millionaires' row and added a number of multimillion-dollar buildings to produce a magnificent physical plant. A $22 million expansion program is in progress for the Pasadena campus alone, and similar improvements are underway on the Ambassador campuses at Big Sandy, Texas (founded 1964), and St. Albans, England (1960). Present combined enrollment of twelve hundred has been projected to a maximum of 2100 (700 at each location) when these expansion projects have been completed.

But Ambassador's prime assets are not physical. The philosophy of the institution impressed Smith favorably. He especially liked "the noticeable absence of hippie-type students" and of student-faculty protest marches and riots. Ambassador claims to provide education's "Missing Dimension . . . the teaching of the very principles of right living—of the way to peace, happiness, abundant well-being; the building of right character, with a right sense of moral, spiritual and intellectual values."

Upon examining the catalog Smith did notice several items that tended to cool his enthusiasm. The seven-man board of trustees was composed entirely of members of the college's Pasadena faculty and staff. At Pasadena the proportion of faculty with advanced degrees was small: only 22 per cent had doctorates and 39 per cent had no degree beyond the baccalaureate. Figures for the Texas campus were even lower: 16 per cent having doctorates and 51 per cent no graduate degree whatever. Furthermore, the catalog did not mention the institutions from which the faculty members received their degrees. Smith discovered that Ambassador itself confers doctor's degrees in philosophy, theology, and education, although it is not listed among accredited institutions of higher learning in the United States.

For some time now, Smith had seriously considered bolting his denomination. He was critical of the church's "leftist" pronouncements on social issues, concessions to militant pressure groups, and curtailment of evangelistic and missionary programs. Despite some reservations, he felt that he had more in common with the Armstrong movement than with his own church. Communications from the Pasadena headquarters had offered to send a personal representative to call upon request. He wondered if one of their churches was within convenient driving distance. He decided to inquire. By return mail he received a "Visit Information Form" on which he was asked to supply pertinent data about himself: address, telephone number, "mate's first and middle names," and race. A cover letter carefully explained, "We ask you to indicate your race only because of growing racial tensions in many areas, . . . to prevent any unnecessary problems from arising when we visit." He was assured that "one of the true representatives of God we have stationed throughout the United States and in other parts of the world" would arrange an interview as soon as his busy schedule would permit.

About three weeks later Smith received a phone call from a pleasant young man who set a date for a meeting in Smith's home. Smith prepared carefully for the interview, poring over the Armstrong literature and compiling an extensive list of questions about some Armstrong teachings that seemed to differ from historic Christian beliefs. Among these were denial of the Trinity and the personality of the Holy Spirit, insistence on the seventh-day Sabbath and compliance with Jewish feasts and dietary laws, denunication of Christmas and Easter as pagan holidays, and the belief that the "lost ten tribes" of Israel have survived to the present day, and that the Anglo-Saxon people of England and America are the lineal descendants of Ephraim and Manasseh.

When the appointed evening arrived, the minister appeared punctually, accompanied by an elderly male member of his congregation. Neat in appearance and friendly in manner, the young man, a recent graduate of Ambassador College, apologized for the delay in setting up the visit. He had been swamped by requests relayed from Pasadena, and had a 75-mile radius to cover. With the introductions out of the way, the conversation focused on Smith's list of questions. The Armstrong representative deftly disposed of each in turn, referring frequently to a well-marked Bible. Invariably, his biblical quotations were prefaced by a statement such as, "I can *prove* it to you out of God's Word."

The discussion went on about three hours. Smith remarked that he had checked the church directories in several city newspapers, without being able to find the Armstrong church. He asked, "Is there a congregation in this area I might visit?"

"I hope you won't misunderstand, sir," replied the minister; "but we deliberately refrain from advertising our services. Frankly, we don't want people dropping in out of curiosity—or for the purpose of criticizing. We tell our people not to invite their friends and neighbors to worship with us. We want them to know something about us first. Then, if we are satisfied that they really mean business—and if they seem to have a sincere interest in being baptized into God's True Church, we gladly welcome them into our fellowship. Don't get me wrong. We're not a closed church or a secret organization. It's just that we want to be sure those who come to us are sincerely motivated."

Smith tried to assure the minister that he was sincerely motivated, even though he still had a number of questions and reservations about the movement. "Well, I'll tell you what I'll do," the visitor offered. "I'll check with the district superintendent and see what he thinks." He divulged that the Armstrong meetings are usually held in schools or other public buildings, which are rented for this purpose on Saturdays. Baptisms are held in private swimming pools, lakes, or streams. The rapid growth of the organization makes it unwise to erect church buildings; they would be outgrown almost as soon as built.

A few days later Smith received a phone call from the minister. He was told that he could attend a service the next Saturday at 2 p.m. in the local I.O.O.F. Hall. Smith arrived at the hall on Saturday about fifteen minutes early. He was surprised to see the parking lot already well filled. At the door he was stopped by two men, who he later found out were deacons. They asked him his name and if he had received permission to attend. When he answered affirmatively, they smiled and became very friendly. Smith was later told that such security precautions are necessary because of antagonistic individuals who sometimes try to break up the services.

Inside the hall about 250 people were milling about and talking. It seemed that every man had a briefcase, and everyone from teen-agers up carried a large Bible with a pen and notebook. This was something Smith had never seen at a church service before. Several people came up to him and introduced themselves, all cordially. Smith took a seat near the back until a deacon requested that he move forward.

The service was a simple one. The ministerial assistant led the congregation in three rather spirited hymns taken from a hymnal with which he was not familiar, in which most of the songs were written by a Dwight Armstrong. A prayer by one of the men of the congregation was followed by a duet. After another hymn, the assistant spoke for about ten minutes on the need to be more organized in one's personal affairs, using Old Testament examples of men who had been eminently successful in this regard. He pointed out that many people are careless in attending to such details and need to improve. Most of the congregation busily took notes and turned to the cited verses in their Bibles.

Following another song, the minister arose to speak. His sermon, which lasted about 50 minutes, dealt with ways in which the Worldwide Church of God is different from other churches. He stressed Sabbath (Saturday) observance, abstaining from pork, not observing "pagan" holidays such as Christmas and Easter, observance of the annual Jewish holy days, trusting God for healing rather than going to doctors, and the authority in the church from God's apostle and direct representative, Herbert W. Armstrong, on down through the ranks. He particularly emphasized the last point, using several Old Testament examples of rebellion by God's people against his ministers. He went on to point out that the churches of the world are in confusion, their members believing many things contrary to the Bible. This is not so in the Worldwide Church of God, he explained, because God has anointed Herbert W. Armstrong as his latter-day apostle to lead his true people in the few remaining years before the end of the age.

After a few announcements, a final song, and closing prayer, the congregation rose and began to visit with one another. One member greeted Smith cordially and introduced his wife and three children. They began to discuss the sermon, and Smith inquired about the apostleship of Mr. Armstrong. The member told him that he should ask the minister, since he was the one God had appointed to teach others the gospel. He explained that he personally believed God spoke through Mr. Armstrong and that in a few years all would come to recognize this worldwide. He told Smith that if he were really seeking the truth, God would reveal to him that this was his true church.

The conversation then switched to nontheological topics. Smith was favorably impressed by the children, who seemed very quiet and submissive. He observed that many parents were accompanied by their young children, all of whom were well behaved. The smaller ones had slept on blankets on the floor during the service. Smith left the hall with a generally favorable impression. The congregation had been friendly and cheerful. The members were clean and neat, but many appeared to be poor.

The minister called Smith the next week to suggest that they arrange another visit to answer any questions. What concerned Smith most of all was the teaching that Herbert W. Armstrong is God's personal representative, directly under Jesus Christ, appointed to lead God's "one true Church" in the last days. The minister said he knew this was hard for Smith to understand, but explained that God has raised up men to lead his people in every generation and Herbert W. Armstrong is God's man in our day. Surely God would not leave his people without a leader in the most critical days of the earth's history. Smith asked if members believe that Mr. Armstrong receives actual revelations from God. The minister replied that Herbert W. Armstrong has never claimed any direct messages in the form of dreams, visions, or audible voice. Nevertheless, God does guide him in his study of the Bible, and whatever he and the other ministers agree on is binding on the whole church.

Smith was somewhat puzzled. He had often heard Garner Ted Armstrong say that one must prove things for oneself—from the Bible—with the freedom to arrive at his own conclusions. This had been the very foundation of the Reformation. It seemed to him that the government of the Worldwide Church of God was set up contrary to that principle. The minister explained that "there has to be real authority from the top down. The sheep can't feed themselves; they need the ministers to do this for them. This is God's way."

Smith began to realize that the key requirement for joining the Worldwide Church of God is willingness to submit to Herbert W. Armstrong as the last-days apostle of God. He told his two visitors that he did not see how one man's interpretation of the Bible could be considered final. Whereupon the minister replied that if God were really calling him, he would come to see that Herbert W. Armstrong is right and that the Worldwide Church of God is the only true church. Most people, he explained, have been purposely blinded by God and will not comprehend his truth until the millennium. The minister suggested that Smith not attend services again but continue Bible study and the quest for God's truth. Should he come around to the persuasion that Herbert W. Armstrong *is* the prophet God has raised up in these latter days, he need only telephone for a new invitation to attend the meetings.

Smith thanked him, but decided to let the matter drop. The more he thought about it, the more he became convinced that he should not leave his church, despite tendencies of which he disapproved, but work within it and pray for a recovery of its evangelical commitment and vision. Much as he concurred with the Armstrongs' indictment of American society, stress on personal morality, and insistence on scriptural authority, their departure from the historic creeds of the church bothered him.

Some months later Smith learned that the Jones family, who had been active in his church for many years, had pulled up stakes and joined the Worldwide Church of God. It had been Smith himself who had introduced Mr. Jones to Herbert W. Armstrong. It happened the first Sunday he had quoted *The Plain Truth* in the men's Bible class. Jones, impressed, had asked to borrow Smith's copy, so that he could examine the magazine more closely.

TWO:
The Man Behind the Legend

The life of Herbert W. Armstrong began inauspiciously "in a red brick two-apartment flat on the northwest corner of E. 14th and Grand Avenue"[1] in Des Moines, Iowa, on July 31, 1892. His parents, Horace and Eva Armstrong, "were of solid Quaker stock," his mother being "something like a third cousin" to Herbert Hoover. He notes in his autobiography that his "ancestors came to America with William Penn," and he claims to have genealogical records linking him to King Edward I of England, "and through the British Royal genealogy, back to King Herremon of Ireland, who married Queen Tea Tephi, daughter of Zedekiah, King of Judah."[2] From earliest childhood he was "kept regularly in the Sunday School and church services of the First Friends Church in Des Moines," and as a lad had the job of pumping the pipe organ. From his father Herbert inherited his resonant baritone voice, for Horace not only was "the main bass in the choir" but also sang in the church male quartet, which was "in constant demand . . . all over the city."[3]

When Herbert was six the family moved to Marshalltown, Iowa, where his father became a partner in a flour mill. The following year the family returned to Des Moines, only to move again the next year to Union, Iowa, where the senior Armstrong entered the hardware business briefly. Returning to Des Moines, he opened a small factory and began to manufacture an improved type of furnace featuring an "air-circulating jacket" that he himself had invented.

Two years after Herbert's birth, he was joined by a sister, Mabel, who died at the age of nine. A brother, Russell, was born when Herbert was eight, and four years later a twin brother and sister. The brother, Dwight Leslie, later was to compose a large number of hymns for the *New Bible Hymnal*, published by the Radio Church of God.

Herbert's boyhood was typical. He was especially fond of ice skating, football, baseball, wrestling, and bicycle riding. He confesses that a couple of times during his pre-adolescent years he experimented with tobacco in a cave which he had dug with some other boys. But smoking didn't become a habit until he was 19—and even then, "never a heavy habit." The practice continued until his conversion at the age of 35.[4] At North High School in Des Moines he participated, but did not excel, in football and track. At 135 pounds, he was "too light to make the team" but qualified for a uniform and sat with the football team during home games. A five-minute miler in track, he wasn't fast enough to be entered in the state meet.

Early in life Herbert learned the discipline of work. He carried papers, ran errands for a grocery store, delivered orders for a dry goods store, and worked summers in his father's furnace factory. At the age of 16 he got his first job away from home, waiting on tables in a "semi-resort hotel" in Altoona, a few miles east of Des Moines. Encouraged by his employer, he became convinced that he had the potential for success.

> I had never realized before [he wrote in his autobiography] that I possessed any abilities. Actually I had never been a leader among boys. Most of the time I had played with boys older than I who automatically took the lead. But now, for the first time, I began to believe in myself. This hotel owner aroused ambition—created within me the desire to climb the ladder of success—to become an important somebody. . . . Actually, this flowered into grossly over-rated self confidence and cocky conceit. But it impelled me to *driving* effort.[5]

Armstrong describes himself as "just an average student in school," explaining that until his "awakening" at sixteen he never seriously applied himself. Even so, he succeeded by "real heavy cramming" to achieve 90 per cent or better in "all final exams."[6] Uninspired by the prepackaged high school curriculum, he nevertheless had an insatiable appetite for learning, which drove him to the city library for avid reading in philosophy, biography, and business administration. He recalls, "I began to study Plato, Socrates, Aristotle, and Epictetus. It was at this time that I first read Benjamin Franklin's Autobiography."[7] He commenced dating girls a year or two older than himself, but if they "could not discuss intelligently the philosophies of Plato, Socrates, and Epictetus," he lost interest. The dates were merely "occasional," and usually he "spent evenings in study while other young men were seeking pleasures."[8]

A self-analysis test he discovered in a book entitled *Choosing a Vocation* pointed him to advertising. His father's younger brother Frank was "the most prominent advertising man in Iowa," and he turned to him for counsel. Frank Armstrong advised against college, and told Herbert he should get a job in the want-ad department of the Des Moines *Daily Capital.*

> I could not have remotely dreamed I would be called into God's ministry, and that I was now being launched on the *very identical training* and *experience* needed for God's ministry! Nor could I then have had the slightest conception that the Eternal God was purposely protecting me from becoming conformed to the groove into which this world's institutions of higher learning had descended, in order that in due time I might be used as His instrumentality in founding and building God's own college—a college unfettered by the errors of tradition, and with a clear vision to recapture the true values.[9]

Quitting high school at the end of his sophomore year, young Herbert strode into the office of the want-ad manager of the *Daily Capital* to announce his intention to join his staff. This he succeeded in doing, at a salary of $6 per week. "In those days," he confesses, "I had developed a very excessive case of swelled-head. I was snappy, confident, conceited, yet *sincere*, and intending to be completely honest."[10] Under his uncle's tutelage, he eagerly devoured advertising books and trade journals and polished his writing style. At first assigned to rooming house ads, he was soon promoted to real estate and his salary raised to $8 per week.

Then he learned of an opportunity to work as time-keeper and paymaster at a sawmill in Wiggins, Mississippi. In January 1912 he made the train trip south. His new employer offered some advice that was to help shape his future career: always travel Pullman and stay at the best hotels, for mingling with successful people will influence one's own success.[11]

At his boarding house in Wiggins Herbert enjoyed entertaining fellow diners with ragtime and jazz on the piano. But the long hours and unpleasant working conditions soon took their toll. Herbert wound up in a hospital in Hattiesburg after six months, a typhoid victim. Returning to Des Moines at the advice of physicians, he was steered by his uncle to a job with *The Merchants' Trade Journal.* Though the starting salary was only $10 per week, the practical experience in writing and designing ads was invaluable. Herbert remained there for three years, most of the time as a roving "idea man." Journeying south to the Gulf of Mexico and east to the Atlantic coast in search of ideas and materials for articles, he was involved in extensive interviewing of merchants and Chamber of Commerce secretaries. He thus believes himself to have been the originator of public opinion polls.[12]

When he resigned from the *Journal* in 1915, his salary had doubled to $20 per week. During the succeeding months he drifted from one temporary job to another—selling motor club memberships in South Bend, Indiana; doing a business survey in Danville, Illinois; and attempting to sell pianos for the Benjamin Piano Company of that city. He confesses that he "never sold a single piano!"[13] Bailed out by his Uncle Frank, he returned to Des Moines to sell ads for new bank buildings. But interest soon faded, and after two months, in late fall of 1915, he moved to the heart of Chicago's Loop and opened an office as a publisher's representative for "a string of nine principal bank journals of the nation."[14] This office he retained for the next seven years. At a time when banks were reluctant to lend money to farmers for the purchase of tractors and other newfangled automotive equipment, Armstrong hit on the idea of selling advertising space in bank journals to the manufacturers of farm machinery by way of gaining confidence for their products. The idea caught on—and, according to Armstrong, "put me in the $25,000-a-year income class (in terms of *today's* dollar) while still a youth in my twenties."[15] He began to move in circles of wealth and prominence. He recalls with evident satisfaction, "My work now brought me into contact with many of the nation's leading bankers."[16]

During this time he returned to Iowa, where he met his third cousin Loma Dillon, whose father owned the general store in the village of Motor, thirty miles south of Des Moines, where Loma taught school. Herbert was immediately attracted to her. Unsophisticated and naive, "she had that innocent, completely unspoiled freshness of a breath of spring."[17] He invited her to Des Moines for lunch and a movie. A second date followed the next day. When the star-struck youth returned to Chicago, the two began a correspondence. During a subsequent visit of Herbert to Iowa the couple became engaged. On Herbert's 25th birthday, July 31, 1917, they were married in Chicago. A Dr. Brown, pastor of the Oak Park Baptist Church, performed the ceremony. Only two others were present as witnesses.

Several months before the wedding, the United States had declared war on Germany. Although he had not attended college, Armstrong had procured letters from influential businessmen to gain acceptance as an officer candidate, though he was twice passed over for active duty due to an oversupply of applicants. On his draft questionnaire he had indicated "Quaker" as his religious affiliation, but added that he did not seek exemption on the basis of his pacifist church ties. Nevertheless, he was classified as a noncombatant; providential protection, he later supposed, from military service for the work to which he was called.[18]

During the first three years of married life the Armstrongs changed living quarters ten times! Two daughters, Beverly Lucile and Dorothy Jane, were born to them.

Herbert's business was prospering. Working in spurts, only "four or five days a month," his tractor ads netted him more than $11,000 in 1920. Soon he "knew and was known by almost every advertising agency in Chicago"[19] and enjoyed the enviable reputation among the agencies of being "one of the two most promising and effective young advertising solicitors" in the city.[20]

Then came the depression of 1920. "Every one of my big-space advertisers in the tractor and similar industries went into economic failure in that flash depression of late 1920. It wiped out my business and source of income—literally!"[21] For two years Herbert remained in Chicago, trying in vain to keep his struggling business alive:

> I didn't know, then, that God the Eternal was intervening to take from me and destroy my idol—the god I was placing before Him! That false god was the vanity of desiring to be considered "important" and to reap and accumulate a big share of this world's material goods. . . . From that time on I became like King Midas in reverse. Everything I touched, as a business enterprise, turned to failure, and always by causes totally outside my control! It was frustrating, humiliating, and exceedingly painful.[22]

In July 1922 the Armstrongs were forced to give up their apartment. Loma and the girls returned to Iowa, while Herbert rented a single room in a Chicago suburb. Then followed what he describes as "perhaps the blackest and most discouraging three months" of his life.[23] Lonely and crushed by his financial woes, he and two other advertising men sought escape through alcohol, frequenting neighborhood bars and nightclubs until one or two in the morning. At last, in desperation, he returned to Iowa to help on his father-in-law's farm. During this period he regained a measure of self-confidence by coaching his brother-in-law Walter to victory in the Simpson College oratorical contest. Walter Dillon went on to win the state contest, and later became Ambassador College's first president and speech instructor.

After spending the winter of 1922-23 at his father-in-law's farm, Herbert did a couple of business surveys. Offered a job as advertising manager of *The Des Moines Register*, he turned it down. Oddly enough, the man who was destined to direct a $50 million global enterprise involving thousands, considered himself unqualified to supervise an office force of merely eight men.

Herbert's parents had moved west a dozen years earlier, and in the summer of 1924 he and Loma decided to travel to Salem, Oregon, where the elder Armstrong was employed as a heating engineer. Walter and Bertha Dillon accompanied them in the Dillons' Model T, as did the two Armstrong children. They slept in a rented tent, averaged two hundred miles in a 12-14-hour driving day, and at one point suffered eight flat tires within a single mile. Enroute, they visited some of Loma's relatives in Weiser, Idaho.

Just after their departure from Weiser Mrs. Armstrong cried out suddenly that she had a premonition of danger. Since the feeling was shared by her brother Walter, they turned back to Weiser, discovering as they approached the city that they had lost their brakes. When they arrived in Salem they learned that Herbert's mother had felt so strong a foreboding that the travelers were in danger—at the precise time of the near-tragedy—that she had gone into a bedroom to pray for their safety.[24]

When Walter and Bertha returned to Iowa in the Model T, Herbert and Loma remained in the Northwest. A newspaper advertising job with the Vancouver (Washington) *Columbian* was followed by a brief venture into the laundry advertising field. However, the national organization of laundry owners joined in a nationwide promotion, leaving Herbert with just one $50-per-month client—and an abundance of spare time for intensive reading and study.

In Salem Loma had become acquainted with an elderly neighbor of the Armstrongs, Mrs. Ora Runcorn. When they moved back to Salem from Vancouver in April 1925, the friendship with Mrs. Runcorn was renewed. Loma had been an active Methodist prior to her marriage, and in Chicago she and Herbert had joined a Methodist church, though "the friendship there had been more social than spiritual or Biblical."[25] Now, under Mrs. Runcorn's tutelage, Loma became convinced that the God-ordained day for rest and worship is Saturday—the Jewish Sabbath—rather than Sunday. Herbert was infuriated by his wife's "fanaticism," and even threatened divorce. It was agreed that she would give up this belief if her husband could prove her wrong. "And so," he explains, "it was that at this time—crushed in spirit from business reverses not of my making—humiliated by wifely religious fanaticism—I was goaded into the study of the Bible for the first time in my life. . . . I set out on this study with angered and indignant zeal."[26]

Not long thereafter, Herbert locked horns with Walter Dillon's wife Hertha, a recent college graduate, on the subject of evolution. Hertha accused Herbert of ignorance for condemning evolution without ever having studied it. Herbert recalls:

> Her words stabbed deeply into what was left of my ego—and there was still an enormous amount of it left. "Hertha," I said, "I am just starting a study of the Bible. I will include in my research a thorough study of the Biblical account of creation, and also I will make a thorough study of evolution. I'm sure I'm going to find that it is *you* who are ignorant, and in error, and if and when I do, I am going to make you eat those words!"[27]

Tackling the evolution question first, Herbert delved into the Bible and numerous scientific works in the Portland Public Library. He "soon learned that the real dyed-in-the-wool evolutionists all were atheists. Evolution *could not* honestly be reconciled with the first chapter of Genesis!"[28] The outcome of the study: "I had *disproved* the theory of evolution. I had found proof of creation—proof of the existence of God—proof of the divine inspiration of the Bible."[29]

Next he turned his attention to the Sabbath. "I spent a solid six months of virtual night-and-day, seven-day-a-week study and research, in a determined effort" to disprove the seventh-day Sabbath notion.[30] Instead, he became convinced that Sabbath observance on the seventh day not only is valid but absolutely binding on God's people. Those who refuse "to obey the true God thus [prove] they are *not* His people!"[31]

Now he had to confront the inescapable consequence of his enlightenment. "To accept this truth meant to throw in my lot for life with a class of people I had always looked on as inferior. I learned that God *looks on the heart*, and these humble people were the real salt of the earth."[32] Crushed by business failure, humiliated by being forced to admit he was wrong, facing the sacrifice of money, social position, and influence, "I realized I had been a swell-headed egotistical jackass. Finally, in desperation, I threw myself on God's mercy. I said to God that I knew, now, that I was nothing but a failure, a burned-out hunk of junk." If God could do anything with his life, "He could have it—I was willing to give this worthless self to Him—I wanted to accept Jesus Christ as personal Saviour!"[33] He made a complete surrender—and "found unspeakable joy in accepting Jesus Christ. . . . I began to pray, and knew that in prayer I was talking with God."[34]

His six months of personal study, unaided by prior training, led Armstrong to seven fundamental conclusions, which he took to be the result of divine revelation:

> 1. God does exist.
> 2. Evolution stands disproved—an error—a false theory.
> 3. The Bible (in its original writings) is the inspired instruction book of the Creator God to mankind—infallible.
> 4. The Sabbath is binding today, the sign that identifies God to us, and identifies us as His people.
> 5. . . . The annual Holy Days and Festivals of God are also binding. . . .
> 6. . . . The wages of sin is death, not eternal life in hell fire . . . it is eternal punish*ment*, not eternal punish*ing*.
> 7. . . . Eternal life is God's gift by His grace, imparted to us by His Holy Spirit. . . .[35]

Having laid the foundation, he was ready to build on it. The next doctrinal question he investigated was water baptism. After unsatisfying sessions with Seventh-day Adventist, Quaker, and Church of God preachers, he called on a Baptist minister.

> [He] had the best and clearest explanation, and was warm and friendly, and, I felt, more spiritual in a sane and sensible way. So I asked him to baptize me, not into his church, but into Christ. . . . On being baptized I *knew* God then and there gave me His Holy Spirit.[36]

The baptism did not occur until "May or June 1927."[37] Meanwhile, convinced that there could be only one "true Church," he had begun an exhaustive search for that authentic Body of Christ. He had determined from Scripture that this "one true Church" must adhere to all of God's commandments, including that regarding the Sabbath. A large number of churches that worshiped on Sunday were thus ruled out automatically. The search was narrowed to three—the Seventh-day Adventists, the Seventh-day Baptists, "and a little, almost unheard-of church called the Church of God, which maintained a small publishing-house headquarters at Stanberry, Missouri."[38] The Seventh-day Adventists he rejected because he felt that they rely on an authority other than Scripture—the writings of Ellen G. White (which the Seventh-day Adventists deny). The Seventh-day Baptists were eliminated because he found them to be almost identical with other Protestant denominations, especially Baptists, except for the day of worship. Nor do they identify themselves by the correct God-appointed name, "the Church of God," a name used twelve times in the New Testament.

By process of elimination, then, this left the Church of God, Stanberry, Missouri. Armstrong was confused. The church was small, with less than 2000 members scattered in rural areas. None of its churches had as many as a hundred members. In the entire State of Oregon there were fewer than fifty members. Its pastors, even its leaders, were men of little education. But had not Jesus referred to his church as a "little flock"? Moreover, this tiny fellowship "*had more Bible truth* than any church" he could find.[39] The Armstrongs had been introduced to the Stanberry group by the Runcorns. During the three-and-a-half years following his conversion, they began to seek out small congregations of the denomination in Oregon. Armstrong articles began to appear on the front page of the church's periodical, *The Bible Advocate.*

Before seeking official membership, Armstrong decided to subject the church to a dual test. He submitted a lengthy article refuting a minor point of the church's doctrine to see whether the leaders would change their position. Although the *Advocate* editor acknowledged the mistake, he refused to publish a correction, lest the members' faith be shaken.

The second test was a 300-page manuscript, based on "exhaustive study and research," which "proved that the so-called 'lost Ten Tribes' of Israel had migrated to northwestern Europe, the British Isles, and later the U.S.—and that the British were the descendants of Ephraim, younger son of Joseph, and the U.S. modern-day Manasseh, elder son of Joseph." Armstrong maintains that the editor/head of the denomination admitted that his thesis was right but refused after six months' delay to announce the doctrine. Armstrong was again bewildered by the leader's action: "Here was the key to understanding of one third of the whole Bible. But this Church refused then to accept it or preach it or publish it . . . though their leader frankly confessed it was truth and a revelation from God!"[40]

In summer 1928 Armstrong preached his first sermon at a Church of God worship service. A month later he tangled with a visiting minister about divine healing, in which he had come to believe quite fervently. His presence increasingly became a source of controversy in the denomination. For a time his opponents halted publication of his articles in *The Bible Advocate*, but an indignant protest from an influential member resulted in their reinstatement. Still, Armstrong continued to preach at Sabbath services and special evangelistic meetings in various communities, though he was not ordained or even a member. More trouble arose when he baptized four converts during an evangelistic crusade in December 1930. Shortly thereafter he was ordained by the Oregon Conference of the Church of God, an offshoot of the Stanberry denomination which he had a part in forming in November 1930.[41]

Fired with an intense zeal to get his family "saved," Armstrong realized that he had to practice what he preached. Troubled by his use of tobacco, he turned to the Bible for guidance: "Why do I smoke? To please others—to help others—or only to satisfy and gratify a desire of the flesh within my own *self*?" The answer was obvious, and he stopped smoking immediately.[42]

Soon after her husband's conversion, Loma Armstrong had been seriously ill. Tonsilitis, quinsy, and blood poisoning from a finger infection caused by a rose thorn, brought her to the very threshold of death. A physician issued the gloomy prediction that she could not live another day. Then a couple came to the house and offered to pray for Mrs. Armstrong with the laying on of hands. Overcoming his initial resistance, Armstrong gave his consent. The couple anointed his wife with oil and prayed for her. "She slept soundly until 11:00 a.m. next day. Then she arose and dressed as if she had never been ill. She had been healed of *everything*, including some long-standing internal maladjustments." Convinced of the efficacy of prayer, Armstrong claims never again to have called on a doctor for any illness in the family.[43]

Thanks to Loma's healing, it was again possible for her to bear children. Richard David was born in October 1928; Garner Ted joined the family on February 9, 1930. The Armstrongs were then in such dire financial straits that they could not pay their rent and utilities, and they were reduced to a near-starvation diet.

A job selling aluminum ware through demonstration dinners introduced Herbert to a new topic of interest: diet and health foods. To families on whom he called Armstrong recommended fasting, to eliminate "stored up toxins and poisons." This, followed by proper diet, he prescribed as a sure cure for "rheumatism, constipation, colds, and many other chronic ailments or diseases." When invited to do so, he would pray for those who were sick—and "several were healed."[44]

A more promising job opportunity took Armstrong to Astoria, Oregon, as advertising manager of a new morning paper, *The Astoria Messenger.* He hit upon several ingenious promotional schemes, which proved profitable for both the newspaper and its clients. Soon envious competitors were knocking on Armstrong's door to seek his services. But the paper's shaky financial foundation caused "the Morning Mess," as it was nicknamed, to fold. "I had kept it alive for 15 months," Armstrong asserts in his autobiography.[45]

In July 1932, two-and-a-half-year-old Garner Ted, previously afflicted with dumbness from a fall on his head before his first birthday, was stricken with pneumonia. His anxious father prayed for his son's healing, and the fever left quickly. "The very next day he was able to say a number of single words. In about three days he was talking in whole sentences."[46]

Armstrong refers to his time in Astoria as "the last detour from the true life purpose" to which God had called him."[47] Returning to Salem, he agreed to preach in the Oregon Conference for $3 per week plus garden produce and other commodities. In April 1933 his father died, a day before his scheduled baptism in the river at the edge of his farm.

During revival meetings in Salem Armstrong became soured on Pentecostalism. Priding himself on his clear-headed, rational approach to Christianity, he was repelled by the noisy and emotional demonstrations of the Pentecostals who attended his services. Moreover, the mistrust between him and the Church of God evangelists with whom he worked was growing. His ecclesiastical enemies tried to oust him from the ministry on the trumped-up charge that his wife was a poor housekeeper. Failing, they next accused him of "baptizing people on repentance of faith, *before* they had been given a complete education about God's Law, and before they had been instructed against eating pork." Reprimanded for this allegedly unscriptural practice, Armstrong wrote to the authorities canceling his salary. He stresses that he did not resign from the conference, nor was he expelled. He merely refused further salary. Later he was to realize that this was the "turning point of my whole life."[48]

THREE:

The Legend Behind the Man

In the summer of 1933, Herbert W. Armstrong held a series of evangelistic meetings in response to an invitation from Mr. and Mrs. Elmer E. Fisher, prominent farmers near Eugene, Oregon. The services, held in a one-room school eight miles west of Eugene, were later to be looked on as the origin of the Worldwide Church of God.

The beginnings were unpretentious. On opening night 27 of the 35 seats were filled. The highest attendance was 64; the average 36. When the meetings closed in August, more than twenty people (including ten members of the Fisher and Ellis families, who had previously been members of the Oregon Conference) decided to establish a new Sabbath-keeping Church of God.[1]

In September, the opportunity developed for Armstrong to conduct fifteen-minute morning devotional services on a Eugene radio station. The manager of the tiny station was impressed by his radio voice and delivery. At his suggestion, Armstrong began half-hour worship services each Sunday morning for the token charge of $2.50 per program. When a second congregation was organized in October, its first decision was to underwrite the broadcast.[2] In April Armstrong had begun publishing a paper, *The Bulletin of the Churches of God in Oregon.* This paper, the broadcast, and preaching services constituted his threefold ministry in those early days.

"Surely nothing could have started smaller," Armstrong observes. "Born in adversity in the very depths of the Depression, this Work of God was destined to grow to worldwide power." But it was not until many years later that the full significance of this modest undertaking was to dawn upon him. "I did not realize its destiny then. There were no illusions of grandeur. It was not through any planning of mine that the little three-point campaign then being launched was to expand into its present global scope and influence."[3] Because a worldwide ministry developed from these humble beginnings, he was led to the conviction that he himself was God-chosen and his ministry God-ordained: "Jesus Christ (Revelation 3:8) was opening the gigantic mass-media door of radio and the printing press for the proclaiming of His same original Gospel to all the world!"[4]

As plans for the broadcast advanced, he developed further the vision of publishing a magazine. Years before he had made up a dummy copy of the proposed periodical and written some articles for it. This was to be a magazine for the public—"the unconverted and unchurched—an evangelistic-type publication to bring to the world God's truth—making it plain!"[5] The first mimeographed issue of *The Plain Truth*, dated February 1, 1934, was mailed to 106 listeners who requested it.[6]

In the beginning, "The Radio Church of God," as the 10:00 Sunday morning half-hour program was called, featured special music and a 22-minute message by Armstrong. Geared to a churchgoing audience, it was, in effect, a condensed church service. But Armstrong felt increasingly that he should aim his talks at the secular, unchurched public. So the worship format was dropped and the music gradually reduced and finally eliminated. Armstrong had learned that it was the message, focusing on "news analysis, prophecy, a dynamic educational Message of interest to the non-religious and non-church people, or in other words, the whole of the public," that attracted listeners.[7]

Armstrong continued to hold evening church services and additional public meetings as time and opportunity afforded. Three county-schoolhouse churches were now functioning. In May 1935 the Armstrongs moved to Eugene into a "little church house," for which they paid only $500. There the rural congregations united to become the "mother church of the 'Philadelphia' era of the true church which Christ himself built and still directs, rules, and blesses."[8] In a windowless room in the Hampton Building, an office rented for $5 per month, *The Plain Truth* was published. Stencils were typed on a $10 used typewriter and copies run off on an old second-hand Neostyle, also procured for $10, which Armstrong describes as a "predecessor to the mimeograph."[9]

Armstrong's work was supported by a Gideon's band of perhaps two dozen "co-workers."[10] He asked for $50 a month from his followers, and when they failed to pledge that much, he desisted from expanding. It was two years before a second radio station could be added. But early in his ministry Armstrong abandoned the conservative policy of waiting for funds before undertaking anything new. He decided to launch forth into the deep by faith. "We had to learn, by experience, that when God opens doors for Christ's Gospel, He expects us to start walking on through, in faith, trusting Him to supply our every need!"[11]

Basic to the faith principle is the practice of never soliciting money from the general public and never charging anything for literature. Members, however, are reminded that tithing is "one of God's laws" (besides, "Experience proves it *pays* to tithe!")[12] and are admonished to contribute to God's work not only tithes but offerings as well.

By March 1935 *The Plain Truth* mailing list had grown from the original 106 names to 200—and the radio audience was now estimated at eight thousand. Herbert and Loma Armstrong still constituted the entire office force. The antiquated duplicating machine could be fed only one sheet at a time, and the pages had to be slip-sheeted to avoid smearing. Since the Armstrongs were too poor to own an automobile, Herbert, who preached at various locations six to nine times a week, had to hitch-hike or rely on friends for transportation. In 1935, thanks to a letter distributed by three recent converts, enough money was donated to purchase a 1929 Graham-Paige for $85.[13]

The poverty of those early years was dire. One member

took Armstrong to a Montgomery Ward store to buy him a new suit for $19.89. A couple of years later, when this one was threadbare, friends raised $35 to buy another. Mrs. Armstrong was forced to accept hand-me-down clothing from her sister. She even repaired the runs in silk stockings which were given to them—a gift that provoked one listener into cutting off her contributions with the irate complaint, "I'm not going to let any of *my* tithes go to buy silk stockings for those Armstrong girls." Armstrong later observed that such remarks "soured and prejudiced our children against God's truth. It required a real miracle from God to convert our sons and bring them into His ministry."[14]

The financial struggle was such that it was decided to suspend publication of *The Plain Truth* in July 1935. By November, monthly receipts were up to $40 or $45 a month, enabling the Armstrongs to move into a small church-owned house in Eugene. The following spring they acquired a 400-seat tent for nightly evangelistic services, but soon had to trade it in for one seating only fifty. A third radio outlet (in Salem) was added in fall 1936; a fourth (in Portland) in September 1937. Later that year an opportunity to buy an 800-seat tabernacle in Portland was refused. The decision signaled the rejection of a local church ministry in favor of a continued mass-media approach. Through the loyalty of his $5-per-week secretary, Armstrong was able in December 1937 to replace his worn-out 1929 automobile with a 1934 model. On her own initiative, Mrs. Helen Starkey wrote all co-workers requesting a love offering for this purpose. Enough money came in to begin monthly payments on the "new" automobile, which was made to last until 1941.[15]

After a lapse of two-and-a-half years, *The Plain Truth* resumed publication on January 1, 1938, with a mailing list of about a thousand. Expenses had soared to $300 per month, and only one in ten of those on the mailing list made any contribution toward expenses, a ratio that was to persist as the operation expanded into its present huge proportions.[16] Income was not sufficient to publish every month, and there were just seven issues in 1938. But a thousand new requests for free subscriptions were received during March and April 1939.

Maintaining the monthly budget of $300 proved difficult. Most of the office work was done by the Armstrongs and their daughter Beverly—and family living expenses were held to $85 per month. In a letter to co-workers dated April 2, 1940, Armstrong wrote:

> One of my daughters has had to stop school. We are about to lose our home. We have gone without badly needed clothing. . . . We are willing and glad to make any sacrifice. But the point is, we have now come to the *end,* unless substantial help comes at once. . . . For the work's sake I must appeal to our helpers. I would starve before I would ask one cent as charity for myself. But I'm willing to humiliate myself in any way for the Gospel's sake.[17]

Shortly thereafter things began to break. It was not until May 1940, he relates, that "God had begun to bring into my mind a glimpse of the future world-wide destiny of this work." Broadcast time was obtained on a 1,000-watt station in Seattle, and "the work began rapidly to take on new life."[18] The mimeograph gave way to the printing press, beginning with the August-September 1940 issue of *The Plain Truth.* Each eight-page issue now cost $100 for printing and mailing to the three thousand subscribers. Within three-and-a-half months, circulation had risen to four thousand—and by May it was up to five. The radio audience was estimated at a quarter of a million.[19]

The expanding operation required more office space, and after seven years, Armstrong bought his first desk. To handle the increased office chores, the staff was augmented by a girl "who couldn't use shorthand or type" and a corps of volunteers. Hand-copied mailing lists were reduced to stencils, but a 1¢ stamp still had to be glued on each copy of the magazine with flour-and-water paste mixed by Mrs. Armstrong. A secretary was added to the staff to help answer the two to three hundred letters that came in from radio listeners each week.

His enlarged ministry subjected Armstrong to a grueling routine. The network of three Oregon stations had required only one performance on his part; with the addition of Seattle, he had to make a 320-mile drive from Eugene each Saturday, arriving about 1:00 a.m. Sunday. Rising at 5:00 a.m., he would make his preparations, deliver an 8:30 broadcast, race back to Portland for a 4:00 p.m. broadcast, and then hurry to Eugene for a 7:30 evening service. He continued this frantic pace until the spring of 1942.

Furthermore, after the war started, his scripts had to be submitted for censorship before each broadcast. Many of the talks were based on current news items, which added to the pressure of producing typescripts in advance.

> I did not dare deviate from the script. Today neither Garner Ted Armstrong nor I use much script. We do like to have the first two or three sentences typed in script form to get us off to a start, but from there on our daily programs are nearly altogether ad-libbed. Of course we have notes, clippings and, always, a Bible in front of us. We never quote the Bible from memory—that is always read directly from the Bible.[20]

The long drive to and from Seattle each weekend was proving too strenuous, and Armstrong began to make the trip north by train, returning by plane. Flying for the first time from Seattle to Portland on December 7, 1941, he learned from a member of the crew that Japanese planes had that morning bombed Pearl Harbor. He hurriedly revised his script to interpret the tragic event to his listeners on the 4:00 p.m. broadcast.

In 1941 Armstrong accompanied his daughter Dorothy to Los Angeles for a meeting with her fiancé Vern Mattson, as he left for Marine duty in the Pacific war theater. During this trip arrangements were made to air the broadcast on station KMTR, Hollywood, Sunday morning at 9:30 o'clock. "The time had come to drop the church-service type program altogether," and the title "Radio Church of God" was changed to "The World Tomorrow."[21] The program was announced by one of the most famous voices in radio, Art Gilmore. Availing himself of Hollywood's top-quality facilities, Armstrong began to transcribe his broadcasts for multiple distribution, thus greatly reducing his work load.

Now a new phase of the radio ministry began. Mail

response to the Hollywood Sunday morning program was double that of the stations in the Northwest, and the California station offered Armstrong additional time at 5:30 p.m. for daily weekday broadcasting. The management wanted a reply within 24 hours. The decision was not an easy one. "It meant at least *doubling* the entire expenses of the whole Work—in one sudden jump!" Herbert telephoned Loma in Eugene and learned that there was just enough money in the bank to pay for one week of daily broadcasting. After that? "I decided that was God's problem and responsibility. I committed it to Him, and wrote out a check for every dollar we had in the bank. Now we were on the air, in Southern California, seven days a week! That was by far the most tremendous leap ahead so far!"[22]

Despite the financial dilemma, Armstrong maintained his policy of not asking over the air for money. But there was a sharp increase in mail—and money—addressed to Box 111, Eugene, Oregon.[23] In July 1942 Armstrong decided to make another leap of faith. He spent $175 to rent the Biltmore Theater in Los Angeles for a Sunday afternoon lecture. To his amazement, 1750 people appeared. Those wishing to contribute were invited to leave their donations in two boxes placed in the lobby. When the money was counted, Armstrong says, there was exactly one cent more than enough to defray expenses. For the next two Sundays, double meetings were held each afternoon. About two thousand individuals attended each week, with between 1300 and 1400 at each service. Since many of the first congregation remained for the second program, Armstrong preached two separate sermons.[24]

After four profitable months in Hollywood, Herbert decided to return to Eugene. While he was in California, the number of "co-worker" contributors had doubled, enabling him to expand the radio ministry to Spokane and San Diego—and finally to the 50,000-watt station WHO, in Des Moines, with its nationwide outreach, on Sunday night, August 30, 1942. Letters began to come in from all 48 states, one WHO program alone drawing 2200 responses.

The Plain Truth was reaching every state and province in the US and Canada, and boasted a circulation of 35,000. Printing costs had risen to $1000 per issue; radio time was costing $250 per week. Armstrong made occasional incursions into Southern California for daily broadcasts and Sunday afternoon services, but a small church established in Los Angeles, with 23 baptized members, soon disintegrated.[25]

Despite the fact that the "Work" was enjoying a 30 per cent annual growth, "doubling in scope and power every 2 years, 7½ months,"[26] the winter of 1944 confronted Armstrong with "the most serious financial crisis faced so far." The January-February issue of *The Plain Truth* had to be canceled. The supply of Armstrong's booklet *The United States and the British Commonwealth in Prophecy* was exhausted, and back orders for 10,000 copies had accumulated. Threatened with the loss of several radio stations, Herbert and Loma decided to sell their home and "put the money in the work." Placing their furniture in storage, they began moving "from one auto court to another" every few days. After several months of this pillar-to-post existence, they managed to rent two upstairs bedrooms in a rooming house—but they had to take their meals in restaurants, which turned out to be as costly as it was inconvenient.

Herbert W. Armstrong looks on 1946 as "the *year of beginnings*, as an organized major national and world-wide Work." Significantly, twelve years had elapsed since the start of the broadcast and the magazine—and twelve is "God's number of spiritual *organizational* beginnings."[27] The Radio Church of God began its own printing operation in 1946, headed by daughter Beverly's husband James A. Gott. Three powerful radio stations beamed the broadcast at "early prime time" throughout the entire North American continent six nights a week. Armstrong himself embarked on his first baptizing tour in 1946. And it was in that year that the idea of Ambassador College first occurred to him.

Armstrong determined that Ambassador College must not be a Bible school or theological seminary, for "the one profession no man is free to choose for himself is Christ's ministry. The true Ministers of Jesus Christ are chosen by Him—just as He chose His original Apostles. . . . The students in this school *must not* come with the expectation of becoming a minister." Besides, "in today's world . . . only an *educated* ministry can adequately represent Jesus Christ." The college he envisioned was a liberal arts school, "a general cultural education, with Biblical and theological training offered as *one* of *several* major courses." A Graduate School of Theology was projected "for those who . . . appeared as possible or probable future ministers chosen by the living Christ."[28]

Arriving in Southern California after an extended baptizing tour, Armstrong learned of the availability of "a small mansion of some 18 rooms . . . on Pasadena's 'millionaire row.' " The price was $100,000; but an attorney arranged for purchase of the property through $1000 monthly payments. After nine payments Armstrong was to take occupancy, and after 25 payments he was to be awarded the deed.[29]

Elated over the acquisition, Herbert sought the advice of his brother-in-law, Walter E. Dillon, who had "the technical experience for academic organization" that Armstrong lacked. Even before the Pasadena institution was established, the idea of a European campus began to evolve. On February 20, 1947, accompanied by his wife and a "Dr. B.," owner of the estate Armstrong was buying, he set sail for Europe on the *Queen Elizabeth* to examine a prospective site in Switzerland. However profitable the trip may have been otherwise, it failed to accomplish the desired goal.

On his return to the United States Armstrong invited his brother-in-law to assume the presidency of Ambassador College (he himself became Chancellor). Dr. Hawley Otis Taylor, whose distinguished academic pedigree included teaching positions at Harvard, MIT, Cornell, and the chairmanship of the Physics Department at Wheaton College (from which position he had recently retired), was appointed Dean of Instruction and Registrar. He, along with other faculty and student applicants, had responded to an appeal in the January 1947 issue of *The Plain Truth.* Four women instructors were included in the original faculty of eight. (For reasons not made clear, he decided after the first year to hire men only as instructors, except for teaching "music, Home Economics, etc.")[30] After some frustrating delays and the completion of extensive remodeling and rewiring, at a cost of another $30,000, Ambassador College opened its doors on October 8, 1947, with four students and a faculty of eight. The four students plus eight faculty members added up to "God's organizational number" of twelve.

The growth of the work and the decision to move to California to start a college, led some of the more parochially minded members of the little church in Eugene to become "disgruntled and cynical." About half of the members left to form a splinter congregation. But, opposition by these diehard critics notwithstanding, the move to Pasadena appeared to be God-ordained. Miraculously, it seemed, a real estate agent procured for the Armstrongs a fourteen-room residence at half the advertised price with no down payment required. "After 28 years of virtual poverty, [God] was beginning to *add*, by His grace, a few material blessings."[31]

But the enormous expense of starting and operating a college precipitated a new financial crisis. Two powerful radio stations had to be dropped. The college fell in arrears in paying faculty salaries, resulting in two or three resignations and a threatened lawsuit. The second year began with a half schedule, classes meeting only three days a week. On December 27, 1948, an indebtedness totaling $17,000 (in taxes, insurance, and interest) was to fall due, and daily receipts were averaging only $500 or $600. Then, on December 1, $3000 came in! The next day's mail produced the same amount. So it continued throughout the month, until the December total exceeded $50,000. "There was only one explanation," says Armstrong, "God sent it!"[32]

Financial problems were not the only difficulties. Given

Armstrong's evolving self-image of apostleship, his radical views of religion and education, and the increasing involvement in his work of talented individuals of considerable education and experience, differences and personality clashes were inevitable. Armstrong discovered that his course in theology, which he considered "the real foundation course of the college," had been listed in the catalog by the president and dean as a "two-hour *minor* subject." His response was decisive.

> I immediately decreed that faculty members, as well as students, must attend all my classes. I taught entirely by the lecture method. I did this, not so much as a retaliatory measure, but as a means of getting the new college off to a start as the very *kind* of college God was building. . . . I constantly used the Four Gospels to demonstrate that the current concept of Jesus' teachings was at total variance with the inspired record. I took great pains to make my lectures so rational and factual as to leave no room for refutation. [33]

Objection to the compulsory feature by Dean Taylor resulted in a compromise. "I saw to it that the theology courses were three-hour majors (the next year). One of them I designated as my own forum period, at which attendance of all faculty members was required."[34] But the third year, the attendance requirement for faculty was dropped. And in the continuing tradition of the weekly forum, students and faculty were "free to speak and voice opinions."[35] Dr. Taylor, described by Armstrong as a "fundamentalist," never came to accept his chancellor's peculiar doctrines, and persisted in writing him "occasional pointed barbs" critical of his beliefs and practices. At length Armstrong called a halt to the diatribes by issuing to Dr. Taylor a warning which was tantamount to an ultimatum. The notes ceased, and Taylor remained as dean and registrar until his death at 77 in April 1954.

When the fall term opened in 1950, Armstrong was teaching four different classes in theology, each meeting three times a week, speaking on his half-hour radio broadcast seven days a week, and still writing every word for *The Plain Truth.*[36] Not surprisingly, only four eight-page issues of the magazine appeared in 1950. Circulation had grown to more than 50,000. Some changes in the operation were inevitable. Ambassador graduates Herman Hoeh and Roderick Meredith, tutored by Armstrong in his rapid-fire, exclamatory style, began writing for the magazine—as did Dick and Garner Ted Armstrong. Additionally, some advanced students and graduates provided editorial help.

In December 1952 Armstrong ordained "the first ministers to assist me." The list included Richard David Armstrong, Raymond Clifford Cole, Herman Louis Hoeh, Dr. C. Paul Meredith, and Roderick C. Meredith. Following their graduation the next month, Marion Joel McNair and Raymond Franklin McNair brought the number of ministers to a biblically significant seven.

This fascination for numbers is a repeated feature of Armstrong's autobiography. Seven, for example, is seen as God's number of perfection and completeness. Armstrong's experience of deep repentance began at 28 (4 x 7); at 35 (5 x 7) he was actually converted. After his years of study and preparation, "God *opened the door* of radio and the printing press" when Armstrong was 42 (6 x 7). After seven lean years, during which Armstrong was "weaned completely from worldly economic ambitions," in 1941 "the door was opened for the Work to launch out on a *national* scale." Purchase of the original property for the Ambassador College campus was consummated in 1948, at the close of the next seven-year period—and "the future of the expanding Work became assured."[37]

The parallels drawn between himself and Jesus Christ—and between *his* "Work" and Christ's—leave little doubt concerning Armstrong's self-image as God's uniquely trained apostle, called to revive true Christianity in an age of rank apostasy in preparation for the end-time. "First, Jesus Christ began His earthly ministry at about age 30. God took away my business, moved me from Chicago, started bringing me to repentance and conversion preparatory to inducting me into His ministry, *when I was 30!* Second, Jesus began the actual *teaching and training* of His original disciples for carrying His Gospel to the world in the year 27 A.D. *Precisely 100 time-cycles later*, in 1927 He began my intensive study and training for carrying His same Gospel to all the nations of today's world."[38] He explains, "One revolution of the earth around the sun is a solar *year.* But the earth, the sun, and the moon come into almost exact conjunction only *once in 19 years.* Thus 19 years mark off one complete time-cycle!"[39] Christ instructed his disciples for three-and-a-half years; he likewise instructed Armstrong for the same period. The disciples were ordained and empowered on the Day of Pentecost A.D. 31;[40] Armstrong's "ordination took place at, or very near, the Day of Pentecost, 1931."

For one 19-year time-cycle, Armstrong says, the proclamation of the gospel was confined to Asia. Then in the year 50 Paul carried the message to Europe. Similarly, it was "exactly one time-cycle" after the first "mass proclaiming of His original true Gospel" on Sunday, January 7, 1934, that Radio Luxembourg began broadcasting the Armstrong program to Europe, on Monday, January 5, 1953.

The second cycle of the apostolic era ended with the Jewish revolt (conveniently pinpointed by Armstrong at A.D. 69, though it actually began in 66),[41] which culminated in the destruction of Jerusalem in A.D. 70. The second cycle of what might be called the Armstrong era is prophesied to end with "the Great Tribulation and the Day of the Lord climax." But Armstrong safeguarded himself against the possibility that World War III (Armageddon) and Christ's return would not transpire in 1972—nineteen years after the cycle began. "*We do not set dates.* Even the date of 1972 as a possible date for finishing this present Work of God is an *indicated*—but by *no* means certain—date."[42]

In the spring of 1955 Armstrong made his debut on television. Daughter Beverly and son Garner Ted sang solos on the program, but later, as had occurred on radio in the 1930s, music was abandoned to devote more time to news analysis. Film clips of actual news events were screened as background for the commentary. But the weekly telecast was costly; it required much time and energy to produce; and besides, Armstrong discovered that "radio was *not* dead, after all." So it was decided to suspend the TV series and to concentrate instead on daily broadcasting over large radio stations, which, though expensive, brought a mail response ten to fifty times greater than smaller ones.[43]

Incorporated into the Armstrong life story, as it appeared in *The Plain Truth*, is an account by Loma Armstrong of the couple's first visit to the Holy Land. Considerable attention is given to a discussion of the sites of the birth, trial, crucifixion, and resurrection of Jesus. Much of this is seemingly designed to assure the readers that these sites are not in Catholic hands, though the traditional locations—long since covered by churches built atop the debris of the centuries—are established on the basis of much better evidence than the sites favored by the Armstrongs.

The report is also revealing in the distinct bias it displays against the Arabs, who are caricatured as "filthy" and "beggars." Crossing into Israel from Jordan was "like suddenly entering into a new world. . . . It was such a relief to be out of the Arab country. . . . These [Israelis] were more like the people of our country."[44] In Israel they visited Megiddo. The caption under *The Plain Truth's* photograph of that ancient site reads, "It is called Armageddon, meaning 'armed Megiddo.' "[45] Any standard biblical reference work, however, will reveal that the Hebrew prefix *Har* means "mountain," so that Armageddon probably means "the mountain of Megiddo."[46]

Armstrong was to discover that one of the prices required of him for his break with traditional Christianity was the friendship of former close friends and relatives. After one particularly trying experience he warned his readers,

> When God really gets hold of one's life—when that life becomes *changed* by the indwelling of God's Holy Spirit—one's contacts, friends, and especially relatives will chill decisively. Actually it is not the converted human they resent. It is the Living Jesus Christ—now living *His* life within the converted one, who is the real object of the hostility.[47]

The year 1956 saw further expansion with the acquisition of the multi-million-dollar four-acre Merritt estate, and the conversion of the lavish mansion into a classroom building renamed Ambassador Hall. The purchase of Manor Del Mar for a student residence for men further enhanced Ambassador's expanding facilities. Eventually, the campus was to encompass a twelve-block area. That fall Garner Ted Armstrong joined the faculty as a teacher of theology, speech, and journalism.[48]

Garner Ted had always attracted more attention than his older brother Dick. Outgoing and aggressive, and gifted with a splendid baritone voice, Ted had early ambitions of singing in night clubs. Much more than his brother, with whom he had once sneaked cigarettes, Ted was hostile toward his parents' religion as a youth. After high school, when Dick began his studies at Ambassador, Ted joined the Navy for four years. Not until the spring of 1953, as a freshman at Ambassador, had he begun seriously to read the Bible for himself.

Once that happened, Ted soon surpassed Dick "in God's Work." Ted became convinced that " 'Dad's religion' was not, after all, Dad's—that is, not one 'Dad' had thought up, devised, or obtained from some sect or cult, but the religion of Jesus Christ, and of the apostle Paul, and of the other original apostles, and of the Bible!"[49] Thus persuaded, he threw himself into the work with energy and enthusiasm. By 1957, a youthful 27, he was doing a good share of the broadcasting work; and in November of that year he was elevated to the vice presidency of Ambassador College.

Tragedy struck in July 1958 when Dick, less than a year after his marriage, was out on a "baptizing tour." Driving north of San Luis Obispo he suffered a head-on collision. A week later he died of kidney failure brought on by the accident. The day after his death was the Armstrongs' 41st wedding anniversary; the day after that, the funeral. Overcoming a desire to retreat into solitude, Herbert Armstrong preached at his son's funeral and at the next Sabbath afternoon services. It was, Armstrong said, "perhaps the most severe test I had ever been called on to experience"—then he adds, "But of course I knew where to go for strength, wisdom, and help."[50]

By January 1958 Armstrong's radio program reached every continent on earth, with an estimated four to five million listeners a week. By October *The Plain Truth*, which had gone to two colors in February 1957, increased to 32 pages. Circulation was now 175,000 copies.

"The Work" in Britain began with Herbert W. Armstrong's lecture tour in 1954, during which he addressed audiences in Belfast, Glasgow, Manchester, and London. Large crowds were part of the harvest from the Radio Luxembourg broadcasts, which had begun the previous year. In 1956 the first church was organized in Britain. By 1959 additional office space was needed, and Herbert and Ted, on tour in Europe, flew to London to assist the European director in locating suitable facilities.

After two or three days of futile search, a real estate agent took the trio to examine a large estate north of London. It seemed unlikely, but the discouraged seekers were getting desperate. Arriving at dusk, they were impressed by the appearance of the stately mansion and its spacious lawns, now overgrown with weeds. Returning the next morning to examine the estate in daylight, and to survey the interior, they suddenly thrilled to the realization that this was the property to which God had led them.

> Almost in unison, we all exclaimed, "This is providential! This means God wants another full liberal arts co-ed college in England, just like the one in Pasadena!" . . . It was like recognizing a revelation straight from God. . . . This may seem preposterous to some readers, I know. But we are engaged in God's Work. We have learned how God works. It was like God had flashed a message straight from heaven like a sudden bolt of lightning.[51]

And so a second Ambassador College campus—at Bricket Wood, near St. Albans, Hertfordshire—came into being. Four years later, in 1964, a third educational institution bearing the name Ambassador was established at Big Sandy, Texas, a hundred miles east of Dallas. The college opened with 100 students—a far cry from the enrolment of four when Ambassador College had been launched in Pasadena in 1947. Six years prior to the Big Sandy opening, "the largest 'church auditorium' in Texas," with a seating capacity of 8,000, to accommodate congregations at the annual Feast of Tabernacles, had been constructed on the future campus site.

Chapter 76 of the Armstrong autobiography, which appeared in *The Plain Truth* for February 1968, ends on a tantalizing note, promising to inform the readers "in the next installment" how the magnificent estate at Bricket Wood—the mansion, its elegant gardens, cedars of Lebanon, aviary, greenhouses, and miscellaneous out-buildings—"all finally came to us for £8,000 ($22,800)." Readers of *The Plain Truth* are still awaiting that "next installment" and information about his life and work from 1960 until the present, including the record of Mrs. Armstrong's death in 1967, just three months short of their 50th wedding anniversary; the global meanderings of Armstrong to visit heads of state in such nations as Japan, Indonesia, India, and Israel; Ambassador College's joint participation (with Hebrew University) in archeological excavations in the Temple area of Jerusalem; increase of *The Plain Truth*'s circulation to over three million, and of radio-television coverage of "The World Tomorrow" to more than four hundred radio and TV stations worldwide; the toppling of Garner Ted Armstrong from his several exalted posts, followed by his restoration to full influence and power in 1973; the growing backlash in the ranks of Worldwide Church of God membership in the early seventies.

Paul's biographer, Luke, leaves the story of the apostle dangling at the end of the Book of Acts—imprisoned in Rome, his fate unreported. So Herbert W. Armstrong leaves the story of his life and work at loose ends, with much of interest and significance remaining to be told.

FOUR:

"A True History of the True Church"

Herbert W. Armstrong's theology was not delivered to him on stone tablets like the Decalogue to Moses. Writing in *The Good News*, a magazine for members, Armstrong relates, "I had to come into God's Truth a single doctrine, or a single bit of Truth, at a time. It was not all laid out *in order*, in a clear-cut, plain, well-organized pattern—as it is today for you!"[1] As noted in the second chapter, he began with the Sabbath and evolution questions and arrived, after six months of intensive study, at a seven-point doctrinal foundation, including the existence of God, the falsity of evolution, the infallibility of the Bible as the inspired instruction of God, the binding nature of the Sabbath and annual holy days and festivals, eternal *death* (not eternal *dying*) as the wages of sin, and eternal life as God's gift of grace.

Having laid this doctrinal foundation, he proceeded to build on it. Immersion baptism, divine healing, heaven and hell, the kingdom of God, the millennial reign of Christ, and the eschatological prophecies of Daniel next received his concentrated attention. During the first six months of his quest a Florida minister wrote that "unless I knew of the identity of the United States and the British as the Birthright people of Israel—heading the so-called 'Lost Ten Tribes,' I was ignorant!"[2] Sifting out the many errors that he discovered, he was persuaded by what he found in the Bible that "our identity" was "proved." "This was the needed key to unlock all the prophecies!"[3]

He proceeded to investigate Church of God and

Seventh-day Adventist literature, rejecting some doctrines, accepting others. The process was one of weighing the various teachings, digging out the truth little by little. Opposing views—at first from the leadership of the Church of God (Stanberry)—could only be interpreted as an effort to hinder God's work.[4] A similarly belligerent stance later was adopted toward opponents within his own organization. Authority is still emphasized—authority from the top down; and the top is, under God, the man who considers himself God's only true apostle, the only channel through which he has seen fit to communicate his truth to the last generation of his people, the one to whom he has committed the task of restoring his church in preparation for the windup of history. "Trouble-makers, bent on dividing and breaking up God's Church, are not tolerated."

Such a full-blown vision of Armstrong apostleship was not apparent at the outset. During the lean years of the thirties and forties, it was only dimly perceived; but its evolution rapidly accelerated as success fed the fires of his imagination and ambition. It was the "leap" into Europe via Radio Luxembourg in 1953, marking the beginning of the "second 19-year time-cycle," that led him fully to comprehend his apocalyptic role in God's plan.[5]

Armstrong's conviction that he had been called on to reconstitute the "one true Church" led naturally to the belief that all other churches are spurious, even Satanic. Again and again in his autobiography he recounts friction with fellow evangelists and other religious leaders. In every instance, to hear him tell it, truth and justice were entirely on *his* side, and his theological and ecclesiological foes were exposed as charlatans, hypocrites, or (at best) incompetent and deluded. The Armstrong mentality knows no compromise, no meeting of minds. Always he is *totally* right; those who disagree with him, *totally* wrong. (The sole exception seems to be his original position on the first subject of his study in the quest for truth. Once having converted to the seventh-day Sabbath, this and all subsequent insights he has ascribed to the illumination of his mind by the supernatural light of God.)

This self-understanding is fundamental to Armstrong's

concept of "the one true Church." If the revelation to him is true, all contrary teaching is false. If the church he brought into being is of God, all others are of Satan. These two assumptions—that there is but one divinely revealed body of doctrine and one God-ordained body of believers—must pertain not only to modern times but to all of Christian history.

There are seven criteria by which the remnant church, from the days of the apostles until the present, has been identifiable: (1) observance of the seventh-day Sabbath; (2) keeping the Passover and other Jewish feasts (while renouncing Christmas, Easter, and other "pagan" religious holidays); (3) compliance with Old Testament dietary laws; (4) rejection of the Trinity in favor of the "God is a family" doctrine (also held by the Mormons); (5) practice of immersion baptism for adults only; (6) nonparticipation in politics; and (7) use of the designation "Church of God."

Citing twelve New Testament passages[6] in which the phrase "Church (or churches) of God" appears and noting that twelve is "God's complete number," an Armstrong pamphlet declares:

> These verses prove the name of the true Church. Denominations *not* bearing this name could *not* be God's true church. And of all the churches that do bear the name, *only one* could be the *true* Church of God—that one which obeys all the commandments of God and maintains the faith delivered once for all time—the one which *grows* in truth. All others are counterfeit, even though they may have the knowledge about the true name of God's Church.[7]

None of the twelve passages, in fact, so much as hints that the official and exclusive name of Christ's church shall be "the Church of God." Furthermore, it would seem that God is breaking his own rule in inspiring Paul to refer to "churches of Christ" (Rom. 16:16) and to "the body of Christ" (Eph. 1:23; 5:23; Col. 1:18, 24). Finally, there are 109 New Testament passages in which the word church (Gr. *ekklesia*) is found; yet only twelve (ten in the RSV) employ the phrase "church (or churches) of God."

As Armstrong developed the notion that there can be

only "one true Church" from apostolic times to the present, and as the criteria for it were gradually "revealed" to him, he began to apply the one-true-Church principle to his study of church history. The results of that study are recorded by Ambassador College dean Herman L. Hoeh in a booklet entitled *A True History of the True Church*, as well as in Lessons 49-53 of the *Ambassador College Bible Correspondence Course.* The history is long on fancy, short on documentation. Occasionally, it is demonstrably false.

As we have seen, the 19-year time-cycle receives a good deal of attention in Armstrong's analysis of church history. Arbitrarily fixing the date of Christ's crucifixion as A.D. 31, two years later than the generally accepted date, he comes up with "two 19-year cycles in the history of the apostolic church during which the Gospel was carried to the old world."[8] The first began with Pentecost, A.D. 31; the second with the penetration of Europe by the gospel, A.D. 50. The latter cycle ended with the flight of the Jerusalem church across the Jordan River to Pella, A.D. 69, allegedly in obedience to a supernatural voice suggesting "Let us remove hence!", heard during an earthquake as Christians met in the Temple to observe the Feast of Pentecost.[9] The next year Jerusalem was destroyed, the Temple razed, and the work of the apostolic church there ended.[10]

"For nearly a century Church history is blank! . . . The True Church of God had faded from view! *Another* church was on stage!"[11] Armstrong, however, purports to declare "the astounding, but little known facts" concerning "the True New Testament Church of Jesus Christ"—not only during that "blank" period, but through subsequent centuries to the present day. With the congregation at Pella as headquarters and those at Antioch and Ephesus as secondary centers, the authentic Christian witness was preserved. "*Rome,*" it is emphasized, "*was never the parent or Headquarters church.*"[12]

Armstrong interprets the seven churches of Asia Minor, addressed in Revelation 2 and 3, as microcosms typifying seven stages of church history. Although the Lord rebuked the Ephesian church for abandoning the love it had at first (Rev. 2:4), the Asian churches were the most faithful among the Gentiles, in contrast to those apostatizing churches whose headquarters quickly gravitated to Rome.[13] Quoting from standard reference works, Armstrong establishes that the "True Church" adhered to the Mosaic requirements of circumcision, Sabbath observance, kosher foods, celebration of Passover instead of Easter, and the like. Polycrates is quoted to the effect that the Apostles John and Philip, as well as Polycarp, "all kept the Passover on the fourteenth day of the month." Although Paul is not even mentioned in the quoted sources, Hoeh affirms, "Here is proof that both the apostles to the circumcision *and Paul*, the special apostle to the Gentiles, taught the true Church to observe the passover on the 14th of the first month of God's sacred calendar"[14] —an apparent contradiction to Paul's warning to the Galatians: "if you receive circumcision, Christ will be of no advantage to you. . . . every man who receives circumcision . . . is bound to keep the whole law" (5:2-3), which implies that the ritual demands of the Mosaic Law have been rendered obsolete by the *new* covenant of grace.

Apparently the Ephesian church failed to repent (Rev. 2:5), and the church's headquarters moved to Smyrna about 135. The bishop Polycarp presided over the churches of Asia until his martyrdom in 155; then it fell on Polycrates to defend the faith against the "vast Easter-keeping organization" based in Rome. With his generation "the True Church in the Greek-speaking world had virtually *disappeared.* With Polycrates, its last candle flickered out. The Synagogue of Satan was now triumphant in the world."[15] What was the "Synagogue of Satan?" The Armstrong history identifies it as "the great apostate church" of Rome—adding that Rome's "many Protestant daughters . . . are also Satan's churches."[16] The Roman church had been founded not by Simon Peter but by Simon Magus, the Samaritan convert rebuked by Peter for trying to buy the Holy Spirit (Acts 8).[17]

The "little flock" of genuine Christians gradually succumbed to the tribulation that was prophesied to be the lot of God's people during the Smyrna era. "Some apostatized; some were martyred. But *most migrated*—going north and east into Armenia and Cappadocia."[18] The Council of Nicea in 325 had decided "that Easter *must* be celebrated on Sunday and that the Passover must be forbidden!" Those who continued to be faithful to the "truth" were enjoined from holding their "superstitious and senseless meetings" either in public or in private. Applying the "year-for-a-day prophetic principle," the 1260-day flight into the wilderness predicted in Revelation 12:6 is seen to typify a 1260-year retreat of the true church into the valleys and mountains of Asia Minor and Europe before the onslaught of Roman persecution.

The letter to the church at Pergamum (Rev. 2:12-17) warns against those who "hold the teaching of Balaam," the prophet who cursed the Israelites (Num. 22–24). Armstrong finds it significant that Balaam came from Pethor (Num. 22:5): "*Who*, today, in the same office, is headquartered in (St.) Peter's?!"[19] During this era, the true Christians were known as "Paulicians," meaning "in its original Armenian. . . 'a follower of wretched little Paul.' "[20] The sect's writings were banned; only a recently discovered volume entitled *The Key of Life* survives to tell of Paulician beliefs and teachings, including immersion baptism, Sabbath-keeping, Passover observance, and the laying on of hands for the "reception of the Spirit." The Paulicians recognized the validity of ordination, and "consistently emphasized Jesus' authority over *apostolic succession*."

With most of its adherents Paulicianism was only a *form* of religion, and false teachings grew up in this group too.[21] Persecuted by Rome, some vacillating Paulicians sought help from the Saracens, instead of relying on Jesus. A hundred thousand were killed.[22] Hoeh offers a moral to the story: "Satan . . . caused many to take part in worldly politics in the hope of safeguarding themselves. Mixing with the politics of this world is called 'fornication' in Revelation 17:2."[23] How that interpretation is derived from the text in Revelation is not made clear.

Paulician cloth merchants took the gospel westward into

northern Italy and southern France in the late tenth century, Armstrong says, setting the stage for the Thyatira era. As usual, the leaders of the "one true Church" were persecuted by the Catholic hierarchy. "The *Work* of the Thyatira Era went into temporary eclipse. . . . Then Christ acted. The man He chose to become His apostle was a wealthy *merchant* in Lyons."[24] His name: Peter Waldo. He financed a new, literal translation of the Scriptures in the language of the people, and gave the rest of his money to the poor. Since he preached the true gospel, "the humble remnant of the Church of God listened to him." His disciples, known as "Waldenses," were given missionary training and traveled throughout western Europe proclaiming the good news of Jesus Christ and condemning Catholic heresies.

Roman vengeance was merciless, and scores of Waldenses were burned at the stake. Armstrong identifies "Jezebel, who calls herself a prophetess and is teaching and beguiling my servants to practice immorality and to eat food sacrificed to idols" (Rev. 2:20), with the Roman Catholic Church. One of her sinful practices was worship on Sunday, the "chief day" of Thyatira's principal deity, the sun god Apollo. By participating in the Catholic mass, compromising Waldenses were guilty of eating food sacrificed to idols. In ancient Thyatira, the people had also eaten food used in the worship of local idols.

Scattered by persecution, Waldenses came to the Netherlands, where they were disparagingly referred to as Lollards—from a Flemish word "meaning to sing or speak softly, or to mumble—because of their practice of memorizing the Scripture, in the vernacular, by mumbling it to themselves or to one another."[25] In 1315 Walter the Lollard took the gospel to England, and succeeded in spreading "the Waldensian doctrine" across that land until his martyrdom in 1322. "Through the preaching of Lollard and other helpers, hundreds were repenting. Thousands were learning for the first time that baptism means immersion—that the world's religious holidays came from paganism and that Sunday was not the Sabbath."[26] In the late fourteenth century, armed with John Wycliffe's new English translation of the Bible, Lollards went two by two throughout England, distributing the Scriptures and evangelizing. But "few real Lollards . . . constituted the Church of God," and "lack of total obedience caused the Church of God in the late Middle Ages to become powerless."[27]

The church in Sardis is described in Revelation as having the name of being alive while being in reality dead (3:1), though a few members of that congregation are commended for not having "soiled their garments" (3:4). At the beginning of the Sardis era, in the fourteenth and fifteenth centuries, the "True Church" had been reduced to a few small colonies of "God's people" scattered about Europe—some in countries as remote as Russia and Scandinavia. The prophetic period of 1260 years was drawing to a close.

Only a handful of "saints" remained in the "True Church." At this point Jesus Christ "raised up a new era of God's Church," choosing England as the locale. By the middle of the seventeenth century, due to the tireless missionary efforts of those Lollards who had remained faithful to the Waldensian gospel, there were enough converts to form several Sabbath-keeping congregations. They called themselves the "Church of God." But again the quality of faith was diluted in transmission to succeeding generations. By the end of the eighteenth century many Sabbath-keepers were electing their ministers, as the Protestants did, "instead of relying on Jesus Christ to select them."[28] They even went so far as to abandon the name "Church of God" and to call themselves "Seventh-day Baptists."

In 1664 "the true Church of God" took root in the New World, when a congregation was established by Stephen Mumford at Newport, Rhode Island. Other congregations were to be constituted in New Jersey, Connecticut, and Pennsylvania. In America, too, there was corruption by Protestant doctrine. In 1818 nearly twenty of these churches united to form the Seventh-day Baptist General Conference, and by this action they "ceased to be the true Church of God. Soon they began teaching the pagan Trinity doctrine and the immortality of human souls!"[29] Ten or twelve congregations, however, refused to affiliate with this apostate church. They became the surviving remnant of "the one true Church of God."

William Miller, dubbed by Hoeh as "uninspired,"[30] was to lead the one true church into its next byway. A Sunday-observer (and thus in Armstrong's eyes fundamentally mistaken), Miller predicted the return of Christ for October 22, 1844. When that failed to materialize, some of Miller's followers became Sabbatarians. They rejected the name "Church of God," however, and formed the Seventh-day Adventist General Conference in 1860. "Once again men forgot that they cannot organize themselves *into* the Church of God. They can only organize themselves out of the Church of God."[31]

Though the Adventist organization showed that the church was continuing to fall apart, there was a small remnant to fulfil the promise of Revelation 3:4—"you still have a few names in Sardis, people who have not soiled their garments." A group of the faithful, most of them in Ohio, Iowa, and Missouri, organized "the General Conference of the Church of God" in Stanberry, Missouri. In a pattern that was becoming familiar a schism arose in this group in 1933. The seceders formed the Church of God (Seventh Day) with headquarters in Salem, West Virginia; today they number seven churches and two thousand members. The original group headquartered in Denver; they report 76 churches and five thousand members today.[32]

Prior to that schism, in 1927, Herbert W. Armstrong had made contact—though he never affiliated formally—with the Stanberry group in Oregon, as related in Chapter 2. It seemed to Armstrong and others that one of the problems with the Stanberry group was its espousal of the principle of elected leadership. It was decided to reorganize after the New Testament pattern also adopted by the Mormons: twelve apostles to look after the spiritual affairs of the church, seven deacons to oversee financial matters, and seventy elders to "go forth two by two" doing evangelistic work. At the reorganization meeting in November 1933, the fortieth name in the drawing for the seventy elders was that of Herbert W. Armstrong. The Worldwide Church of God's interpretation of this is not surprising:

> No one knew it then, least of all Mr. Armstrong, who was not present at the meeting, but *Jesus Christ had made His choice*—with the number forty—of a man to revive His Work in the end time. Forty signifies the completion of testing. Now the time of trial and test for the Sardis Church had run out.[33]

Unfortunately, in Armstrong's view, the 1933 meeting was a "reorganization by men," consequently foredoomed to failure. "In just a few years that Church had permanently disintegrated into several ineffective fragments, neglecting much of God's truth."[34] The Sardis era had ended. The Philadelphia era was about to begin.

The letter to the Philadelphia church begins,

> "The words of the holy one, the true one, who has the key of David, who opens and no one shall shut, who shuts and no one opens. I know your works. Behold, I have set before you an open door, which no one is able to shut; I know that you have but little power, and yet you have kept my word and have not denied my name" (Rev. 3:7-8).

The open door Armstrong claims to be the " 'door' of radio," which was opened "by Christ" with the inauguration of "The World Tomorrow" broadcast in January 1934. "And now," he adds, "the message goes out also on television—an even *greater* 'door.' "[35]

> "Behold, I will make those of the synagogue of Satan who say that they are Jews and are not, but lie—behold I will make them come and bow down before your feet, and learn that I have loved you" (vs. 9).

The significance of this prophecy comes from Armstrong's identification of the "synagogue of Satan" with the Roman Catholic Church, of which the Reformation churches are her Protestant daughters.

> "Because you have kept my word of patient endurance, I will keep you from the hour of trial which is coming on the whole world, to try those who dwell upon the earth. I am coming soon; hold fast what you have, so that no one may seize your crown" (vv. 10-11).

Believing himself and his followers to be the only contemporary saints who have kept Christ's word of patient endurance, Armstrong is confident that only they will enjoy this divine protection from the imminent holocaust of Armageddon. A defensive and suspicious posture toward the "Satanic" denominations can be justified in the light of the warning to "hold fast what you have, so that no one may seize your crown." Fidelity to God's call holds the promise of rich and eternal dividends in the lush, secure, and beautiful "World Tomorrow":

> "He who conquers, I will make him a pillar in the temple of my God; never shall he go out of it, and I will write on him the name of my God, and the name of the city of my God, the new Jerusalem which comes down from my God out of heaven" (vs. 12).

Only in the light of these interpretations can the exalted claims made by Armstrong and his disciples be fully understood. Herman Hoeh describes the inauguration of the Armstrong ministry with typical expansiveness: "Jesus chose Paul, who was highly educated, for spreading the Gospel to the Gentiles. He later raised up Peter Waldo, a successful businessman, to keep His truth alive during the Middle Ages. In these last days when the Gospel must go around the world, Jesus chose a man amply trained in the advertising and business fields to shoulder the mission—Herbert W. Armstrong."[36]

Armstrong himself, despite his carefully detailed review of the history of the faithful remnant, seems at times so preoccupied with the magnitude of his divinely appointed task that he forgets even the role played by men like Waldo. "What is the one and *only* Gospel of Jesus Christ?" he asks. "The world does not know! It has not been preached for 18½ centuries, strange as that may seem."[37] From apostolic times until the present

> all worldwide organized proclaiming of *Christ's* Gospel was stamped out by the worldly popular, professing "Christian" churches! But Christ also foretold that, *just before* the end of *this* world—*this* age—*this* man-built society rejecting the laws and ways of God—His very *same* Gospel of God's Kingdom "shall be

> preached" (Matthew 24:14) and also *published* (Mark 13:10) "in all the world for a witness unto all nations."[38]

Now "the 'true way' is being heard or read by more than 150 millions, worldwide. Untold thousands of human lives have been changed, enriched, made more useful and happy."[39] Ultimately, he predicts, "This 'Work' will finally result in not only *changing the world*, but also in *saving the world*!"[40]

Armstrong is unaffected by scholarly criticism of his reading of the history of Christianity, which focuses on him and his "Work" as its grand climax—just before the end. Indeed one era of church history remains—the Laodicean era. Christ admonished the church of Laodicea:

> "I know your works; you are neither cold nor hot. Would that you were cold or hot! So, because you are lukewarm, and neither cold nor hot, I will spew you out of my mouth. For you say, I am rich, I have prospered, and I need nothing; not knowing that you are wretched, pitiable, poor, blind and naked" (Rev. 3:15-17).

Laodicea symbolizes soft, luxurious, complacent living. It was only natural that such a climate would breed "some famous *Skeptic* philosophers!" A pagan temple and "a great *medical* school" were located near the ancient city of Laodicea. It follows, Armstrong surmises, that "the *modern* 'Laodiceans' will be products of this *modern* age of skepticism, unbelief, creature comforts, medicine and permissiveness."[41] Only through their suffering in the Great Tribulation will they be "finally shaken out of their lukewarmness."

What will be the fate of "God's people" when the Tribulation comes? Most of them will be taken to a place of refuge in the wilderness, probably "southeast of Jerusalem . . . beyond the Dead Sea."[42] A "remnant" will be left behind to maintain the lukewarm witness of the Laodicean era, which will last perhaps three-and-a-half years.

The time is short. The call to "the true Church of God" is to faithfulness in fulfilling its mission. Young men must be prepared for God's ministry. Just as in the time of Elijah there were three schools for training the "sons of the prophets," "it is significant that today the Philadelphia Era of God's Church trains students on *three* campuses!"[43] The awful responsibility of the Worldwide Church of God in these latter days is to prepare those who can reach the world with the good news of God's coming Kingdom. No wonder the urgency of this task is repeatedly impressed on the membership: "Think how much depends on you—on *your* prayers—*your* efforts—*your* tithes and offerings!"[44]

FIVE:

"The United States and British Commonwealth in Prophecy"

"The events prophesied to strike the American and British peoples in the next four to seven years are sure! That is why events of the next four to seven years may prove this to be the most significant book of this century." So stated Herbert W. Armstrong in the introduction to the 1967 edition of *The United States and British Commonwealth in Prophecy*. The failure of these events to materialize on schedule resulted in the substitution of the word "several" for "four to seven" in the 1972 edition.

The importance of British-Israelism to Armstrong's theology is clear from his own writings, and is recognized in a number of books written about the Worldwide Church of God.[1] It is Armstrong's contention that the gospel of Jesus Christ was not preached to all the world from the year 69 until its proclamation on "The World Tomorrow" beginning in January 1934. He claims to have rediscovered the "lost master key" that alone can unlock the meaning of that third of the Bible classifiable as prophecy, ninety per cent of which relates to the latter half of the twentieth century.[2] "The one central master key to prophecies as a whole is *the identity of the United States and the British nations* in these prophecies for today!"[3] The clear implication is that the so-called master key was divinely revealed to Armstrong—and to him alone. Roger Chambers tells of hearing Garner Ted on a broadcast "shrug off the charge that he was preaching British-Israelism with a 'whatever that is,' "[4] conveying the impression that British-Israelism was completely unfamiliar to him, and that his father's "master key" doctrine is in no way related to or derived from it.

Armstrong's claim to be *the* latter-day prophet to whom has been revealed the long-hidden secret of the identity of the "Lost Ten Tribes" collapses under the most superficial examination. Decades before Armstrong's "master key" announcement, disciples already in possession of it numbered approximately two million in Great Britain and the United States. According to *The Encyclopedia of Religion and Ethics*,

> The earliest suggestions of an Israelitish ancestry of the English are to be found in John Sadler's *Rights of the Kingdom* (1649). . . . The modern movement owes its foundation to Richard Brothers (1757-1824), a half-pay officer of eccentric habits in the English navy. . . . He described himself as a "nephew of the Almighty," and claimed descent from David.[5]

The author of fifteen volumes on the subject, Brothers prophesied "imminent restoration of Israel to the Holy Land, and the elevation of himself as prince of the Hebrews and the ruler of the world." Not surprisingly, "in July, 1795, he was committed to an insane asylum, after demanding that King George III surrender the crown to him, and he died in obscure poverty in 1824."[6]

Although Armstrong does not acknowledge dependence on other sources in *The United States and British Commonwealth in Prophecy*, he admits in his autobiography that it was only "after exhaustive study and research" that he "found it proved that the so-called 'Lost Ten Tribes' of Israel had migrated to northwestern Europe, the British Isles, and later the U.S."[7] Prior to his "discovery" a letter from an unnamed man in Florida first acquainted him with the tradition. The "study and research" whereby he "proved" the theory to be "true" evidently focused on a 1917 edition of J. H. Allen's *Judah's Sceptre and Joseph's Birthright*, first published in 1902. The volume is stocked at the Ambassador College bookstores. There is a close correspondence between Armstrong and Allen. Some material has been rearranged, abbreviated, or expanded; but the basic outline is followed to such a degree as to make it unlikely in the extreme that the latter source was written independently of the former.

The heyday of British-Israelism was nineteenth-century England. Britain's far-flung colonial possessions gave rise to the boast that the sun never set on the British Empire. During that era, Armstrong observes, "the British and American peoples had acquired more than two thirds—almost three fourths—of all the cultivated physical resources and wealth of the world!"[8] But in the aftermath of two world wars, as Britain's wealth and influence declined, British-Israelism also waned. The rug had been pulled out from under the theory that Great Britain, as *Ephraim redivivus*, was divinely destined to dominate the kingdoms of the world. In order for the legend to survive, a new vitality had to be injected. Ephraim must give way to Manasseh (the United States). Both, ultimately, had to go down to oblivion at the hands of a German-led United States of Europe, within "four to seven years" of 1967. "The United States," Armstrong says gloomily, "has won *her last war*—even little North Vietnam holds her at bay, and, with many other nations, *saps America's national strength* . . . as God long ago foretold!"[9]

The United States and British Commonwealth in Prophecy, Armstrong's exposition of his "master key," indulges in unwarranted assumptions, exaggerations, misstatements, dubious interpretations of Scripture, and imaginative speculations. Its racist tone is never far beneath the surface, as in Armstrong's remark early in the book that "our white, English-speaking peoples—*not* the Jews—have inherited the national and physical phases of [God's covenant] promises!"[10]

In the remainder of this chapter we shall examine some of the strange contentions in which Armstrong indulges himself in this book.

1. Armstrong points to the covenant promise to Abraham, who would be the "father of *many* nations" (Gen. 17:4). The Jews, he says, "have never been more than *one nation*. . . . So here is an amazing prophecy . . . that could not be fulfilled in Christ, in Christians, nor in the Jews. We must look for a number of nations apart from either the

Church or the Jews."[11] But (as Armstrong himself admits) the Jews are *not* the only nation to descend from Abraham. Abraham's son Ishmael was the progenitor of the Arabs, who themselves are divided into "many nations." Furthermore, Genesis 25 reports that Abraham sired six additional sons, at least one of whom, Midian, fathered a great desert tribe. During the loosely structured days of the Judges, when the Israelites had no central government, each of the twelve tribes could, in a sense, be viewed as a separate nation—corresponding to the seven Canaanite nations which inhabited the Promised Land at the time of the Conquest. Following the death of Solomon the one nation of Israel became two. The "many nations" prophecy hardly requires linking Abraham with the peoples of northern Europe, England, and America to vindicate God's promise.

2. Quoting Genesis 15:18, which defines the limits of the land promised to Abraham, Armstrong identifies the "river of Egypt" as the Nile. It is accepted by students of the Bible that the river of Egypt here "was not an Egyptian stream at all, but a little desert stream near the borderland of Egypt, a *wady* of the desert, and, perhaps, the dividing line between Canaan and Egypt."[12] The error is perhaps trivial, but it is an illustration of carelessness that hardly befits one who makes the interpretative claims Armstrong does. He goes on to quote Genesis 28:14, in which Jacob is promised that his seed would spread "abroad to the west, and to the east, and to the north, and to the south," as evidence that the Promised Land was to extend far beyond the limits of Canaan. The assumption is entirely without justification. The geographical boundaries of Abraham's inheritance are given precisely in Genesis 15:18, and that promise was fulfilled to the letter when David conquered all the territory between the river of Egypt and the Euphrates (I Chron. 18).

3. To justify further the interpretation of biblical prophecies in terms of the British Commonwealth, Armstrong points to the prediction that Abraham's seed would become as numerous as "the grains of sand on a seashore, and . . . the stars—uncountable for multitude."[13] But even

prior to the conquest of Canaan Moses had told Israel, "The Lord your God has multiplied you, and behold, you are *this day* as the stars of heaven for multitude" (Deut. 1:10). In the time of Solomon, their numbers having greatly increased, "Judah and Israel were as many as the sand of the sea" (I Kings 4:20). And Isaiah wrote:

> O that you had hearkened to my commandments!
> Then your peace would have been like a river,
> and your righteousness like the waves of the sea;
> your offspring would have been like the sand,
> and your descendants like its grains;
> their name would never be cut off
> or destroyed from before me (48:18f.).

The Lord is here reminding Judah that his promises are not unconditional but contingent. It is unnecessary to postulate the many additional nations, lands, and millions of people assumed by Armstrong in order to validate the promises made to Abraham and his descendants.

4. Armstrong reads Genesis 24:60 — "And they blessed Rebekah, and said to her, 'Our sister, be the mother of thousands of ten thousands; and may your descendants possess the gate of those who hate them' " — as a prophecy that the nations who descend from Abraham will possess the gates of their enemies. "A gate," he explains, "is a narrow passage of entrance or exit. When speaking nationally, a 'gate' would be such a pass as the Panama Canal, the Suez Canal, the Strait of Gibraltar."[14] There is no reason whatever to believe that these words — spoken by Rebekah's brother and mother as a blessing prior to her departure to marry Isaac — were intended as divine prophecy. And the word "gate" (Hebrew, *shaar*) means precisely the gate of a city, which was especially vulnerable to attack. "To 'possess the gate' was to possess the city." [15] By Armstrong's account, the fulfilment of this prophecy "is a test of the inspiration of the Bible and of God's power to rule this world!"[16] A more likely view is that the credibility of Armstrong's interpretation, not of the Bible, is at stake.

5. Armstrong sees a sharp distinction between the *sceptre* promise given by Jacob to his son Judah and the *birthright* promise to Joseph and his sons.

> The *spiritual* promises—the promise of the "*one* seed," Christ, and of salvation through Him—the Bible calls "the sceptre." But the *material* and *national* promises relating to many nations, national wealth, prosperity and power, and possession of the Holy Land, the Bible calls the "birthright." . . . The astonishing truth . . . [is] that the Birthright promises were never given to the Jews![17]

Armstrong believes that only the descendants of Judah are Jews. The sceptre, it is said, will not depart from Judah (Gen. 49:10), but the birthright is Joseph's (I Chron. 5:2). "This knowledge about the birthright is the pivot of this entire truth which will prove the key to the understanding of all prophecy!"[18]

The birthright had been denied Ishmael, spurned by Esau, forfeited by Reuben. Finally it was conferred on Joseph, and thence to his sons Ephraim and Manasseh. Ephraim, the younger, was to receive the superior blessing. As quoted by Armstrong from the King James Version, Jacob's prophecy in Genesis 48:19 reads, " 'he [Manasseh] *also shall become a people, and he also shall be great:* but truly *his younger brother shall be greater than he*, and his seed shall become a multitude (or company) of nations.' "[19] Armstrong reads into this prophecy the coming to pass of the British Commonwealth (Ephraim—the "company of nations") and the United States (Manasseh—the "great single nation"), for, he says, "these promises never were fulfilled . . . in times of Bible history."[20]

But Joshua 21:45 states that God delivered the land of Canaan into the hands of the Israelites, and that "not one of all the good promises which the Lord had made to the house of Israel had failed; all came to pass." Manasseh did become a great people, with more territory allotted to it than to any other tribe. Ephraim did become greater than Manasseh, and rivaled Judah for supremacy. The northern kingdom of Israel was often referred to as Ephraim—37 times in the prophecy of Hosea. And since cities in patriarchal times were considered nations, it can truly be said that Ephraim fathered a "company of nations."

6. In unraveling the mystery of the lost Ten Tribes Armstrong often insists that "while all Jews are Israelites, most Israelites are *not Jews*!"[21] Biblical support for this

idea he finds in Genesis 48:16. Blessing the sons of Joseph, Jacob says, "Let my name be named on them. . . ." Since Jacob's name had been changed to Israel, the assumption is that Jacob was thus conferring the name Israel on Joseph's sons Ephraim and Manasseh. But this isolates a portion of a single verse from its context and so subverts the intended meaning. The full sentence reads, "Let my name be named on them, *and the name of my fathers Abraham and Isaac*; and let them grow into a multitude in the midst of the earth." The blessing included not only the name of Jacob or Israel, but the names of Abraham and Isaac as well. In other words, Joseph's sons were now to be accepted as Jacob's sons, to become beneficiaries of the blessings promised by the Lord to Abraham, Isaac, Jacob, and their descendants.

Why such emphasis on this seemingly minor point? Because Armstrong's theory demands that the "real Israel" of today — the British Commonwealth and the United States — be identified with Ephraim and Manasseh, which he considers to be separate tribes, cut off entirely from their southern cousins in Judah. These tribes, he says, were deported to Assyria in 721 B.C., where they were removed from all contact with their kinsmen from Judah (the Jews). Lost to history for hundreds of years, they nonetheless retained their national identity and reappeared as the Saxons of northern Europe, who invaded the British Isles and then divided, Ephraim remaining in Britain, Manasseh migrating to America.

History, including that found in the Old Testament, is not kind to this hypothesis. Consider some of the evidence. Soon after the division of the kingdoms, King Jeroboam I instituted idol worship. The Levites soon left his realm and joined the southern kingdom of Judah, as did "those who had set their hearts to seek the Lord God of Israel . . . *from all the tribes of Israel*" (II Chron. 11:16). A similar migration when Asa was king of Judah is recorded in II Chronicles 15:8-9, this time specifically mentioning persons from Ephraim and Manasseh.

Nor is it the case that the entire population of the northern kingdom was removed to Assyria during the captivity. The Assyrian conqueror Sargon weakened the nation of Israel by exiling its leadership and mixing with the native population immigrants from other lands he had conquered (II Kings 17:24). The best available evidence would suggest that about two per cent of the Israelites were actually removed to the land of Assyria. Sargon's Display Inscription claims that he led away 27,290 captives after the fall of Samaria.[22] During the religious reforms of Hezekiah, king of Judah, some years after the Assyrian conquest, letters were sent "to Ephraim and Manasseh, that they should come to the house of the Lord at Jerusalem" (II Chron. 30:1). During Josiah's reforms, a hundred years later, the Passover was celebrated nationally, and the celebrants included some from Israel (II Chron. 35:18).

Armstrong arbitrarily denies the judgment of numerous reputable scholars about the Samaritans of Jesus' day: that they were "a people of mixed origins, composed of the peoples brought by the conqueror from Babylon and elsewhere to take the place of the expatriated Israelites and those who were left in the land."[23]

It is unlikely (but required by Armstrong's view) that the exiles from Judah, beginning in 605 B.C., had no contact with the descendants of the exiles from Israel deported by Assyria. The notion that the ten tribes had been "lost" (as early as the days of Daniel, according to Armstrong), comes from the noncanonical and nonhistorical book of II Esdras. When Nebuchadnezzar conquered Nineveh, the Assyrian capital, in 612 B.C., and defeated Egypt in 605 B.C., Babylon gained control of the entire Fertile Crescent, including what had been Assyria. There is no reason to suppose that the Israelite captives were segregated from those transplanted from the kingdom of Judah. When Cyrus allowed the exiles to return seventy years later, Armstrong contends — without any basis — that his decree applied only to refugees from the southern kingdom.[24]

The words "Jew" and "Israelite" are used synonymously in the later books of the Old Testament. Isaiah 48 begins, "Hear this, O house of Jacob, who are called by the name of Israel, and who came forth from the loins of

Judah. . . ." Ezekiel, the exiled prophet from Judah, is told by the Lord to bring a message to his fellow-exiles—the "house of Israel" (3:4-6). Likewise, in the New Testament, the word "Jew" appears 174 times, "Israel" 75, with no difference in meaning or reference. The cumulative evidence makes it clear that the term Jew does not always connote membership in the tribe of Judah—nor does the word Israel uniformly signify descent from one of the ten northern tribes.

7. Armstrong's speculations about Esau and the tribe of Edom which he fathered, depend on the King James Version of Genesis 25:23, where God prophesies to Rebekah about her unborn sons. His case is built on a faulty translation of the Hebrew. "And the Lord said unto her, Two nations are in thy womb, and *two manner of people* shall be separated from thy bowels; and the one people shall be stronger than the other people; and the elder shall serve the younger." Armstrong interprets, "Their descendants, then, were to become two different manner of people. Esau was hairy and red, but Jacob was white (verse 25)."[25] The mistranslation is corrected in both the American Standard and Revised Standard Versions, where "two manner of people" becomes "two peoples." Armstrong's description of Esau as "hairy and red" accords with all three translations, but (despite his parenthetical reference to verse 25) there is no textual evidence whatever for describing Jacob as "white." The implication is that Isaac's two sons had different racial characteristics. Obviously both infants, being Semitic, bore the same racial traits. By noting that Esau was "hairy and red," Genesis 25 in no way implies that Jacob was racially identical to the white Anglo-Saxon "Israelites" of later generations. If anything, it is likely that Jacob was darker than his brother, since red skin would suggest a fairer complexion than usual for the normally swarthy Semites.

Armstrong understands prophecies that use the name Edom as referring to the Turkish nation of today. He claims that "the sparse records of history, with other proofs, show that many of the descendants of Esau became known as Turks."[26] Later he reminds the reader that the Turks occupied Palestine for four hundred years before 1917, when the British took over. "Esau's descendants always have lusted for that land, central promise of the Birthright! The Turks have truly lived by the sword!"[27]

If the ancestry of the Turks is indeed traceable to Esau, the burden of proof rests on Armstrong, who offers not so much as a hint about those "sparse records of history, with other proofs" that support his thesis. Reliable and accepted historical records attest that the Edomites inhabited the wild desert country south of Palestine until 300 B.C. Moving northward, they occupied southern Judah, which became known by the Greek name *Idumea.*

> Hebron, their chief city, was taken by Judas Maccabaeus in 165 B.C. . . . Antipater, governor of Idumaea, was made procurator of Judea, Samaria, and Galilee by Julius Caesar. He paved the way to the throne for his son Herod the Great. With the fall of Judah under the Romans, Idumaea disappears from history.[28]

8. The prophet Jeremiah played an important role in transplanting Judah's "sceptre" from Jerusalem to Ireland, Armstrong believes. The crux of this argument is Jeremiah 1:10, rendered with typical Armstrong emphasis, " 'See,' said God, 'I have set you this day *over nations* and over kingdoms, *to pluck up and to break down, to destroy and to overthrow, to build and to plant.*' "[29] Referring to the prophecy that the Davidic dynasty was "to continue through all generations forever," he declares,

> The faithfulness of God is at stake. The inspiration of the Holy Bible as His revealed Word is at stake. But note it!—see it in your own Bible!—Jeremiah was divinely commissioned to pull down, and to overthrow that very throne of David in Judah—but notice the second half of the commission . . . to build and to plant! To build and to plant what? Why, naturally, that which he was used in "rooting out" of Judah—the throne of David which God swore He would preserve forever.[30]

As Armstrong sees it, "that throne was divinely commissioned to be planted and rebuilt by the prophet Jeremiah—during his lifetime!"[31] Matthew Henry, taking the verse in its context, discovers an entirely different meaning—one that relates to the local situation at that particular moment in history:

> He [Jeremiah] must attempt to reform the nations, to *root out, and pull down, and destroy* idolatry and other wickednesses among them, to extirpate those vicious habits and customs which had long taken root, to *throw down* the kingdom of sin, that religion and virtue might be *planted* and *built* among them. . . . He must assure those who persisted in their wickedness that they should be *rooted out and destroyed*, and those who repented that they should be *built* and *planted.*[32]

It is entirely possible, of course, that more is intended than Henry's interpretation would indicate. Jeremiah *did* predict the overthrow of Judah—and Judah's future restoration. But there is nothing in Jeremiah's prophecy to support the theory that the throne of David was to be moved to another geographical location.

At the fall of Jerusalem and exile to Babylon in 586 B.C., Jeremiah decided to remain with those left behind in Judah. When Gedaliah, Nebuchadnezzar's appointed governor of Judah, was assassinated, a delegation of Jewish leaders headed by Johanan came to Jeremiah for God's direction. His advice was to remain in the land, where no harm would befall them. If they sought refuge in Egypt, he said, they would be destroyed by "sword, famine, and pestilence" (Jeremiah 42:22). Rejecting the word of the Lord, the commanders took "all the remnant of Judah," including Jeremiah and his scribe Baruch, and fled to Egypt. Jeremiah's eventual fate at the hands of the pursuing Babylonian army is unknown. Some early church fathers report "that he was stoned to death at Daphne by the Jews. . . . However, this report is not well founded. The same is the case with the rabbinical tradition, according to which he, in company with Baruch, was taken from Egypt to Babylon by Nebuchadnezzar, and died there."[33]

On the basis of the flimsiest of evidence, Armstrong tries to prove that Jeremiah and Baruch escaped from Egypt with one of the daughters of Zedekiah (last king of Judah) and returned to Judah. There the royal princess married "the son of the king of Ireland who had been in Jerusalem at the time of the siege." Their son accompanied them—including Jeremiah and Baruch—to Ireland.[34]

To defend his noncanonical sequel to Jeremiah, Armstrong calls on two witnesses—the Scriptures and the "ancient annals of Ireland." Among the Jewish remnant taken to Egypt by Johanan were "the king's daughters" (Jer. 43:6). Jeremiah had prophesied that a few would return from Egypt to Judah (44:28); and Isaiah had earlier revealed that "the remnant that escaped of the house of Judah shall again take root downward and bear fruit upward" (37:32, 31). Armstrong comments, "This, indeed, is thrilling! This remnant with Jeremiah—at least one of the king's daughters—shall *take root downward!* That is, be replanted! And then *bear fruit upward!* Be builded!"[35] Thus Armstrong tries, by reversing the order of verses 31 and 32, to make it appear that the "rooting downward" and "bearing fruit upward" were to occur after the remnant had gone from Jerusalem, and in so doing to establish that the legend of Jeremiah's migration to Ireland is rooted in inspired prophecy.

Another passage Armstrong cites is the parable in Ezekiel 17, which he claims had never been understood until his "master key" unlocked the symbols:

> Thus says the Lord God: "I myself will take a sprig from the lofty top of the cedar, and will set it out; I will break off from the topmost of its young twigs a tender one, and I myself will plant it upon a high and lofty mountain; on the mountain heights of Israel will I plant it, that it may bring forth boughs and bear fruit, and become a noble cedar; and under it will dwell all kinds of beasts; in the shade of its branches birds of every sort will nest (vv. 22f.)

Most commentators take the cedar allegory to be messianic. The Lord himself would break off a tender branch (the Messiah) and plant it on a high mountain in Israel (Zion). There it would grow into a mighty cedar (the messianic kingdom) and provide shelter for all varieties of beasts and birds (mankind). Armstrong, however, notes that the chapter opens with the Lord's instruction to Ezekiel to address these allegories to the house of Israel (vs. 2). This identification, he asserts, can *only* refer to "Ten-Tribed Israel."[36] Quoting from the King James Version, he singles out verse 22 for particular comment:

"I will crop off from the top of his young twigs a *tender* one, and will plant it upon a high mountain and eminent," continues the Almighty! Ah! "A tender young twig"! The twigs of this highest branch represent the children of King Zedekiah! Certainly a tender young twig, then, represents a daughter! " . . . and will plant it." Could symbolic language say plainer this young Jewish Princess is to become the royal seed for planting again of David's throne? Where? " . . . upon a high mountain and eminent," says the Eternal! A "mountain" in symbol always represents a nation. "In the mountain of the height of Israel will I plant it," answers the Eternal! David's throne now is to be planted in Israel, after being thrown down from Judah! Could language be plainer?[37]

"Israel," he insists, could not possibly refer to "Judah." Long before the "Mysterious Commission" of Jeremiah, "lost" Israel had migrated northwestward across Europe to the British Isles—so now *that* nation had become *Israel.* Armstrong even goes so far as to say that at the time of Ezekiel's prophecy, "Israel had already been independent in Ireland for centuries. . . . Israel in Ireland had already a kingly line onto which Zedekiah's daughter was grafted. . . . The Irish Israelites were an ancient colony and had not gone into Assyrian captivity."[38]

Armstrong seeks support for this supposition not only in Scripture but in ancient Irish annals. From this extensive material, Armstrong sifts out the "legendary" by keeping "the facts of Biblical history and prophecy in mind."[39]

Long prior to 700 B.C., a strong colony called "Tautha de Danaan" (tribe of Dan) arrived in ships, drove out other tribes, and settled there. . . .

Then, in 569 B.C., an elderly, white-haired patriarch, sometimes referred to as a "saint," came to Ireland. With him was the princess daughter of an eastern king and a companion called "Simon Brach," spelled in different histories as "Breck," "Berech," "Brach," or "Berach." The princess had a Hebrew name "Tephi"—a pet name, her full name being "Tea-Tephi."[40]

The royal party included the son of the king of Ireland, who had married the Hebrew princess in Jerusalem, and their twelve-year-old son.

Beside the royal family, Jeremiah brought with them some remarkable things, including a harp, an ark, and a wonderful stone called "lia-fail," or "stone of destiny." A peculiar coincidence (?) is that Hebrew reads from right to left, while English reads from left to right. Read this name either way—and it still is "lia-fail."

Another strange coincidence—or *is* it just coincidence?—is that many kings in the history of Ireland, Scotland, and England have been coronated sitting over this stone—including the present queen. The stone rests, today, in Westminster Abbey in London, and the Coronation Chair is built over and around it. A sign beside it labels it "Jacob's pillar-stone" (Genesis 28:18).[41]

The stone referred to is that used by Jacob as a pillow at Bethel during his flight from Esau; as he slept he beheld the vision of a heavenly ladder. When he awoke "he took the stone which he had put under his head and set it up for a pillar and poured oil on the top of it" (Gen. 28:18). There is no biblical evidence for the removal of this stone from Bethel. Furthermore, according to *The New Century Dictionary*, "The Stone of Scone [is] a famous stone, formerly at Scone, Scotland, upon which the Scottish kings sat at coronation: now beneath the coronation chair in Westminster Abbey."[42] After examination of the stone in 1865, Professor A. C. Ramsey of the Geology Department of London University described it as "calcerous sandstone of a reddish or purplish colour and (containing) heterogeneous pebbles" and judged it to be of Scottish origin. "This report has been confirmed by every subsequent examination by reputable geologists."[43]

9. Another flight of Armstrong fancy has to do with "the Hebrew meaning of the names of the British people."

The Hebrew word for "covenant" is *beriyth*, or *berith*. . . . The Hebrew for "man" is *iysh*, or *ish*. . . . In the original Hebrew language vowels were never given in the spelling. So, omitting the vowel "e" from *berith*, but retaining the "i" in its Anglicized form to preserve the "y" sound, we have the Anglicized Hebrew word for covenant, *brith*. The Hebrews, however, never pronounced their "h's." . . . So the Hebrew word for "covenant" would be pronounced . . . *brit*. And the word for "covenant man," or "covenant people," would, therefore, be simply, "Brit-Ish." And so is it mere coincidence that the true covenant people today *are called the* "British"?[44]

Since the Lord told Abraham, "In Isaac shall thy seed be called," it does not surprise Armstrong that the latter-day

Israelites (dropping the "I," since vowels are not used in the Hebrew spelling) should be called "Saac's sons," or in shortened form, "Saxons!"[45]

According to Ernest Klein "Britain" is derived from the Old English word *Bret*, and is of Celtic origin. "Saxon" is from the Old High German *sahs*, meaning "knife, short sword, dagger." Saxons were "those armed with knives."[46] Anglo-Israel philological speculations are ingenious, but utterly devoid of etymological and symbolical significance.

10. The tribe of Dan is alleged by Armstrong to have left "waymarks" along the road from Assyria to the British Isles. The prophetical basis for this phenomenon is the Armstrong reading of Genesis 49:17: "Dan shall be a serpent's trail." "Trail," he volunteers, is "another translation of the original Hebrew"[47]—a translation not supported by a single English version. The verse reads, in the RSV,

> Dan shall be a serpent in the way,
> a viper by the path,
> that bites the horse's heels
> so that his rider falls backward.

Dan was to be a subtle and menacing foe to his enemies. But there is not the slightest hint that Dan would blaze a serpentine trail to a distant destination.

"It is a significant fact," Armstrong says, "that the tribe of Dan . . . named every place they went after their father, Dan." He reminds the reader again that vowels are not included in the spelling of Hebrew words; thus the English equivalent could be found in any name with the combination "Dn," "Dan," "Den," "Din," "Don," or "Dun."[48] Given that principle, he finds reminders of Danite occupation throughout Europe—"*Dans*-Laugh," "*Dan*-Sower," "*Dun*-dalke," "*Dun*-drum," "*Don*-egal Bay," "*Don*-egal City," "*Dun*-glow," "Lon-*don*-derry," "*Din*-gle," "*Duns*-more."[49] The Danites who had moved to northern Israel early in their history migrated northwestward from Assyria, leaving such "waymarks" as the "*Dn*ieper,"

"*Dn*iester," and "*Don*" (he apparently overlooks the *Dan*-ube) rivers, and so on to "*Den*mark" ("Dan's Mark"). This branch of the tribe of Dan made their way to Scotland, where "they set up the 'waymark' names of *Dun*-dee and *Dun*-raven."[50]

Even if it could be established that the "D-n" places were authentic "waymarks" of the Danites, the question would remain, What bearing does all this have on the destiny and identity of the "Anglo-Saxon" tribes of Ephraim and Manasseh?

11. Exegesis of the King James Version of Ezekiel 21:27 enables Armstrong to find further proof of British-Israelism. The chapter begins with the Lord's instruction to Ezekiel to prophesy against "the land of Israel." The prophecy, of course, concerns *Judah*, since the northern kingdom had long since gone down the drain, and the terms Judah and Israel had come to be used interchangeably. The "prince of Israel" mentioned in verse 25 is really the king of Judah, Zedekiah: for it was he who reigned during the time of Ezekiel's prophecy. The crucial verses (25-27) are:

> And you, O unhallowed wicked one, prince of Israel, whose day has come, the time of your final punishment, thus says the Lord God: Remove the turban, and take off the crown; things shall not remain as they are; exalt that which is low, and abase that which is high. A ruin, ruin, ruin I will make it; there shall not be even a trace of it until he comes whose right it is; and to him I will give it.

Armstrong, for reasons that will be clear, prefers the King James "overturn" to the RSV "ruin" in verse 27: "I will overturn, overturn, overturn it: and it shall be no more, until he come whose right it is. . . ." "What was to be overturned?" he asks. "The diadem, and the throne. Not once, it is to be overturned three times."[51] This does not mean, he says, that the crown will cease to exist, but refers to its transfer from Israel to Ireland to Scotland to London. Thus, when "Christ returns to earth to sit on that throne, He shall take over a live, existing throne, not a nonexistent one (Luke 1:32)."[52]

But clearly Ezekiel 21:25-27 means—whether the word

"overturn" or "ruin" is used in the translation—that Zedekiah's throne was to be *overthrown*—cut off without a trace—until the coming of the Messiah, when it would be restored. As a look at the *Oxford English Dictionary* will show, "overturn" meant, for the King James translators, "destroy," and it is repeated three times for emphasis.

12. British-Israelism is further supported by Psalm 89:3-4, which is taken as proof that David's throne was to continue without interruption until the coming of Christ:

> I have made a covenant with my chosen one,
> I have sworn to David my servant:
> I will establish your descendants forever,
> and build your throne for all generations.

"All generations" Armstrong takes to include those between Zedekiah and the birth of Christ. This he offers as rationale for the continuous existence of David's throne. "If the throne of David ceased with Zedekiah," he reasons, "then it does not exist today. And if it does not exist, *how shall Christ sit upon a nonexistent throne?*"[53]

But Acts 15:16, quoting from Amos 9:11, clearly refers to "the dwelling of David, which has *fallen*." Moreover, God's promises are contingent on the obedience of those to whom they are given. And within a generation of the promise of David that his throne would endure "to all generations," the Lord qualified that prophecy in these words to Solomon,

> If you turn aside from following me, you or your children, and do not keep my commandments and my statutes which I have set before you, but go and serve other gods and worship them, then I will cut off Israel from the land which I have given them; and the house which I have consecrated for my name I will cast out of my sight (I Kings 9:6-7).

Solomon failed to meet these conditions, the promised blessing was revoked, and the dire consequences of his apostasy were imposed on Israel. The premise that Christ could not (in his first coming) and cannot (in his second coming) "sit upon a nonexistent throne" is thus refuted. Christ's power to rule is in no way dependent upon the presence of a Davidic king sitting upon a man-made throne at the time of his coming to establish his reign.

13. When Jacob blessed Joseph's sons, the aged patriarch crossed his hands so as to place the right hand of superior blessing on the head of the younger brother Ephraim. Joseph objected, but his father insisted: "I know, my son, I know; he [Manasseh] also shall become a people, and he also shall be great; nevertheless his younger brother shall be greater than he, and his descendants shall become a multitude of nations" (Gen. 48:19). Armstrong prefers the word "commonwealth" to "multitude," in support of the theory that Ephraim eventually became the British Commonwealth. "The proof that we [the United States] are Manasseh is overwhelming," he avers. "Manasseh was to separate from Ephraim and become the greatest, wealthiest single nation of earth's history. We alone have fulfilled this prophecy. Manasseh was, in fact, a *thirteenth* tribe. . . . Could it be mere coincidence that it *started*, as a nation, with thirteen colonies?"[54] The coincidence is, of course, just that—even on Armstrong's terms; for his claim is not that the thirteen colonies represented all the tribes (eleven sons of Jacob and two of Joseph), but only Manasseh.

The notion that Manasseh was to become "the greatest, wealthiest single nation of earth's history" is Armstrong's way to circumvent the prediction that Ephraim would be greater than Manasseh. Britain's loss of vast colonial possessions is a source of considerable embarrassment to the British-Israel movement.

To say the least, it is odd to believe that captive Israel retained its individual tribal identities and that the bulk of Joseph's descendants are Anglo-Saxons, who populated the British Isles. There is no evidence that such a tribal separation between Ephraimites and Manassehites was involved in the 17th- and 18th-century migrations of British citizens to North America. And what of the host of immigrants from every nation in the world? The mingling of these peoples with the Anglo-Saxon settlers to make America a "melting pot" does *not* invalidate the Manasseh theory, Armstrong argues, but confirms it.[55] Did not Israel make a practice of absorbing Gentiles, "who became Israelites through living in Israel's land and intermarrying"? Did not Amos prophesy, "For, lo, I will command, and I will sift the house of Israel among all nations, like as corn is sifted in a sieve, yet shall not the least grain fall upon the earth" (Amos 9:9, KVJ)?

> Many . . . of Manasseh who had filtered into and through other nations did not leave them until they came, as immigrants, to the United States after the New England colony had become the separate nation. This does not mean that *all* foreigners who have immigrated into this country are of the stock of Manasseh, but undoubtedly many are.[56]

Additionally, "there is ample evidence" (none of which is produced) that the other eight tribes inhabited "such northwestern European nations as Holland, Belgium, Denmark, northern France, Luxembourg, Switzerland, Sweden, Norway. The people of Iceland are also of Viking stock."[57] "The tribe of Reuben settled in the country that is France today."[58]

14. Why were the birthright promises made to Israel withheld for so long? Why was it not until about 1800 that Britain and the United States came into prominence in fulfilment of the blessing of Jacob? The clue is in Leviticus 26. This chapter teaches the consequences of Israel's obedience and disobedience: "If you will not hearken to me, and will not do all these commandments . . . I will do this to you: I will appoint over you sudden terror . . ." (Lev. 26:14-16). Three times (vv. 18, 24, 28) a "sevenfold" punishment is pronounced. Following the King James Version, Armstrong interprets "sevenfold" as "seven times," and asserts that the "seven times" means seven "prophetic 360-day year" periods. Instead of seeing the Lord's chastisement as sevenfold in intensity, which the context suggests, Armstrong multiplies seven times the 360-day prophetic year to arrive at a figure of 2520 days of punishment. Interpreting each "day" as a year, he postulates a period of withheld promises dating from the Israelite exile in 721 B.C. to about the year A.D. 1800. Beginning in that year, Armstrong recounts,

> God did cause the Birthright nations [Ephraim and Manasseh]—and them *only*—to become *suddenly* the recipients of such national wealth, greatness and power *as no nation or empire ever before had acquired!* Together then—the British and Americans, descendants of only *one* original tribe, Joseph—came into possession of more than two thirds—almost three fourths—of all the cultivated resources and wealth of the whole world![59]

"It sounds incredible!" he exclaims. Indeed!

15. Armstrong goes beyond the nineteenth-century version of British-Israelism, appropriated without credit, to deal with the decline and fall of the British-American empire. "*Why* is the United States now discredited, despised, hated, throughout so much of the world? *Why* could we not *win* the Korean War? *Why* can't the United States whip little North Vietnam?"[60] His answer is that God is no longer obligated by his promise to maintain Israel's modern descendants in world domination, wealth, and greatness. Since God has kept his promise to Abraham, all future blessings are conditional and will be revoked in the event of rebellion and disobedience, as Leviticus 26 states. Indeed, the threats of that chapter are now in process of fulfilment. Great Britain is no longer great, and the United States is soon to lose her greatness. "Today even little nations dare to insult, trample on, or burn the United States flag—and the United States, *still having* power, does no more than issue a weak protest!"[61]

Continuing to unfold the mysteries of Leviticus 26, Armstrong discloses that "seven times more plagues" will fall on these nations because of their sins (vs. 21). Previously he had interpreted this phrase as 2520 years, but his eschatological timetable does not allow for 2520 more years of punishment. So the "seven times more plagues" switches suddenly to mean intensity rather than duration of punishment.

But if he has corrected one error of interpretation, he leaves another: the warnings of Leviticus 26 are clearly addressed to Old Testament Israel. Armstrong selects the verses that suit his purpose and ignores some that do not fit in at all; for example, verse 29: "You shall eat the flesh of your sons, and you shall eat the flesh of your daughters." Cannibalism seems a remote possibility for England and America, and certainly did not occur within the four to seven years that Armstrong predicted (in 1967) would see the fall of the United States. So he ignores the verse. But the prophecy did come true in the time of Elisha, when a woman in famine-ravaged Samaria boiled her son and ate him (II Kings 6:29), and during the siege of Jerusalem, as reported by Jeremiah (Lam. 2:20).

The lesson of Leviticus 26 about the consequences of sin is surely applicable to every century. But if its specific predictions apply to the twentieth century, it is capricious to pay heed only to those that fit a predetermined scheme, and to ignore the rest.

The downfall of the American and British Commonwealth peoples, predicts Armstrong, is to come at the hands of a restored Holy Roman Empire in the form of an alliance of ten European nations, whose chief instigator will be the Roman Catholic Church.[62] Scriptural foundation for this speculation is characteristically imaginative. The ten nations, of course, come from Revelation 17. Significance is attached to the phrase "daughter of Babylon" in Isaiah 47:1:

> Not the Babylon of ancient days. Not Nebuchadnezzar's Babylon of 600 years before Christ—but a daughter of that Babylon, now, in our 20th century. In prophecy a woman, or a daughter, means a church—a religious organization.[63]

The "lady" of this prophecy is described in Revelation 17 as a "great whore," whose name "is there given as 'mystery, Babylon the Great, the mother of harlots and abominations of the earth.' "[64]

The identity of Rome with Babylon is more than figurative, according to Armstrong. Simon the Sorcerer, rebuked by Peter for trying to buy the power of the Holy Spirit (Acts 8:18-24), was in fact, Armstrong says, the "leader of the Babylonian mystery religion, with the title of Pater or Peter, meaning Papa." This Simon "actually appropriated the name of *Christ*, and the Christian principle of grace, which he turned into license, doing away with God's law (Jude 4), started what is today called 'Christianity'." This falsely labeled religion "is not, and never was, the outgrowth of the Church of God, founded by Jesus Christ and His Apostles!"[65]

Not only did the ancient Babylonians migrate to Italy to launch the Roman Catholic Church, but Israel's ancient nemesis Assyria traveled northwestward and settled in Germany.[66] Prophecies about Assyria thus relate to Germany. Just as ancient Assyria destroyed ancient Israel, so modern Assyria, heading a ten-nation united states of Europe, will crush the United States and Britain. Why ten? Because the beast of Revelation 17 is described as having ten horns, which are explained as prefiguring "ten kings who have not yet received royal power." And so "Germany will try it once again—World War III. And this time, Germany will be allowed to succeed!"[67]

Armstrong insists that Ezekiel 6:6 ("in all your dwelling places the cities shall be laid waste") must apply to the twentieth century, because such wholesale devastation requires nuclear warfare.[68] The history and archeology of the Holy Land, however, demonstrate that from the time of the conquest on, through centuries of Old Testament history, cities were "laid waste" again and again. The Palestinian landscape is full of heaped-up ruins, called "tells," consisting of several layers of successive occupations. These tells bear silent but eloquent testimony to the ancient fulfilment of Ezekiel's prophecy—a fulfilment that did not need to await the era of the H-bomb.

The British-American nations will go down to ignominious defeat at the hands of the German-led confederacy because of their disobedience and apostasy. Chief among the manifestations of that apostasy is rejection of the Lord's appointed Sabbath. "The Sabbath Command," Armstrong points out, "is the only one of the ten which is a sign identifying who are the real and true Christians today! *It is the real test Command!*"[69] Only those who keep the seventh-day Sabbath are "God's people." But, as Richard Marson wonders, why did the Lord then restore the birthright to Anglo-Saxon Christians (modern "Israel)," who generally observe the "wrong" day of worship?[70]

"Those in the true Body of Christ" (meaning the baptized members of the Worldwide Church of God), Armstrong promises, will be removed to "a place of safety" during the Tribulation, "due to erupt in the next four to seven years."[71] Those not included in this select group are doomed to suffer the unspeakable horrors of World War III, which will *start* with nuclear devastation unleashed on London, Birmingham, Manchester, Liverpool, New York, Washington, Philadelphia, Detroit, Chicago, Pittsburgh, without warning.[72] After Armageddon, "God's people" will enter into the everlasting bliss of the newly re-created "World Tomorrow." All others, if they persist in their repudiation of the gospel, will be annihilated.

"By God's direction and authority," Armstrong admonishes, "I have laid the truth before you! To neglect it will be tragic beyond imagination! To heed it will bring blessings, happiness and glory beyond description! The decision is now yours!"[73]

SIX:

"The Wonderful World Tomorrow"

The seven days of the Genesis creation account form a microcosm of world history, Herbert W. Armstrong suggests. The first six typify six thousand years in which man is allowed to go his own way; the seventh day of rest prefigures the thousand years of Christ's rule. Creation is pinpointed at 4025 B.C. (21 years earlier than Ussher's classic date of 4004 B.C.).

By this interpretation of history, time is rapidly running out for the human race. The last generation of man is now living on planet Earth. Cataclysmic events destined to destroy the present civilization loom on the horizon. The descendants of Israel's "Lost Ten Tribes"—Great Britain, the United States, and the peoples of northwest Europe—will soon be devastated by a reconstituted Roman Empire, under the aegis of the Roman Catholic Church and headed by Germany.[1] The armies of this confederacy, after crushing their western foes, will be frightened by the threat of a Russian invasion into moving their headquarters to Palestine. There, within a few years, the terrible battle of Armageddon will transpire. Christ will intervene to destroy all wicked and rebellious nations and usher in an era of peace, prosperity, and righteousness.

Writing in 1966, the Armstrongs predicted that this "Wonderful World Tomorrow" would come to pass "in just ten or fifteen short years."[2] Even apart from biblical revelation, they warn, numerous signs of the times point to civilization's demise within the foreseeable future: air, water, and food pollution; weather changes producing droughts and floods—resulting in mass starvation and disease epidemics; the population explosion; acceleration of " 'the three L's'—Leisure, Luxury, and License"; the moral and spiritual wasteland of modern education; the failures of technological, political, and religious forces to stem the onrushing tide of crime, poverty, strife, and war.[3]

The *only* authoritative source of enlightenment concerning these end-time events is God's latter-day apostle, Herbert W. Armstrong. Introducing a lesson in the correspondence course, C. Paul Meredith writes:

> No other Bible course in this world even *dares* to reveal the future as does this Course. Why? Because only this Work—which *God* had to raise up to carry His message—dares to preach the true gospel of His Kingdom to the world as a final "*witness*" (Mat. 24:14). This Work has proven itself willing to be corrected by the Bible—and that's why only this Work really understands Bible prophecy![4]

Only the Armstrong key can unlock the meanings of mysterious passages that have baffled Bible scholars for centuries.

The seven seals of Revelation Armstrong considers to be parallels of the seven apocalyptic signs mentioned by Jesus in Matthew 24: false teaching, wars, famine, pestilence, tribulation, earthquakes, and, at the same time, the universal proclamation of the gospel. Crucial to that proclamation is the Armstrong "Work"—especially "The World Tomorrow" broadcast and *The Plain Truth* magazine.

The horrors of the end-time are predicted in considerable detail, according to Armstrong's complicated and literal reading of the visions in Revelation. A war-making revived fascist power (the locusts of Rev. 9:7), a Communist Eurasian army of 200,000,000 men (the cavalry of Rev. 9:16), and the revived Roman Empire with the false (Roman Catholic) church and her daughters (the Protestant churches of the Reformation)—all figure in this apocalyptic drama. The battle (erroneously called Armageddon)[5] of the great day of God Almighty will climax a horrendous war that will leave the earth desolate. The site will be Megiddo, northwest of Jerusalem; the immediate cause will be evil spirits emanating from the mouths of the dragon (Satan), the beast (the political leader of the revived Roman Empire), and the false prophet (the religious leader of the "United States of Europe").

Christ will return at the same time as God's final judgments are being poured out on the fornicating ecclesiastical system. Overcoming his fascist foes, Christ will establish a throne in Jerusalem and reign forever, casting the beast and the false prophet into a lake of fire.

The invasion of Palestine from the north, described in Ezekiel 38 and 39, will occur after the return of Christ, "after the Great Deliverer has come and rescued our people and restored us to Palestine. . . ."[6] By "our people" Armstrong means the members of God's one and only "True Church," the Anglo-Saxon survivors of the onslaught of the revived Holy Roman Empire, who will have been brought to Palestine "from a dispersion and captivity and slavery, gathered out of the nations where we had been scattered, now once again rich and increased with goods!"[7]

But what of this new invasion? Listen to Armstrong again: "It is conclusively proved, as *all* students of prophecy know, that 'Gog' in the land of 'Magog' is Russia. 'Meshech' is Moscow, 'Tubal' is Tobolsk. The margin says 'Prince of Rosh' which is Russia."[8] Similarly simple explanations of other prophetic symbols used by Ezekiel "prove" that Russia will be joined by Oriental allies. Armstrong concludes, from Ezekiel 38, that "it is Russia, not Japan, who shall finally succeed in marshalling all the yellow races into a gigantic invasion upon our people. . . . But our people shall not *have* to fight in that battle. We shall have learned by then that God fights our battles for us!"[9]

At Christ's coming, "the dead in Christ . . . will rise in a gigantic resurrection, made immortal. . . . Those who have the Spirit of God, then living, shall be instantaneously *changed* from mortal to immortal (I Corinthians 15:50-54), and together with those resurrected, shall rise to meet the descending glorified Christ (I Thessalonians 4:17) in the clouds in the air."[10] As immortal spiritual beings, they, under Christ, will rule the nations consisting of the mortals who remain on the earth after Christ's return.

Only those who are faithful members of "God's true Church" (i.e., the Worldwide Church of God) will be translated from mortality to immortality at Christ's coming. It is not God's purpose to save many in the present age. Christ himself "didn't try to convert everyone!"[11] The task to which he has called Armstrong and his church is not to convert but to witness. This is not the only day of salvation. The vast majority of people will have their first and only chance for salvation at a later time.[12]

Those who are in the Armstrong "Work" are the only ones to have "an absolute *guarantee* of safety" in the coming trials.[13] In fulfilment of the promise of Revelation 12:14, a wilderness retreat is being prepared in Petra, the rock-walled city of ancient Edom. To Petra, at the proper time, the Lord "will *supernaturally* bring His people" to preserve them from the genocide perpetrated on the race by the warring nations and the vengeance Christ will visit on the wicked. Thus saved, the members of the "one True Church" will be prepared to assume leadership roles in the government of the "World Tomorrow."

Already they are being trained for this purpose. "Prepare Now to be a King!" is the title of a typical *Tomorrow's World* article (November 1971). The kingdom, however, will be a government from the top (God) down. There will be no elections or political parties. All its officials will be appointed. "Some resurrected saints will rule over ten cities, some over five (Luke 19:17-19)."[14] "*All* saints will be priests and will, in *addition*, have other offices, such as rulership and judgeship."[15]

Armstrong admits that it is unclear exactly how this coming

> World Super Government will be organized. Yet He has given us the general pattern. He has told us specifically where 14 high executives (including Christ) will fit in. And from them we may deduce a great deal of the remaining governmental structure.[16]

The throne of Christ on earth will be subordinate to that of the Father in heaven. David will be resurrected as king over the twelve great nations formed from literal descendants of the tribes of Israel. Each of the twelve apostles will be a king. Abraham will outrank David, as he is the "father" of both Gentile converts and Israelites.[17] And since Abraham, Isaac, and Jacob are frequently grouped together in the Bible, it is clear to Armstrong that they "will function as a topflight team, with Abraham as 'Chairman' of the team, next under Christ in the coming world Government of God!"[18]

Church and state will be one under Christ. The organizational consequence of this is that under Christ and his top "team" (Abraham, Isaac, and Jacob), Moses will be in charge of national and international government and Elijah in charge of organized religious and educational activity.[19] Armstrong recalls that Elijah organized schools at Bethel, Jericho, and Gilgal (II Kings 2:3, 5; 4:38), which (he says) have been shown to be "not mere 'religious schools,' but full-education Liberal Arts colleges!"[20] (No hint is given as to the source of this unusual information.)

Everyone in the World Tomorrow will be prosperous, but not equally so. At the top will be the nations descended from Ephraim and Manasseh; next, the nations descended from the other tribes; finally, the Gentile nations. The king over the Gentile nations will probably be Daniel, the prophet trained for top-level government authority in the world's first great empire.[21] (Armstrong considers it "an interesting possibility" that Daniel's three friends Shadrach, Meshach, and Abednego "might serve as a team directly under him" just as Abraham, Isaac, and Jacob will serve directly under Christ.) Next in line will be Paul, the apostle to the Gentiles, aided by his co-workers Barnabas, Silas, Timothy, Titus, and Luke.

The descendants of Ephraim and Manasseh are, of course, the white Anglo-Saxons from Great Britain and the United States. Their position in the World Tomorrow will be enhanced by the policy of racial segregation that will be in effect. Administering that function in the divine government will be one uniquely experienced to deal with it—the patriarch Noah:

> In Noah's day, the chief cause of the violence and chaos of world conditions was racial hatreds, racial intermarriages, and racial

> violence caused by man's efforts toward integration and amalgamation of races, contrary to God's laws.

These difficulties previewed the "race wars, race hatreds, race riots, and race problems" that plague today's world. A better world is coming, however, through a resurrected and powerful Noah:

> Noah merely preached to people in his human lifetime. But Noah in the resurrection, immortal, in power and glory, will be given the power to enforce God's way in regard to race. . . . It seems evident that the resurrected Noah will head a vast project of the relocation of the races and nations, within the boundaries God has set. . . . This will be a tremendous operation. It will require great and vast organization, reinforced with power to move whole nations and races. This time, peoples and nations will move where God has planned for them, and no defiance will be tolerated.[22]

Armstrong does not try to reconcile this divinely ordered racial segregation with Paul's teaching that in Christ "there cannot be Greek and Jew, circumcised and uncircumcised, barbarian, Scythian, slave, free man, but Christ is all, and in all" (Col. 3:11).

Armstrong goes on to place other biblical figures in important slots. Joseph, once the leading food administrator in the world's most powerful nation, will head the economy of the World Tomorrow, wiping out poverty and hunger.[23] Job, whom Armstrong alleges (without proof) to have built for Pharaoh Khufu the Great Pyramid ("the largest and tallest building ever built on earth, until the Woolworth Building"),[24] will be director of urban renewal, assisted by Zerubbabel, the builder of Judah's Second Temple. John the Baptist will assist Christ and Elijah in ruling the church and controlling the educational system.[25]

Finally, Armstrong believes that there will be important posts for the great women of the faith—though he does not seem to have many openings left after assigning all the chief roles to men. Paradoxically, though, he asserts that women will enjoy equality with men in the World Tomorrow.[26] Sexual distinctions will be eradicated, apparently, even though racial ones remain.

When Christ returns, he will "rule all nations 'with a rod

of iron.' "[27] Rebellious mortals, under the tutelage of righteous immortals, will be *forced* into a life of obedience and submission. Satan, permitted to victimize mankind during history's first six thousand years, will be bound during the millennium. Through a program of reeducation, coupled with rigorous discipline, the World Tomorrow's mortal citizens will be compelled to live God's way of obedience, unselfishness, and happiness. "Christ will . . . *force* the world to cease from its labor of wars, sickness, heartache and death! . . . Just imagine—compulsory joy!!"[28]

The context surrounding the biblical "rod of iron" passages (Ps. 2:9; Rev. 2:27; 19:15), however, reveals that the rod will be wielded in executing *judgment* on rebellious sinners, not in governing them during a time of peace and righteousness. The rod of iron will be used to punish and destroy, not to redeem and heal. Such a context seems far removed from the serenity and beneficence of Christ's rule during the millennium.

It is difficult to reconcile Armstrong's exegesis with Jeremiah's prophecy of a new covenant, in which the Lord promises, "I will put my law *within them*, and I will write it *upon their hearts;* and I will be their God, and they shall be my people" (Jer. 31:33). The biblical picture of the messianic age sees it as a time of *voluntary* acceptance of God and his commandments, arising from the inner response of people's hearts. Ironically, Armstrong speaks of Christ's "rod of iron" rule while affirming that "God's way of life is the way of liberty."[29] Perhaps this has political and economic overtones, for assurance is then given that "in the Utopia of tomorrow, God will make private ownership possible for everyone! . . . People will *own* their own property in the Millennium. They will be *liberated* from systems which deprive them of the righteous rewards of their own toil!"[30]

Just what will life be like in that utopian age? Anyone wanting a preview is encouraged to visit one of the three Ambassador College campuses, where " . . . we enjoy a foretaste of the conditions that will obtain in the world of tomorrow!"[31] Not only will the evils of crime, war, disease, famine, and illiteracy be eradicated, but "the social and religious customs will be changed by divine force."[32] No longer will men observe "the pagan days, Christmas, New Year's, Easter, and others, 'which God hateth!' . . . God says He will not accept that kind of observance or worship. It is an abomination to Him—'*which He hateth*' (Deut. 12:30-31)."[33] Instead, all will keep the "seven annual Festivals and Holy Days He commanded to be observed. They pictured God's Master Plan for working out His purpose for humanity. They were established forever."[34] "Those who rebelliously won't keep God's Holy Days now—who sneer at them as 'Jewish,' in scathing contempt, will observe them when Christ returns!"[35]

Payment of tithes to the Lord (presumably also compulsory under Christ's "rod of iron" rule) will result in God's opening "the windows of heaven" and pouring out " 'a blessing, that there shall *not* be room enough to receive it' (Mal. 3:10)."[36] Rich rewards are also in store for those who obediently keep the prescribed feasts, whether by necessity or by choice. "For keeping His *days*, God assures them they will 'ride upon the high places of the earth' (Isa. 58:13-14). They will live in absolute luxury! The Bible is *full* of such promises for obedience."[37]

During the millennium there will be a concentrated effort at reeducation, aimed specifically at German Rationalism and the "atheistic theory of Evolution."

> One of the great problems facing the returned glorified Christ will be that of re-educating the supposedly "educated." These minds . . . have become so perverted with false education that they will be unable to accept truth until they first unlearn error.[38]

Among the problems solved in the World Tomorrow will be the population explosion—though the cataclysms preceding the millennium will presumably decimate the earth's population and eliminate the problem, at least for the duration of that period. God's solution will be

> simply [to] make most of the earth cultivatable! *Reduce* the bare, snow-swept and craggy mountains, *raise up* some of the

> deep, arid desert valleys, change the world weather patterns. Make all the deserts *green*, and fertile! Open up huge slices of the earth. . . . Uncover the deep ice packs and snowdrifts. . . . Then provide good, gentle rainfall, in right balance, just at the right season![39]

It is Armstrong's belief that no human being ever has gone, or ever will go, to heaven. Heaven is reserved for the *heavenly* Father and his angels. Jesus came from heaven to become incarnate for our sakes, after which he returned to heaven to share his Father's throne. During the Battle of Armageddon (the climax of World War III), he will return to the earth to establish his divine government in Jerusalem, where he will reign throughout eternity.

There are, on Armstrong's view, three resurrections, after which those who remain disobedient will be annihilated. Death, he teaches, is the end of conscious existence; there is no immortal soul in man. The first resurrection will be of the righteous who die prior to Christ's return. These immortal spiritual beings, along with living members of the Worldwide Church of God, will be the charter members of the kingdom of Christ on earth. At the conclusion of the millennium, there will be a second resurrection—of those who never had a fair chance to learn about God in Christ. According to Armstrong's interpretation of Isaiah 65:20, these will live for a hundred years, during which century most of them will avail themselves of the opportunity to be saved. The third resurrection—of those who have persisted in resisting God's grace—will conclude the final era of human history. This handful of recalcitrant sinners will be annihilated—cast into the lake of fire; the Father will then move his throne to earth, and the earth will become the eternal center of the universe.

This, of course, conflicts with certain classic Christian doctrines—including the endowment of man with an immortal soul and the existence of hell. Both these doctrines seem to be taught quite explicitly in Jesus' parable of the Rich Man and Lazarus (Luke 16:19-31). Armstrong meets the parable head-on with an interpretation of his own. Lazarus, the parable says, went to Abraham's bosom (vs.

22)—not heaven. "Abraham's bosom" indicates that Lazarus is an heir to the Abrahamic covenant, whose promise was *land*, not heaven.[40] In other words, eternal life on this earth is the reward of the blessed.

Naturally, Armstrong reasons, Lazarus could not come into possession of eternal life before his father Abraham received it. And Abraham will not inherit eternal life until he is brought back at the first resurrection to assist Christ in his millennial reign. So when the parable says that Lazarus was carried by the angels to Abraham's bosom, it means that he was promoted to "the status of a son and heir of Abraham, to inherit the land on this earth, and eternal life upon it. . . ."[41]

Like the Seventh-day Adventists and Jehovah's Witnesses, Armstrong brushes aside the statement of Jesus to the dying thief on the cross—"Truly, I say to you, today you will be with me in Paradise" (Luke 23:43)—as a case of incorrect punctuation. The "today," he argues, should go with "I say to you," which means that Jesus' words say nothing about the survival of a soul past physical death, as they do in the standard reading. However, the formula "Truly [or 'verily'] I say to you" appears 71 times in the New Testament;[42] and it is highly unlikely that it should be modified here alone to read "Truly I say to you today"—especially when the word "today" would be utterly superfluous in such a context.

There are additional passages that supply biblical evidence for belief in a soul that survives death of the body, contrary to Armstrong teaching. Jesus comforts Martha: "whoever lives and believes in me shall never die" (John 11:26). Stephen, dying, calls on Jesus to receive his spirit (Acts 7:59). Paul assures the Corinthians that "if the earthly tent we live in is destroyed, we have a building from God, a home not made with hands, eternal in the heavens" (II Cor. 5:1). Peter speaks of "the salvation of your souls" as the result of faith (I Pet. 3:9). John saw the souls of the martyrs under the altar (Rev. 6:9).

Jesus' talk with his disciples about preparing a place for them (John 14:1-3) is interpreted by Armstrong as a reference to the Lord's setting up the organizational structure for the World Tomorrow. Naturally, since he rejects the traditional notion of heaven, Armstrong has to twist the meaning of "I will come again and will take you to myself" to "After Jesus receives us unto Himself, He will remain on this earth. We shall ever be with Him."[43] This is in contradiction to the interpretation of nearly all evangelical biblical scholars. Alexander Maclaren, for example, says about this verse: "He who went away as the Forerunner has not done His work until He comes back, and, as Guide, *leads those for whom He had prepared the place to the place which He had prepared for them.*"[44]

The Worldwide Church of God teaches that Enoch died like all mortal men, disregarding the testimony of Hebrews 11:5, "By faith Enoch was taken up so that he should not see death; and he was not found, because God had taken him." The translation of Elijah is likewise denied, despite the evidence set forth in II Kings 2:11, "And Elijah went up by a whirlwind into heaven." Armstrong spokesman Herman L. Hoeh conjectures,

> Certainly the whirlwind used by God could not take him beyond the earth's atmosphere. Neither does the Bible account leave Elijah in the air. . . . Elijah is dead in the dust of the earth awaiting the resurrection of the just. Elijah, some years after being removed in the whirlwind, went into the grave, but will rise again to live forevermore.[45]

The millennial views of contemporary Bible scholars, both conservative and liberal, are widely divergent, and consensus is difficult to achieve about details of Christian teaching about the end of time. There are two points, however, at which Armstrong's eschatology can be criticized by interpreters regardless of their millennial doctrines: (1) his tendency to state as dogmatic fact purely personal speculations that are unsupported and unsupportable,[46] and (2) his *ex cathedra* interpretations of Scripture in defense of predetermined doctrines, when in many instances the biblical passages alluded to or quoted obviously have not the remotest bearing on the point he is attempting to establish. Armstrong is far too ready to brush aside the responsible biblical scholarship of the ages in favor of the presumption that to him alone it has been given to interpret the Bible authoritatively in these latter days. All the revered giants of Christendom—Augustine, Luther, Calvin, Wesley, Jonathan Edwards—were, he would have us assume, either frauds or fools.

SEVEN:

Basic Armstrong Doctrines: God, Christ, the Holy Spirit, Satan

A. God

"He who created all matter, force and energy, who created all natural laws and set them in motion, who created life and endowed some of it with intelligence—He is God! He is superior to all else that is called 'God.' He, alone, is God!"[1] Herbert W. Armstrong affirms the eternity of God and denies the eternity of matter, citing radioactive disintegration as evidence. Since matter is not eternal, there must have been a creation—and therefore a Creator, God. David Jon Hill amplifies the definition:

> God is the Creator, the Beginner, the One who caused us to have life—and so is called our Father. He is Benefactor, Provider, Protector. He is Love-giver, Law-giver and Forgiver, Punisher of sins, Rewarder of virtue, Maker of angels (and so *their* Father by creation), true and actual Father of Jesus Christ *the* Son of God.[2]

Thus far the Worldwide Church of God is in agreement with the historic creeds of Christendom. But from this point, deviations occur. Hill quotes various passages that allegedly teach that God's spiritually begotten children are every whit as much his sons (and daughters) as was Jesus himself. Jesus' statement, "I and *my* Father are *one*" (John 10:30) is to be taken *literally*. So, too, all other human beings literally *become God* through spiritual rebirth:

> Paul goes on to explain in verse 29 [of Romans 8] that the purpose of God according to which *true* Christians have been called is that *we might be sons of God as Christ is a Son of God,*

> *born into the Kingdom and Family of God as Christ was born into the Kingdom and Family of God!*[3]

All who attain sonship in God's family are endowed with the same powers the Father conferred on Jesus Christ. Psalm 8, quoted in Hebrews 2:6-8, is offered as evidence. Man is described as made "a little lower than the angels," "crowned with glory and honor," "appointed over the works of [God's] hands," and given authority over "all things," which have been placed "in subjection under his feet." Hill considers this passage to be a direct parallel to Matthew 28:18: "All power is given unto me in heaven and in earth." The reference by Paul [*sic*] in Hebrews is "*not just* the Son of Man (Jesus) . . . but mankind. That God created *mankind* with the ultimate purpose of sharing His own rulership of all things is manifest by these verses. Christ is not the only One to have Sonship in the Kingdom of God—all of mankind was created with that purpose in mind."[4]

It is thought significant that one of God's Old Testament names—*Elohim*—is plural in its form. This is interpreted not as a reference to many gods, but as proof that the one God is "a Kingdom!"[5] "Jesus taught that humans can be born into the *ruling* divine family of God!"[6] As a consequence of this spiritual rebirth, "when we are born of God, *we shall be* Spirit as He is Spirit—immortal as He is immortal—divine as He is divine!"[7]

> The purpose of life is that in us God is really re-creating *His own kind—reproducing Himself* after *His* own kind—for we are, upon real conversion, actually *begotten* as sons (yet unborn) of God; then through study of God's revelation in His Word, living by His every Word, constant prayer, daily experience with trials and testings, we grow spiritually more and more like God, until, at the time of the resurrection we shall be instantaneously changed from mortal into *immortal*—we shall then be born of God—we shall then be God![8]

Traditional Christian theology teaches that there is a difference between the oneness of the divine Father and the divine Son, and the oneness of the infinite Creator and his finite creatures. Father and Son have a unity of *es-*

sence, of *being*. But God's human creatures can aspire to nothing more than a unity of spirit, of mind, of will in this life—and an intimate spiritual *communion* (but not *identity*) with God their Creator in the life to come. Man has indeed been made "a little lower than the angels." In comparison with all the other works of creation he may even be described as "a little lower than *God*" (RSV). But when the Infinite is viewed from the perspective of the finite, the contrast should at least lead us to a sense of man's insignificance and unworthiness before the Creator and King of the Universe.

Not so, the Worldwide Church of God objects. Did Jesus not pray that his disciples might have the *same* unity as that shared by the Father and the Son? The answer is that Jesus and his Father have more than one kind of unity. Not only are they one in essence, but they are also one in mind and spirit. It is the latter type of unity for which Jesus petitioned in his high priestly prayer. Jesus coveted for his church those visible signs of spiritual concord which would demonstrate to the world that the same "personal relationship of mutual love"[9] that binds together the Father and the Son might also unify the members of Christ's Body. The end and object of this unity, Dr. G. Campbell Morgan explains, is the "manifestation of life and light and love . . . that brings conviction and belief into the world."[10]

The God-is-a-Family concept is hardly original with Armstrong. The Mormons held such a teaching for a century prior to the Armstrong "revelations." The doctrine flatly repudiates the teaching that God is triune—Father, Son, and Holy Spirit—which Armstrong brands as a "heretical and false doctrine introduced by pagan false prophets." An Armstrong spokesman sarcastically refers to the Trinity as "the universe's most exclusive club—the clique from which all mankind is utterly excluded . . . a closed Godhead clique of three beings." On the contrary, he declares, "*God is a Family*—not a trinity. . . . This is one group you don't have to be excluded from! You can be put into the greatest group of all. God's Family is open!"[11]

Armstrong caricatures the Trinity as sitting loftily in condescending disdain of lowly humanity. In so doing he brushes aside clear scriptural teaching about the nature of God, the nature of man, and the contrast between the two.

Isaiah's vision of the Lord on the occasion of his call illustrates this awesome contrast. Seeing the Lord exalted on his throne, surrounded by seraphim, Isaiah was moved to exclaim, "Woe is me! For I am lost; for I am a man of unclean lips, and I dwell in the midst of a people of unclean lips; for my eyes have seen the King, the Lord of hosts!" (Isa. 6:1-5). Thereafter, Isaiah commonly referred to God as "the Holy One of Israel." The purging of Isaiah's sin, symbolized by the touching of his lips with a live coal from the altar, by no means gave him the illusion that he had been elevated to the level of deity. The goodness attainable even by regenerated human beings stands in stark contrast to the glory of the Holy One; and Isaiah was moved to observe that not our evil but "our *righteous* deeds are like a polluted garment" (64:6). "O Lord," he acknowledged, "thou art our Father; we are the clay, and thou art our potter; we are all the work of thy hand" (64:8).

The vision of the New Jerusalem in Revelation 21 goes completely against the doctrine that men can become God. The Apostle John describes

> a great voice from the throne saying, "Behold, the dwelling of God is with men. He will dwell with them, and they shall be his people, and God himself will be with them; he will wipe away every tear from their eyes, and death shall be no more. . . . for the former things have passed away" (vv. 3-4).

Far from being identified with God *as God*, the redeemed are described as being in fellowship with God while at the same time remaining distinct and separate beings. Verse seven promises that "He who conquers shall have this heritage, and I will be *his God* and he shall be *my son*"—a flat contradiction of the teaching that the destiny of the faithful is to *be God.*

Unlike the Mormons, who consider God to be a physical being of flesh and bones, Herbert W. Armstrong interprets the God-nature as spiritual. But, paradoxically, "Christ clearly indicated that the Father has the general *form* and *stature* of a mortal man!"[12] In John 5:37 Jesus said of the Father, "His voice you have never heard, his form you have never seen"—which is taken to indicate that he does indeed have both voice and form. Revelation 1:13-16 is interpreted as a literal description of the Lord's appearance:

> . . . one like a son of man, clothed with a long robe and with a golden girdle around his breast; his head and his hair were white as white wool, white as snow; his eyes were like a flame of fire, his feet were like burnished bronze, refined as in a furnace, and his voice was like the sound of many waters; in his right hand he held seven stars, from his mouth issued a sharp two-edged sword, and his face was like the sun shining in full strength.

The possibility that the Bible may intend to pictorialize in concrete physical terms realities that are spiritual and therefore difficult for man to visualize does not seem to have occurred to the Armstrong theologians. The doctrine of God's immanence—which teaches that he is everywhere present throughout the universe—argues against the idea that he is localized in a discernible, even though spiritual, body. His omnipresence is attested by Jesus in Matthew 13:20, "For where two or three are gathered in my name, there am I in the midst of them"; and by Solomon in I Kings 8:27, "Behold, heaven and the highest heaven cannot contain thee; how much less this house which I have built!"

B. Jesus Christ

"Is Jesus God?" So runs the title of a key Armstrong essay first published in 1958. The treatment begins by affirming and scripturally supporting such orthodox teachings as Christ's deity, humanity, and virgin birth, as well as his roles in creation and redemption.

Then Armstrong launches into his teaching that Jesus Christ and Yahweh (he prefers the spelling Yahveh) of the Old Testament are one and the same. The common supposition that "Yahveh" (translated "The Lord" in the

King James and Revised Standard Versions, and "Jehovah" in the American Standard Version) was God the Father he calls a flagrant error. Armstrong's case is weak. "Yahweh" was the sacred, personal, tribal name for God employed by the Hebrews, considered too holy to utter. The term "Father" was not a formal name or title for God in the Old Testament, so there is no reason to assume that Yahweh is *not* the Father. And since the Messiah (Christ) appears in the Old Testament as a prophetic figure, it would seem unlikely that he should be equated with Yahweh. The Greek Septuagint translation of the Old Testament renders the Hebrew "Yahweh" as *kyrios* (Lord), a title frequently assigned to Jesus in the New Testament. But *kyrios* is also used in the New Testament to apply to God in contexts that suggest that God the Father is intended (for example, Matt. 1:20 and Acts 5:19).

Proof of the identity of Yahweh and Jesus, Armstrong says, "is a long study involving hundreds of passages."[13] He offers a few samples—Isaiah 8:13-14; 40:3; 44:6; 48:11-12, etc.—by way of showing that "Yahweh" is used in prophecy to refer to Christ. But the evidence is not convincing, because the term "Yahweh" and its Greek counterpart "kyrios" are ambiguous.

Garner Ted contends that the voice that hailed Jesus at his baptism and transfiguration was not that of his Father—despite the fact that on each occasion it testified, "This is my beloved Son, with whom I am well pleased" (Matt. 3:17; 17:5).[14] After all, he reasons, John 5:37 says that "the Father who sent me [Jesus] has himself borne witness to me. His voice you have never heard, his form you have never seen." What he fails to notice is that in John 5 Jesus was addressing the hostile Jewish leaders, not his disciples. Assuming that no one on earth could hear the Father's voice, Garner Ted suggests that it must have been an angelic messenger who spoke "as one bearing this message from the Father in heaven."[15] Thus is removed a formidable obstacle to the theory that the divine manifestations in the Old Testament were projected not by the Father but by the Son, Jesus Christ.

The distinct functions of Father and Son amount to more than theological split hairs. Apparently minor differences may have serious consequences. Follow Armstrong's reasoning, as evidenced in the *Ambassador College Correspondence Course:*

> The "Ancient of Days" described in Daniel [7:13] is the heavenly Father. The title "Father" was not used because the heavenly Father had not yet begotten the human Jesus. . . . Notice also that "One *like* the Son" appeared before the "Ancient of Days" to *receive* the Kingdom. The *Logos* or "Word" (John 1:1) was *like* the Son of man. He was not yet born as a Son, but since He would become a Son of man through Mary, He was, in Daniel's day, "*like* the Son of man"—the Jesus who would be born of the Virgin Mary![16]

Is Armstrong suggesting that the Father was only *potentially* a Father, and the Son only *potentially* his Son, prior to the incarnation? Indeed that is what he teaches. Commenting on the Virgin Birth, the *Correspondence Course* states, "He thus *became* the 'Son' of God. He called God His 'Father.' And so *began* [emphasis added] the '*Father*'-and-'*Son*' relationship. . . . The 'Father'-and-'Son' relationship of the God Kingdom clearly began when Jesus was *begotten* in His mother Mary by His heavenly Father." Later, reference is made to "the One who *became* the Father!" And again to the "logos—who later *became* Christ." In Lesson 8 this comment appears:

> Before Christ (the *Logos*) was conceived in Mary, He was not the "*Son of God.*" He was one of the two original members of the God Kingdom. He, like the one who became the "Father," had existed eternally. But He is nowhere in God's Word referred to as a Son of God prior to His conception in Mary. His *human* birth was His *first* birth.

Armstrong seems to overlook such commonly accepted messianic prophecies as Psalm 2:7 and Isaiah 9:6. In both passages, written centuries before the birth of Christ, the implication is that Jesus was *already* a son—not one who was to *become* a son on being given.

The fundamental changes in the relationship of the persons of the Godhead to one another as taught by Armstrong militate against the scriptural doctrine that God is a *changeless* Being. This doctrine, clearly taught in Malachi 3:6 ("I the Lord do not change") and Hebrews 13:8 ("Jesus Christ is the same yesterday and today and forever"), is also given explicit statement in the creeds of the church — though for Armstrong, one supposes, that does not count for much. The Westminster Confession, to take one example, speaks of the Son as "eternally begotten of the Father."

The Armstrong view of Jesus' *becoming* the Son of God determines a doctrine of Christ's humanity that is at variance with traditional Christianity.

> Jesus Christ *became perfect* [emphasis added] through the trials and tests of human experience. He overcame the *temptations* of the devil, His flesh and the world around Him. In spite of opposition and temptation, He kept God's commandments perfectly. In so doing He *developed the perfection of spiritual character* which *enabled Him to become* [emphasis added] our Savior and elder brother.[17]

The heresy that Jesus acquired "fallen" human nature from Mary is a belief once held, but later repudiated, by the Seventh-day Adventists. Apparently Herbert W. Armstrong, through his early exposure to Adventist teachings, appropriated and retained this discredited doctrine.

An article in *The Plain Truth* makes explicit what is implicitly taught in the foregoing quotation:

> Christ, one of the beings in the Godhead, had now been *changed* into flesh . . . had become *human*, having human nature with all of its *desires, weaknesses* and *lusts*—and subject to *death* just like any other human. . . .
>
> The Satan-inspired doctrine that Jesus was *not* human, that He did not inherit the human nature of Adam . . . *is the doctrine of the anti-Christ*. . . .
>
> The only *difference* between Jesus and any other human is that He was conceived of the Holy Spirit. . . .
>
> Yes, Jesus had *sinful* flesh. . . .[18]

But what of Hebrews 13:8, "Jesus Christ is the same yesterday and today and forever"? If his nature is constant, what does it mean for him to evolve? Why, if he inherited sinful human nature, did he never offer sacrifices (to atone for his *sin*, even though he committed no *sins*), never pray for forgiveness (although he prayed that *others* might be forgiven), never acknowledge moral weakness or failure? Why does the New Testament depict him as "holy" (Luke 1:35), as one who "knew no sin" (II Cor. 5:21), as "without sin" (Heb. 4:15), as "holy, blameless, unstained, separated from sinners" (Heb. 7:26), as being "without blemish" (Heb. 9:14 and I Pet. 1:19), as one in whom "there is no sin" and who "is righteousness" (I John 3:5, 7)? Guided by these and similar Scriptures, the historic Westminster Assembly framed the following statement:

> The Son of God, the second Person in the Trinity, being very and eternal God, of one substance, and equal with the Father, did, when the fullness of time was come, take upon him man's nature, with all the essential properties and common infirmities thereof, *yet without sin:* being conceived by the power of the Holy Ghost, in the womb of the Virgin Mary, of her substance. So that two whole, perfect, and distinct natures, the Godhead and the manhood, were inseparably joined together in one person. . . . Which person is very God and very man, yet one Christ, the only Mediator between God and man.

What about the resurrection? Garner Ted Armstrong raises a warning flag by declaring, "Jesus Christ died because He bled to death . . . it was His soul that was poured out! . . . The 'soul' is the physical, temporary life of the human body, which can *die* (Ezek. 18:4, 20), be cut off (Exod. 31:14), and sent to the grave (Ps. 30:3)."[19] Thus he denies the survival of life beyond physical death, a belief shared with Jehovah's Witnesses and Seventh-day Adventists. But the Adventists affirm that "Jesus Christ arose literally and bodily from the grave."[20] Jehovah's Witnesses conjecture that Jesus' physical body dissolved or evaporated, and that a "divine spirit being" was resurrected and appeared before the disciples. Armstrong certifies that Jesus arose bodily, but surmises that his resurrection body was not the same body that died and was placed in the tomb. Those who believe that only Christ's *body* died, while His *spirit* continued to live, are pronounced "lost and doomed to eternal punishment! *If Christ* did not die for their sins—if it was only a mortal *body* which died—then we have no Saviour, and we are lost."[21]

> It was Christ Himself who was dead. He was revived. Nowhere does the Scripture say He was alive and active, or that God had

> Him get back into the human body that had died and was now resurrected.
>
> Jesus Christ was dead. . . . but was revived!
>
> And the resurrected body was no longer human—it was the Christ resurrected, immortal, once *again* changed! As He had been changed, converted into mortal human flesh and blood, subject to death, . . . *He was again changed, converted, into immortality*—and He is alive forevermore.[22]

Presumably, then, Jesus Christ, after he had been killed, *ceased to exist* and was re-created by the Father after three days of total extinction. This despite Jesus' assurance to the penitent thief, "*Today* you will be with me in Paradise" (Luke 23:43), and his final words from the cross, "Father, into thy hands I commit my spirit" (Luke 23:46).

Contrary to Armstrong's teaching, the traditional Christian doctrine is that when Jesus' mortal body was "crucified, dead, and buried," his immortal spirit lived on. He kept the appointment with the thief in Paradise *that day*—and returned on the third day to reenter his dead body and restore it to life. If the body in which Jesus made his ten post-resurrection appearances was not identical to that tortured on the cross, what became of the corpse which had been laid in the tomb? Indeed, Garner Ted Armstrong elsewhere cites the fact of the empty tomb as strong evidence that Jesus had arisen. Jesus invited Thomas to handle his wounds as proof that he had in fact risen from the dead—in the very same body that had been nailed to the cross and mutilated by the soldier's spear (Luke 24; John 20). Hence A. H. Strong asserts, "the same body that was laid in the tomb was raised again, although possessed of new and surprising powers. . . ."[23]

Armstrong argues at great length that Jesus was crucified on Wednesday and resurrected on Saturday, the Jewish Sabbath, largely in order to do away with the basic assumption behind Sunday observance—that Jesus arose on the first day of the week. His objections to the Good Friday and Easter observances, almost universal throughout Christendom, provide added incentive to the effort to establish a different Holy Week calendar.

Armstrong is quite insistent about the implications of his central piece of evidence—Matthew 12:40: "For as Jonah was three days and three nights in the belly of the whale, so will the Son of man be three days and three nights in the heart of the earth." What this means, he says, is that either Jesus spent 72 hours in the tomb or he was "an imposter."[24] We know from the biblical crucifixion account that Jesus died in the afternoon and was buried before sunset. In order for him to spend 72 hours in the tomb, then, he must have been resurrected in the late afternoon. Since the women discovered the empty tomb on Sunday morning, Christ must have risen on Saturday afternoon, and, therefore, been crucified on Wednesday.

A more sophisticated and complex version of this argument is developed by Herman Hoeh in a 47-page booklet published in 1959. Again the reasoning rests on interpretations that have been discredited by reputable scholars. During the week of the crucifixion, says Hoeh, there are two "Sabbaths," one of which came on Thursday, the day after the crucifixion. To be sure, the Greek word usually translated "Sabbath" in Matthew 28:1 is plural in form. Most scholars point out that its meaning is nonetheless singular, since this particular Hebrew word needs a plural ending when transliterated into Greek in order to make it more easily pronounceable.[25] But Hoeh takes this as a clear reference to two Sabbaths, and thus as further proof of the Wednesday crucifixion.

Perhaps the best refutation of Armstrong's view comes from Harry Lowe, himself a Seventh-day Adventist, who thus has no interest in establishing Sunday as the proper day of worship. Lowe points out that Christ's death, resurrection, and ascension "clinched the already mounting evidence, and became the supreme sign of Messiahship—*not* the literal number of hours Christ spent in the tomb."[26] If Jesus had considered the "three days and three nights" to be of paramount importance, would he not have emphasized this detail in Matthew 16:4 and Luke 11:29-32 (which parallel Matt. 12:39-40)? On the contrary, the time element is omitted from these passages altogether.

Lowe lists sixteen passages that refer to "three days" or "the third day," all of them pertaining to the resurrection. Only one (Matt. 12:40) specifies "three days and three nights." Two (Matt. 27:63 and John 2:19) predict Jesus' rising "after three days," the latter substituting the word "in" for "after." The other thirteen speak of God raising up Jesus on "the third day." Lowe points out that "day" in Bible times, as in our own, could mean a 24-hour interval, or the period of daylight (as when Jesus said, "Are there not twelve hours in a day?" in John 11:9). If it is reckoned that Jesus was crucified on Friday afternoon and arose Sunday morning, then he did indeed arise on the third day. Lowe reasons that if the Resurrection took place on Saturday (as Armstrong and Hoeh maintain), "it is certain that this tremendous event would have become known to both disciples and guards within a few hours, yet the guards were still on duty at the grave Sunday morning. Matthew 28:2, 4."[27]

Thus Lowe concludes that "the idea of a Wednesday crucifixion finds no support in any of the Gospels. All give the same sequence of events—a Friday crucifixion, a Sabbath rest in the tomb, and a resurrection on the third day, which was Sunday—three days by inclusive reckoning."[28]

C. The Holy Spirit

As noted above, Armstrong rejects the doctrine of the Trinity. He considers the Holy Spirit to be a divine force rather than a separate and distinct personality, a member of the triune Godhead:

> The Holy Spirit is the *one* harmonious, perfect *holy attitude* of mind which is shared by both Father and Son. . . . The Holy Spirit is the very power of God! It *expresses* the unified creative will of the God family. . . . How clear it is that the Holy Spirit is not a *third person* of the Godhead as taught by the pagan "trinity" idea![29]

This attitude is available to man through repentance, faith, and obedience. Ultimately, "at the *resurrection* our spiritual creation will be *complete.* We will then have the *mind* of God *in full!* We'll be *completely composed* of Holy

Spirit, and be the very *sons of God in God's kingdom!*"[30] When this occurs—"when we are changed from flesh to spirit and we become the living Sons of the living God—(we will) become God as God is God, God as Jesus Christ is God."[31]

The well-known Christian theologian A. H. Strong offers a convenient summary of the scriptural evidence that the Holy Spirit *is* God. He is spoken of as God. The attributes and works of God are attributed to him. He receives honor due God alone. He is equally associated with the Father and the Son in both the apostolic benediction and the baptismal formula. Furthermore, Strong argues, the Bible speaks of the Holy Spirit as a person. The masculine pronoun is used for him in the Greek—even though the Greek word for "spirit" is neuter. He is said to perform the sorts of acts that only persons perform—searching, speaking, testifying, convincing, interceding. He is affected in a personal way by the deeds of others: he can be grieved, vexed, resisted. And he manifested himself visibly at Jesus' baptism as distinct from the Father and the Son, yet in direct connection with them.[32]

Far from being a "pagan" doctrine, the Trinity is thoroughly grounded in Scripture and in logic and has been accepted since the early centuries as the orthodox view of the nature of God. The fact that it is not explicitly taught in Scripture in no way invalidates it. The Bible does not purport to be a textbook on systematic theology. It was left to the scholars of the early church to analyze the discourses of Jesus and the writings of the apostles, and on the basis of their study to formulate doctrine. Irenaeus, Origen, and Tertullian, in the late second century, developed the concept of the Trinity—not out of their heads, but out of Scripture. "Under the leadership of Athanasius the doctrine was proclaimed as the faith of the Church at the Council of Nicea (A.D. 325), and at the hands of Augustine a century later it received a formulation, enshrined in the so-called Athanasian Creed, that is accepted by Trinitarian churches to this day."[33]

Since Armstrong disagrees with this long-established tenet, the burden of proof would seem to be on him. But he has failed to refute adequately the interpretations of the devout Christian scholars who developed the doctrine from the New Testament and who have throughout the centuries confirmed it in the thought and life of the church.

D. Satan

Long before the time of Adam, Armstrong believes, the earth was visited by God's wrath as a judgment on its population of "sinning angels" and reduced to chaos. The Hebrew word for "created" in Genesis 1:1, *bara*, implies, Armstrong says, that the creation was originally perfect.[34] It became chaotic, however, as a result of sin. But the sin that caused this chaos could not have been man's, "because there had been no man on earth until the sixth day of that re-creation."[35] It follows, then, that the earth was populated at an earlier time by nonhuman creatures. The key to the mystery is found in II Peter 2:4—"For if God did not spare the angels when they sinned . . . "—and Jude 6—"And the angels that did not keep their own position but left their proper dwelling have been kept by him in eternal chains in the nether gloom until the judgment of the great day."

It was to Lucifer that God had given the responsibility to rule the other angels on the earth. But Lucifer became

> *inordinately proud* . . . because of the unusual *beauty* of his body, which had the brightness of a star. He wanted to exalt himself to a position of rulership *over all* the "stars," or angels of God! . . . Lucifer's strength and influence was so great, that he persuaded *one third* of all the multiple millions of angels . . . to aid him in his revolt!

A power struggle for control of the universe ensued.

> A spectacular battle occurred, the like of which *defies the imagination*! . . . Giant comets were created, tracing gaseous trails in their space-wandering orbits. Huge chunks and masses of smashed planets crashed into the twisted wreckage of other planets. . . . What the astronomers see through their telescopes today is not an evolving universe, but the wreckage of a *titanic battle* waged by spirit beings throughout space—a battle fought long *before* man's creation![36]

Lucifer's effort to "make himself God" failed, and he and his angels were cast down to the earth, with resultant destruction to this planet.

> So *God did not create Satan*, the Devil! God created a cherub named Lucifer—*perfect in his ways*, but with the power of free choice—and Lucifer *transformed himself* into a devil by his rebellion against the government of God![37]

Once again, just before Christ's return to earth, Satan will seek to wrest control of the universe from God. Again he will fail. But Satan and his angels have dominion over the earth and its inhabitants. To prevent men from fulfilling their destiny of replacing him as rulers of the world, Satan deliberately incites them to rebel against God.

Satan's first effort was to persuade Adam and Eve to switch from the seventh-day Sabbath to the first day of the week.

> Satan, the adversary . . . , *lost no time*! He was at once having his own church service—*not* on God's holy commanded Sabbath Day—but on the day *following* God's Sabbath. He was conducting his own "church" service on the *first* day of the week—on Sunday. . . .
>
> God's True Church . . . *refuses* to keep "this present evil world's" first day of the week—tagged by the pagans *Sun*day—the observance of which is *direct disobedience* to God![38]

Those who persist in Sunday worship will receive "the mark of the beast" and be relegated to the lake of fire. The *Correspondence Course* further warns, "Satan supernaturally influences people to form 'churches' to spread his *death*-dealing doctrine of *Sun*day observance and other damning practices which may rid him forever of potential Sons of God." The tirade against Sunday worship continues throughout four consecutive lessons (29-32) dramatizing the belief that it is this "pagan" doctrine which Satan has exploited since Eden to seduce mankind into rebelling against the authority of God.

During the "week of creation," in six literal days "God *remade* the earth, *reshaped*, *refashioned* it, and created human beings upon it. He gave Adam a chance to take the place of Satan the devil." But Adam muffed his opportunity. He obeyed the devil instead of God, and humanity has been "sold down the river to the devil ever since." Not until Christ returns will the devil be displaced.

Armstrong teaches that Satan, unlike man, is an immortal spirit.

> The "churches" [teach that] *man* has an immortal spirit! Christ said an everlasting *fire* awaits Satan and his angels. The churches teach an everlasting fire awaits all "sinners." Satan fell from his attempt to overthrow God. The pagan misconception is that man fell![39]

To assist him Satan has one-third of all the angels. Their chief target is, of course, God's church, the Worldwide Church of God. Those who dare question its doctrines or challenge its policies incur the risk of severe discipline, even excommunication. Those who criticize from without, no matter how gently or constructively, are "persecutors," charged with Satanic motivation.

Satan has free rein during the present dispensation, but with the advent of Christ's millennial rule, he will be bound and cast into an abyss (Rev. 20:1-3). This restraint will last a thousand years, and then "the devil will be momentarily allowed freedom to deceive the nations again (verse 3)!"[40] The separation of the sheep and the goats (Matt. 25:32) "takes place over a period of 1,100 years!—to the end of the 100-year period after the millennium."[41] The "sheep" will be converted into spirit beings upon Christ's return, to rule with him for a thousand years in the "Wonderful World Tomorrow." At the conclusion of the millennium, a second resurrection will occur—that of all people from the beginning of time who have never had an opportunity to know Christ and His gospel. These will be exposed to the gospel—and to the wiles of Satan—for a grace period of a hundred years. Those who decide for Christ will then be converted into spirit beings to enjoy eternal happiness on the re-created earth. The remainder will be cast into the "lake of fire."

Since the wicked will be resurrected as physical human beings, the fire to which they are consigned will completely and instantly destroy them. Not so with Satan and his angels—for "*spirit beings are not affected by fire!*"[42]

Hence, these evil spiritual creatures will enter into an eternity of intense suffering upon being cast into the lake of fire.

The Book of Revelation is full of symbolic figures, and it would seem entirely consistent with its apocalyptic nature to interpret the lake of fire as a metaphor providing a pictorial description of the fate that awaits the wicked. If the lake of fire is symbolic, the line of reasoning by which the Worldwide Church of God establishes that the "goats" will be annihilated—instead of punished eternally—is unfounded.

Garner Ted Armstrong believes that the fire will burn itself out. What then will happen to the evil spirit beings who are indestructible and destined to suffer eternal torment?

> The Bible plainly reveals Satan will be cast into the lake of fire, but the lake of fire will *end* when the new heavens and new earth are established, and Satan is to be tormented unto the *ages of ages*! It also shows his torment *while* in that fire is going to be *mental*, at seeing all he has strived toward, worked for, plotted for, *burned up*. . . . The *exact nature* of their eternal punishment is yet to be decided![43]

By whom?

> The Apostle Paul gives us the amazing answer in I Corinthians 6:2-3! "Do ye not know that the saints shall *judge the world?* . . . Know ye not that we shall judge angels?" There it is! *We shall judge angels!*[44]

Heady wine, this, for members of the Worldwide Church of God. Only *they*—the "little flock" of sixty thousand out of the world's total population of three-and-a-half billion—will be numbered among that elect company whom God is calling out to rule the earth with Christ.

EIGHT:

Basic Armstrong Doctrines: Salvation, Scripture

A. Salvation

"Have you ever attended a 'good old-fashioned revival,' or evangelistic campaign?" inquires Garner Ted Armstrong. "Have you heard a hoarse-voiced, perspiring evangelist in broken, quavering tones, while the measured pulse of the choir softly chants 'Just as I am,' plead emotionally: '*Won't* you come? With every head bowed, with others praying for you, won't you step out into that aisle and come down to the altar? Give your heart to the Lord right now, tonight!' "[1]

Continuing in the same sarcastic vein, he asks, "What about the broken-hearted appeals of religion, today? Have *you* seen the signs on rocks, barns, billboards, and automobiles—'Christ *died to save* sinners'? . . . (But) can a person be truly saved—be given an eternal inheritance, just by confessing he believes Christ *did* live once, and that he died? No, according to the Holy word of your Creator!" We are *reconciled* to God by Christ's death, but "we shall be saved by His life!"[2] This future salvation, unattainable in the present life, requires more than faith; it is contingent on obedience, "overcoming," and baptism. Clearly, the Armstrong system differs radically from traditional Christian orthodoxy with respect to the concept of grace. Salvation, according to the Armstrongs, is a process, not an act, and involves six steps:

1. Repentance
2. Faith

3. Baptism
4. Receiving the Holy Spirit
5. Obedience
6. Resurrection (new birth)

The fifth step of obedience means it is impossible to predict anyone's salvation in advance. We can be converted in this life, but salvation will have to await a future resurrection. The new birth happens not at conversion but at the resurrection of the faithful dead. We were born physically; we must be reborn spiritually if we are to enter the kingdom of God. Jesus was the first to experience rebirth through resurrection, but he was the "first-born among many brethren" (Rom. 8:29)—in other words, many others will duplicate that experience.

In contrast to the orthodox Christian teaching that man was originally formed as a morally perfect being and later fell into sin, thus acquiring a sinful nature, Armstrong holds that God created man at the beginning with a corrupt, sinful nature, to set the stage for his plan of salvation. This was necessary, he teaches, in order for man at last to be reborn as an immortal spirit being, thus fulfilling his ultimate purpose of becoming a member of the God-Family. According to Armstrong's doctrine of conditional immortality, man's only hope for escape from extinction is God's grace. If man already had an immortal soul, the Bible would be false to call eternal life God's gift.[3]

What Armstrong ignores is the possibility that death can mean something more than total cessation of being. That "something more" is related in the account of the raising of Lazarus. When Jesus received news of Lazarus' illness, he waited for two days and then announced to his disciples that Lazarus had fallen asleep (John 11:11). When the Twelve failed to grasp his meaning, he said explicitly, "Lazarus is dead" (vs. 14). Jesus' keen spiritual perception enabled him to see beyond the apparent to the real· Lazarus—though physically dead—was not extinct. He still lived. Later Jesus comforted Martha with the assurance, "I am the resurrection and the life; he who believes in me, though he dies, yet shall he live, and whoever lives and believes in me shall never die" (John 11:25f.).

The Worldwide Church of God likens conversion to conception. It is but the beginning of the process that culminates in birth. The gestation period, rather than covering a set number of months, is a life-long process during which the "fetus" is nurtured in preparation for spiritual birth. Mortal man is flesh, and nothing more. But if he follows the path of salvation, he shall become immortal spirit.

To defend this analogy Armstrong argues that "the original Greek . . . has *only the one word . . . 'gennao'* "[4] to represent the two English meanings of conception (begettal) and birth. Because of this, he charges, "the 'scholars' of our comparatively recent years who translated the Bible into English did not, themselves, *under*stand God's Plan—(and consequently) they often translated the Greek word 'gennao' into the English word 'born' where it actually *meant* 'begotten.' "[5] For example, when the English versions of the Bible say of the children of God (John 1:13) that they were "born, not of blood, nor of the will of the flesh, nor of the will of man, but of God," they should read "*begotten* . . . of God." Armstrong's theology here overrules his acquaintance with Greek, which is limited at best. *Gennao* is not the only New Testament Greek word for conception and birth; there are at least four others. And, as Walter R. Martin has pointed out, the New Testament is full of passages to show that "the new birth . . . is synonymous with spiritual regeneration to eternal life, and the very fact that Jesus Christ and the apostles described the possessors of the new birth as 'saved' decimates Mr. Armstrong's contention that one must wait until the resurrection in order to be born again."[6] To the prostitute in the house of Simon the Pharisee, Jesus said, "Your sins are forgiven. . . . Your faith *has saved* you" (Luke 7:48, 50). Luke records in Acts 2:47, "And the Lord added to their number day by day those who *were being saved.*" Paul wrote to the Roman Christians, "For in this hope we *were saved*" (Rom. 8:24). Salvation is described as an ongoing experience in II Corinthians 2:15: "For we are the aroma of Christ to God among those who *are being saved. . . .*" "By grace you *have been saved,*" Paul declares in Ephesians 2:5. A few verses later he affirms, "For by grace you *have been saved* through faith . . ." (vs. 8). Reference is made to "God, who *saved* us . . ." in II Timothy 1:8-9. And to Titus Paul wrote, "but when the goodness and loving kindness of God our Savior appeared, he *saved* us" (Titus 3:4-5).

Spiritual rebirth is not, as Armstrong contends, reserved until a future resurrection. Peter exclaims in his first epistle, "Blessed be the God and Father of our Lord Jesus Christ! By his great mercy we *have been born anew* to a living hope through the resurrection of Jesus Christ from the dead" (I Pet. 1:3). Six times in First John "born of God" is mentioned as a precondition for victorious Christian living—as in I John 3:9, "No one *born of God* commits sin; for God's nature *abides* in him, and he cannot sin because he *is born of God.*"

Admittedly, those verses that point to salvation as a future reward outnumber those describing it as a past or present experience. But a comparison of all relevant New Testament passages shows that salvation involves all three—past, present, and future. The Christian *has been saved* by the redemptive work of Christ; he *is being saved* through repentance, faith in Christ, and surrender to the control of the Holy Spirit; he *will be saved* when, upon death, he attains everlasting life.

Armstrong appeals to John 3:8 as evidence that the new birth is future. Jesus told Nicodemus, "The wind blows where it wills, and you hear the sound of it, but you do not know whence it comes and whither it goes; so it is with every one who is born of the Spirit." Armstrong argues that since the wind is invisible, and those who are reborn are likened to it, they too will be invisible. "After people are actually born of God, they, too, shall *be* spirit, just as God is spirit. They will be invisible to material human sight, just as angels are."[7] Apparently he misses the point of the analogy completely—as Floyd V. Filson makes clear:

> A physical birth cannot give spiritual life (vs. 6). Sinful man needs a spiritual renewal which only the divine power of the Holy Spirit can bring about. This is a mystery; Jesus conceded that. The

> change is as mysterious and impossible to see as is the wind which can be heard but not seen (vs. 8); but the work of the Spirit, though invisible, is as real as is that of the wind.[8]

As noted above, the first of Armstrong's six steps is *repentance.* To prepare potential converts for the mental shifting of gears required of Worldwide Church of God members, an article in *Tomorrow's World* elaborates broadly on the traditional meaning of this term: "It means to *change* everything—the way we dress, look, act and think. It means rooting out all preconceived ideas about God, Christ and self. It means to actually change in mind and direction."[9]

The sequel to repentance is *faith.* By faith the penitent sinner responds to God's grace in Christ. Armstrong distinguishes between faith in Jesus' death and faith in his life. Through Jesus' death the believer is saved from *past* sins. This provisional salvation in no way guarantees the ultimate reward of eternal life. "You are now under grace—undeserved pardon. You are pardoned from paying the penalty, since Jesus Christ paid it for you! This is not your works. It is Christ's sacrifice. You are now acquitted—justified—the slate is wiped clean of a guilty past!"[10]

But "death cannot impart life."[11] We are delivered from our guilty past by Christ's death. But resurrection into immortality can be accomplished only through his life. Instead of viewing the crucifixion-resurrection as a unified event having a single significance, Armstrong divides the crucifixion and the resurrection into two separate events, each of which has a distinct significance. The former requires a simple response of faith; the latter, faith plus law-keeping.

That the Worldwide Church of God teaches a salvation based partially on works and not entirely on faith is, Armstrong vigorously charges, a slander thought up by "a few persecutors."[12] However, when the sixfold plan of salvation has been completely outlined, it will be seen that without a strictly disciplined obedience to the law, the *gift* of salvation cannot and will not be conferred. Herbert W. Armstrong accuses, "Most professing 'Christians' . . . say there are no conditions—nothing that *we* must do to receive God's glorious grace! They deny that God requires obedience to His Law! They twist the truth around by saying that would be *earning* one's salvation!"[13] "God Won't Accept You 'Just As You Are'!" an Armstrong headline admonishes.[14] If he is right—and millions of orthodox Christians wrong—deathbed repentance has no validity and Jesus was mocking the penitent thief in telling him, "Today you will be with me in Paradise" (Luke 23:43).

Baptism is the third rung in the Armstrong ladder of salvation. It is the "outward sign of our repentance, and *willingness* to surrender our lives *completely* to God—being willing to *bury* the old self."[15] Every individual who wants to become a member of the Church of God must submit to baptism. The only acceptable scriptural method is immersion: "baptism is not valid if it is done by pouring, sprinkling, dabbing with a damp cloth, or cavorting under a fire hose!"[16]

Only those who are mature—truly able to count the cost—should be baptized, and a true representative of Jesus Christ must perform the baptism. It is clear from the Armstrong literature that these "representatives" are the ministers of "the Work," stationed throughout the world.

A corollary to the Armstrong doctrine of baptism has to do with the importance of the *name* of the church one affiliates with. Since true baptism is administered in the name of Jesus Christ, those baptized acquire God's name:

> As the Father's own children, they would naturally also be given His *name* and be called the Church of God. . . . For the *true name of the Church of God* is just that: "the Church of God." . . . And of all the denominations bearing the name "Church of God," only *one* could be the true Church of God—the one that obeys *all* the commandments of God and maintains the faith delivered once for all time.[17]

Step four is *the gift of the Holy Spirit*. For the Armstrong theology, we have seen, teaches that the Holy Spirit is not a person, but a power—chiefly the power "to obey God's Laws."[18]

> God will give His Holy Spirit—with all the powers, abilities and capacities involved—only to those who have demonstrated by

> both attitude and actions that they want to *and will* obey God and His Laws forever. God *first* demands this wholehearted, wholly sincere *desire* to obey His Laws; *then*, and *only then*, will He give us the *power* to actually obey these Laws.[19]

When these conditions are met, all that is necessary is to "follow the simple, straightforward directions of Acts 2:38: one, 'repent'—and that naturally includes 'obey'—and two, '*be baptized.*' . . . then you *shall* receive the gift of the Holy Spirit when God's ministers lay their hands on you after the actual baptism" (Acts 8:17).[20]

The fifth step in Armstrong's plan of salvation is *obedience.* Repentance, faith, baptism, receiving the Holy Spirit—all are rendered null and void by disobedience. Does this imply that we are saved in part by works, and not by faith alone? As noted above, Armstrong is very sensitive on this score. Commenting on James 2:24, "You see that a man is justified by works and not by faith alone," an Armstrong pamphlet insists, "We are saved by faith! But faith functions *with our works* and by works our faith is made perfect! That is living faith!" "What is sin, anyhow?" the booklet asks. " 'Sin is the transgression of the law,' is God's answer (I John 3:4)."[21] Accordingly, the only way to nullify sin—and its penalty of death—is by keeping the law. That requires faith—"faith in the power of God! And, just as your own diligent effort coupled with faith makes faith perfect, so faith coupled with your effort makes perfect obedience!"[22]

But "perfect obedience" is impossible for human beings in this earthly life. Man is sinful by nature, and will persist in sinning until he dies. After he becomes a Christian he stops sinning *deliberately*, but he does not stop *sinning.* His goal is to be "perfect, as [his] heavenly Father is perfect" (Matt. 5:48). But no matter how much he prays and relies on the power of the Holy Spirit, he cannot achieve perfection as long as he remains in the flesh. Armstrong himself admits that only Jesus Christ succeeded in keeping the commandments perfectly—and in attaining salvation. The Christian gospel is *not* "Believe on the Lord Jesus and keep the commandments, and you will be saved." It is simply "Believe on the Lord Jesus, and you will be saved" (Acts 16:31).

The analogy of a drowning man is helpful for explicating the traditional Christian position. His rescue depends not on anything he is able to do for himself, but on the pull of the person at the other end of the rope that is thrown to him. The faith by which he lays hold of the lifeline is merely his response to the free gift (grace) proffered him. In the case of man's salvation from sin, even his faith-response to God's mercy—his "yes" to Christ as Savior—is a gift of the Holy Spirit. Strong explains,

> We are justified by faith, rather than by love or by any other grace: not because faith is itself a work of obedience by which we merit justification,—for this would be a doctrine of justification by works, . . . but because faith, and not repentance, or love, or hope, is the medium or instrument by which we receive Christ and are united to him.[23]

Salvation is not a process that begins with conception (begettal) and ends with spiritual rebirth (resurrection). Armstrong confuses justification (the *act* whereby we receive Christ's sacrificial death in payment for our sins, and so are saved) and sanctification (the *process* whereby we are purified and nurtured toward Christian maturity through the dynamic of the Holy Spirit). To Armstrong, the formula for salvation is *faith* (justification) + *works* (sanctification). Paul's formula is *faith* alone—with works following as an inevitable result or by-product of faith. For Armstrong there can be no "blessed assurance" that one is safe from future condemnation, since salvation is contingent not only on receiving Christ as Savior but also on obedience to his commandments. Not until death can a person's life be evaluated to determine whether or not he qualifies for salvation.

Paul wrote to the Galatian Christians to refute a legalism of this very sort. There were those who wanted to make circumcision a requirement for salvation, in addition to faith. That, Paul said, was a "perversion of the gospel of Christ" (Gal. 1:7). "A man is not justified by works of the law but through faith in Jesus Christ . . . by works of the law shall no one be justified" (Gal. 2:16). With this Herbert W. Armstrong agrees—but there is a catch. He teaches that "justified" has to do only with *past* sins, and that law-keeping is necessary if one ultimately is to be resurrected into eternal life. In the context, however, Paul makes it clear that justification means not only deliverance *from* past guilt, but deliverance *to* eternal life. Otherwise, why should he take issue with the Galatians for burdening Christian converts with the necessity to keep the law? *Adding* to grace destroys grace! If one charges a price, however small, for a gift, it ceases to be a gift.

Armstrong misrepresents the traditional orthodox doctrine of salvation by faith alone. He apparently assumes that anyone who eliminates "works" from the salvation process is motivated by a desire to break the law with impunity.[24] That is simply not true of classical Christianity. Because the Christian is free *from* sin does not mean that he is free *to* sin. Because he is exempt from keeping the law as a means of salvation does not mean that he is exempt from keeping the law altogether. Jesus taught that "No man can serve two masters" (Matt. 6:24)—but neither can he serve none. As Throckmorton has written, "The Christian who is 'under grace' and not 'under law' must *obey*. He has changed masters, but he is not his own master; he is not, therefore, free to sin if he so wishes."[25] And if he does? Then, although he may believe, he does not have saving faith. For "faith apart from works is dead" (James 2:26). Genuine faith produces a life of disciplined obedience to the moral laws of God—just as a living seed, when properly planted and nurtured, inevitably produces fruit.

Armstrong has written,

> Some religious teachers tell you Christ lived a righteous life for you 1930 years ago, and since you "can't keep the law," as they claim, God "imputes" Christ's righteousness of 19 centuries ago to you—by sort of "kidding Himself" that you are righteous, while you are given license to still be a spiritual criminal breaking His Law! God does not impute to you something you do not have.[26]

Here is precisely the parting of the ways between the Worldwide Church of God and traditional Christian orthodoxy. The latter affirms that Christ has imputed to man that which he does not have and cannot possibly attain by his own efforts: righteousness (justification), exoneration, acquittal, reconciliation, atonement, redemption—salvation. Numerous Scripture passages attest this, among them Romans 5:18—"Then as one man's trespass led to condemnation for all men, so one man's act of righteousness leads to acquittal and life for all men"—and Romans 4:23—"For if Abraham was justified by works, he has something to boast about, but not before God. For what does the scripture say? 'Abraham believed God, and it was reckoned to him as righteousness.'" Man's righteousness, his right standing with God, comes through the death of Christ in payment for his sins. As for his acquittal constituting a ground for lawless behavior, Paul's answer is this:

> Consider yourselves dead to sin and alive to God in Christ Jesus. Let not sin therefore reign in your mortal bodies, to make you obey their passions, . . . but yield yourselves to God as men who have been brought from death to life. . . . For sin will have no dominion over you, since you are not under law but under grace (Rom. 6:11-14).

Set free from sin, the faithful are now "slaves of righteousness" (Rom. 6:18).

Armstrong denies that works of obedience performed by the Christian subsequent to his conversion in any way earn his salvation, but he maintains, nonetheless, that the atonement was not completed at Calvary. In agreement with Jehovah's Witnesses and Mormons, Armstrong contends that a lifetime of ritual-observance and commandment-keeping is necessary to qualify the believer for immortality.

> The blood of Christ does not finally save any man. The death of Christ merely paid the penalty of sin in our stead—it wipes the slate clean of past sins—it saves us merely from the death penalty. . . . It is *only* those who, during this Christian Spirit-begotten life, have grown in knowledge and grace, have overcome, have developed spiritually, done the works of Christ and endured unto the end who shall finally be given immortality. . . . So, being, as we say, converted—receiving the Holy Spirit of God—is *merely the beginning!* Then begins a lifetime of living under the government of God—by God's laws which express His will, instead of by self-will and desire.[27]

Paul is not alone in repudiating the heresy of salvation by faith plus works. After feeding the five thousand, Jesus discussed the deeper significance of this miracle with some of the crowd in the Capernaum synagogue. When he offered them "food which endures to eternal life" (John 6:27), they asked, " 'What must we *do*, to be doing the work of God?' Jesus answered them, 'This is the work of God, that you *believe* in him whom he has sent' " (John 6:28f.). In other words, the "work of God" was not something they must be doing; it was a work of grace, to be received by faith. Later Jesus said, "I am the bread of life; he who comes to me shall not hunger, and he who believes in me shall never thirst. . . . All that the Father gives me will come to me; and him who comes to me I will not cast out" (vv. 35, 37). Nothing is said about keeping the law. The grace of God in Christ is to be received simply by faith. Throughout this passage, Jesus presents salvation as a free gift of his grace. To respond in repentance and faith to the symbols of his sacrificial death is to have (in the here and now) eternal life, and to enjoy full assurance (based on Jesus' own promise) of a future resurrection. And there is the further promise that Christ will abide in the believer. Can one whom Christ indwells really be capable, as Armstrong suggests, of using his faith as an excuse for "license to still be a spiritual criminal breaking His Law!"?

Two peculiarities of the Armstrong soteriology are disclosed in a story printed in *The Wonderful World Tomorrow.* A listener in the heart of Africa wrote in to urge that a church be established among his people. But when two ministers from London went to visit the correspondent,

> They found he was the *only* man of any education among them. The others were illiterate savages. They were so ignorant, it was impossible for them to comprehend anything about God, or Christ, or salvation. Sadly, our ministers said such people would have to receive at least elementary education before they could be reached with the Gospel![28]

The Worldwide Church of God offers a "salvation by knowledge" similar to that of the Colossian church of the first century—similar also to the Gnostic cults of Christian

Science, the Church of Jesus Christ of Latter Day Saints, and Jehovah's Witnesses. Each of these requires its own unique brand of specialized knowledge as the key to understanding the Bible and its message. Gnostic heresies of this sort were rife in the early church, and contributed much to the hammering out of doctrines true to the Holy Scriptures, as the apostles and the church fathers sought to combat error with sound teaching. The genius of the Christian gospel is that it is so simple that even a little child can understand it—and only he who has the faith of a little child can receive it.

A second peculiarity is disclosed by the foregoing incident. Abandoning these "illiterate savages" to a continued state of godless ignorance is not as heartless as may appear on the surface. For according to Armstrong theology, those people are not lost. They will die outside of Christ and his salvation, it is true. But because of their ignorance, they will be given the chance to hear and respond to the gospel when they are resurrected as mortal beings following the millennium. This will not be a *second* chance, Armstrong emphasizes, since these benighted people have never had a first chance. Christ's first advent was not for the purpose of saving the world—"If Christ had been trying to 'save' the world, He would have *saved* the world. *It didn't get 'saved'*!"[29] His purpose was to call out a "little flock" (the one and only true "Church of God") and prepare it for the work of evangelizing mortals during the millennium—and those resurrected for their "first chance" at salvation during a hundred-year grace period following the millennium.

The ministry of the "little flock" in this time preceding the millennium is not to convert people, but to witness and to warn. Evangelism will be undertaken in the World Tomorrow by the Headquarters Church, "composed of resurrected Immortals, under direct personal supervision of Christ Himself!"[30] And so there is no missionary challenge in the Worldwide Church of God. They can write off primitive tribes due to their illiteracy, instead of learning the language and reducing it to writing, meanwhile seeking by example and precept to communicate the love and mercy of God in Jesus Christ. Evangelical missionaries have done precisely this in hundreds of such instances.

The gospel of authentic Christianity does not require prior knowledge or education. Even an "illiterate savage" can comprehend the good news that the God who made all things is a loving Father who sent his Son to live, die, and arise from the dead that we, by repenting of our sins and trusting him as Savior, might enjoy abundant life here and hereafter.

B. Scripture

The Worldwide Church of God believes without qualification that "the Bible is God's inspired word!"[31] This doctrine has been repeatedly confirmed by the numerous prophecies in its pages which have been fulfilled.[32]

From the time of his initial Bible study, Armstrong experienced a growing conviction that to him alone had been revealed the true meaning of Scripture, a meaning that had been lost for more than eighteen centuries. "Do you realize," he asks, "God has purposely closed much of the Holy Bible from human understanding *until now?*"[33] Hundreds of sects and denominations have disagreed about what the Bible says because none had been given the keys to open the doors of understanding.[34] This is a fulfilment of Daniel's prophecy: "The words are closed up and sealed till the time of the end" (12:8-9). The carnal mind cannot comprehend spiritual truths, which are revealed only to those who obey God and keep his commandments. Thus it was that Herbert W. Armstrong gained insight into biblical truth denied mankind since apostolic times.

Armstrong lists seven keys to understanding the Bible:[35]

1. *The True Gospel.* Hidden by the powers of darkness for 1900 years is the knowledge of the good news of the kingdom of God. Since "kingdom" means government, the gospel is the message of "government by God's laws."

2. *Salvation is Creation.* To present salvation as God's effort to restore man to a pre-fall sinless state "is a damnable lie." Man was created with the human nature he now

has. Salvation is merely the completion of creation, by which man evolves through faith plus works to immortality.

3. *God's Dual Method.* There is a "dual principle" that runs through all biblical prophecy. A preliminary fulfilment occurs, which is the forerunner of a final climactic fulfilment, which comes at the close of the age (a period that has already begun).

4. *God's Holy Days.* There are seven Old Testament observances which the true church still maintains in the new dispensation, contrary to the apostate sects and denominations who have adapted Roman holidays to their own purposes (for example, the celebration of Christmas).

5. *The Truth About Israel.* Prophecy cannot be understood without the teaching of British-Israelism (discussed in Chapter V above).

6. *Bible Interpretation of Symbols.* The Bible uses symbols to hide, not to clarify, God's true meaning. We must look to the Bible itself for the meanings of these symbols. Armstrong's further claim is that only he of all the biblical interpreters of history has explained Scripture without doctrinal prejudice.

7. *God's Sabbath.* The commandment to remember the Sabbath Day is God's test commandment to identify his people. This is "the basic key to the identity of the true God . . . and to the identity of Israel."

Another member of the Worldwide Church of God lists twelve rules for Bible interpretation and study.[36] As with much of the Armstrong literature, the rules sound impeccably evangelical (for example, "pray for guidance," "check the context," "compare translations"). It would be difficult, however, to show that Armstrong pays much heed to these "rules." In particular, one wonders about his allegiance to rule 2, "Be willing to accept correction"; rule 6, "Check the context"; and rule 9, "Never establish a doctrine by a vague or difficult-to-understand Scripture."

In effect such rules are not meant for Armstrong himself, but for his followers. For all its talk about letting the Bible alone determine doctrine, the Armstrong method assumes the divine revelation of the teachings "discovered" by Herbert W. Armstrong through his personal Bible study. It relies heavily on proof-texting, looking for biblical support for given doctrines instead of letting the Bible speak for itself. Ambassador College's way of dealing with the Bible is narrow, rigid, and authoritarian. Armstrong's students are not encouraged to read widely or to seek counsel from reliable commentaries or to bring their own intellects to bear on the Scriptures. They are told to believe nothing unless they can prove it for themselves out of their own Bibles. What that comes to in practice is, look up the prescribed prooftexts and accept without question their application by the Pasadena hierarchy. The credulous disciple dutifully concurs that the truth of the Armstrong "revelation" is indeed plain. To respond otherwise is to arouse suspicion; to persist in questioning is to invite dismissal. As reported by a former member of the Worldwide Church of God, in Bible studies at Ambassador College Herbert W. Armstrong "is adamant with anyone who asks questions that seem to put down anything that Mr. Armstrong has established as doctrine. The people are required to sign their names to the questions. In that way, they have the name of the individual who dared ask the wrong question. It is a good way of discouraging the people from asking any searching questions at all." On at least one occasion, Armstrong is reported to have denounced an innocent inquirer by telling him he was "on the way to destruction" and "possibly has a demon."[37]

Yet the catalog describes Ambassador's method of biblical study as "scholarly . . . scientific . . . worshipful and spiritual." The *scholarly* aspect is described as "direct, firsthand, intensive personal study . . . involving an exceedingly high ratio of total hours of study under continual caution to lay all preconceived ideas and religious bias on the shelf."[38] "Scientific" study means that "students are taught to approach the Bible with open-mindedness, with due respect for the results of past research, but accepting only that which is proved true, regardless of previously accepted or universally approved theories or doctrines." New scientific findings are examined "without bias. But nothing is accepted unless proved, and every student is emphatically encouraged to think for himself. . . ." The *worshipful* and *spiritual* emphasis includes the obviously false statement in the catalog that "Ambassador College [is] nondenominational. . . ."

A simple illustration of the anti-intellectual bias and *lack* of "scholarly" and "scientific" method that prevail at Ambassador College is found in a *Plain Truth* article on The Lord's Prayer. Regarding the doxology of the prayer ("For thine is the kingdom, and the power, and the glory forever. Amen"), the writer comments,

> Then, as a conclusion, we *again* acknowledge the great power and rulership of the Almighty Creator. . . . Some critics want to leave out this conclusion, but it is a part of the inspired Scripture. *It is those who don't want to acknowledge God's Kingdom who want to leave it out.*[39]

The accusation recorded in the final sentence is grossly unfair. Many devout, evangelical, Kingdom-acknowledging Christians are persuaded that the doxology constitutes an appropriate conclusion to the Lord's Prayer—but are equally convinced that it is not a part of the originally inspired text. This judgment is grounded not on anti-kingdom prejudice, but on the near-unanimous verdict of competent textual scholarship. The doxology is omitted or specially marked in practically every English version of the Bible currently in use except the ancient King James. The solidly conservative *International Standard Bible Encyclopaedia* accounts for the omission as follows: "The doxology . . . is not found in the leading manuscripts and is generally regarded as an ancient liturgical addition."[40] This example of arbitrarily ignoring readily available scholarly data is no isolated instance.

Nor is it true that the Ambassador student "is emphatically encouraged to think for himself." This is strikingly illustrated by a look at the correspondence course. Each lesson follows the same format: an introductory statement (two or three pages), lesson development (ten or eleven pages), a concluding statement (one or two pages), and finally a self-grading quiz. The 16-page booklets are attractively printed and amply illustrated. The lesson development employs leading questions, scriptural references that allegedly provide the answers (to be looked up by the student), followed by commentary.

For example, Lesson 27 of the 1964 series deals with Saturday-Sabbath observance. A subhead announces, "God's 'Sign' Necessary for Salvation Today." The reader is invited to "see what the Bible says." Then follows leading question number one: "Doesn't the Bible plainly reveal that to be a true Christian today one must become a *spiritual* Israelite . . . in order to inherit the *same* covenant promise of eternal life that was made to Abraham and his seed? Rom. 4:16; 9:4 and Galatians 3:28-29." When he has consulted these passages for confirmation, the student is ready for leading question number two: "So today must a spiritual Israelite . . . have to possess God's 'sign' (*keep God's Sabbath*) in order to be 'sanctified'—be set apart to be made holy? Ex. 31:13." The question is phrased in such a way as to preclude a negative answer. Then follows the "clincher" paragraph, in which the conclusion is drawn: "So today every true Christian *must also keep the* (seventh-day) *Sabbath*. . . . He must have the Sabbath 'Sign' in order to be *made Holy*. . . ."

The average correspondence course pupil lacks the biblical orientation and tools of logical thought to cope with the facile arguments of the Armstrong salesmanship. Ironically, he is led to think that the conclusions he has reached have been attained by proving them himself, out of his own Bible.

NINE:

Basic Armstrong Doctrines: Law

Herbert W. Armstrong makes it abundantly clear that salvation depends not only on faith but also on obedience. Two conditions must be met in order for an individual to receive the Holy Spirit:

> 1) real repentance of sin, which means repentance of transgressing God's Law; and which, in turn, means to surrender to obey God's Law; and
> 2) faith in and acceptance of the living resurrected Christ as personal Saviour; and this means a *living* faith coupled with obedience.[1]

Law-keeping, then, is an essential ingredient of Armstrong soteriology. But what laws?

Much of the Old Testament law has been brought by Armstrong into the new dispensation almost intact. Jewish feast days and holy days (except the new moons), the Hebrew Sabbath, the practice of tithing, dietary laws, and the Decalogue, all have been retained. Most of the Israelite civil statutes and the intricate regulations governing priestly garb and duties, as well as animal sacrifice and outmoded Temple rituals, have been dropped.

A. The Annual Feast Days of God

The basis on which members of "God's Church" today are obligated to keep the annual holy days is the example of Jesus. I Peter 2:21, after all, tells us that Christ left us an example, "that we should follow in his steps."[2]

Jesus, however, was reared in a Jewish home. Naturally, he observed the Jewish laws. That does not imply that members of the New Testament church must follow his example in this respect. Before his death and resurrection the old covenant of law was still in force. The new covenant of grace, which he was shortly to inaugurate through the crucifixion and resurrection, had not yet begun. Besides, the "in his steps" passage in I Peter is totally unrelated to Jesus' conformity to the law of Moses. The author is urging Christians to bear unjust sufferings in the same spirit of courage and patience with which Christ bore his. Finally, if we are required to conform to Christ's conduct in obeying the law at one point, we are obliged to obey it at all points. We may not pick only those parts of the law that we find agreeable. As he "kept God's annual Holy Days," so must we. (Armstrong says yes.) As he was circumcised physically, so must we be. (Armstrong says no.) As the Passovers he attended involved animal sacrifice, so must ours. (Again Armstrong says no.)

That Jesus' example of law-keeping is not binding on those living under grace, for whom the law has been declared obsolete, is Paul's teaching in Galatians: "No man is justified before God by the law; for he who through faith is righteous shall live" (3:11). The law "was our custodian until Christ came, that we might be justified by faith. But now that faith has come, we are no longer under a custodian; for in Christ Jesus you are all sons of God, through faith" (3:24-26).

The Worldwide Church of God maintains that the law is *not* obsolete. Quite in line with orthodox Christianity, Armstrong accepts the New Testament reinterpretations of Passover in the Lord's Supper and circumcision as being a matter of the heart (Rom. 2:29). But he diverges when he teaches that believers, by following these modified practices, are still keeping the law in the Old Testament sense—and that the *whole* of the ceremonial law must be kept to the very letter. This is merely the Galatian heresy with slavish conformity to the feasts and holy days substituted for the requirement of literal circumcision as an adjunct to faith. Paul's indictment—with the appropriate substitution—still applies:

> If you receive circumcision, Christ will be of no advantage to you. I testify again to every man who receives circumcision that he is bound to keep the whole law. You are severed from Christ, you who would be justified by the law; you have fallen away from grace. For through the Spirit, by faith, we wait for the hope of righteousness. For in Christ Jesus neither circumcision nor uncircumcision is of any avail, but faith working through love (Gal. 5:2-6).

Furthermore, the Worldwide Church of God does not distinguish between the ceremonial law and the moral law. The former, as Paul emphatically instructed the Galatians, has been abrogated. The latter, Jesus explained in the Sermon on the Mount, still is in effect. "Think not that I have come to abolish them but to fulfill them" (Matt. 5:17). All of the illustrations Jesus presented by way of commentary are from the moral law; none is from the ceremonial law.

Even with respect to the moral law, as Jesus taught through his example (as when he healed on the Sabbath) and teachings (in the Sermon on the Mount and elsewhere), it is the spirit of the law and not the letter that matters most. The new covenant is "not in a written code but in the Spirit; for the written code kills, but the Spirit gives life" (II Cor. 3:5-6). Such an interpretation does not, as Armstrong charges, give basis for lawlessness. To say that the deeper meaning of the sixth commandment is "Thou shalt not hate" is not to say it's all right to kill.

But the whole point of the discussion is that law-keeping is effect and not cause. The Christian does not keep laws, obey rules, and follow instructions in order to be saved, but because he is saved. Obedience is the end, not the means, of salvation. Jesus was talking to his disciples (Judas Iscariot had already left the Upper Room) when he said, "If you love me, you will [not, "you must"] keep my commandments" (John 14:15). And what were Jesus' commandments? To love one another, to perform deeds of compassion, to live sacrificially, to eschew worldly values, and to observe the Ten Commandments—not only in letter but in spirit.

Herman Hoeh reads into I Thessalonians 2:14 an argument that the New Testament churches kept the Old Testament feasts. The verse reads, "For you, brethren, became imitators of the churches of God in Christ Jesus which are in Judea; for you suffered the same things from your own countrymen as they did from the Jews. . . . " Paul is commending the Thessalonian Christians for their willingness to suffer for the sake of the gospel. In *this* respect they imitated the Judean churches. Not one word is written which can be construed as teaching that the Gentile churches were imitating the Jewish-Christian churches in conformity to the law. In his discussion Hoeh conveniently omits the last half of the verse, which makes the intended meaning clear. And from his reasoning about what the Thessalonians did he generalizes that all the "Churches of God in the Gentile world followed their example!"[3]

The appeal to Paul as a defender of Jewish legalism is ironic. Not only did the Apostle to the Gentiles strenuously oppose the efforts of the Judaizers to subvert the gospel of grace (Acts 15), but he expressly dissociated himself from the law: "For though I am free from all men, I have made myself a slave to all, that I might win the more. To the Jews I became as a Jew, in order to win Jews; to those under the law I became as one under the law—*though not being myself under the law*—that I might win those under the law" (I Cor. 9:19f.).

Each year the Worldwide Church of God publishes a booklet entitled *God's Sacred Calendar.* In it, the approved divine calendar (as revealed by God to Moses) is superimposed over the "Roman" calendar, though the latter is condemned as pagan. "Rather than follow the God-given principles, the Roman calendar begins a new year in the dead of the winter, its days in the middle of the night, and its months without reference to the moon."[4] God's way has each year beginning in the spring, each month with a new moon, each day at sunset. "Months have 30 and 29 days alternately with a few minor variations in some years.

Seven years of a nineteen-year cycle have a 13th month called Veadar. The present year [1970-1971] contains but twelve months and a total of 354 days."[5]

Purple, "the color of royalty," has been selected for the numbering of "God's calendar." Commenting on the fact that religious holy days and holidays are customarily lettered in red on "Roman" calendars, the editor states, "The world has chosen scarlet, the color of a fallen woman, for its days—days which have had their origin in Babylon and have been branded upon the Christian-professing world by the daughter of Babylon described in Revelation 17 and Isaiah 47."[6]

(1) The Sabbath

The Sabbath, valid only if observed on the seventh day of the week (sunset Friday until sunset Saturday), is not only significant as "a memorial of creation—but also foreshadows the seventh 1000 years, in which man shall rest from his labors of sin."[7] Sabbath-keeping is considered "a test of obedience. No one shall enter into an eternal rest unless he first, here and now, is willing to enter into the rest of each Sabbath, each seventh day of the week."[8]

Specific instructions for Sabbath observance are delineated in a *Good News* article. The Christian is to desist from ordinary work. Instead of attending to our business, we should be about his business on his day. "The Sabbath gives you extra time to study and meditate about God's course of eternal life, His principles and mode of action."[9] Forbidden are those pursuits

> which you take extra pleasure in doing—hunting, fishing, golfing, swimming, cards, movies, boating—those things which take up the majority of your leisure time. This would also include the many time-consuming hobbies such as the "ham" radio operator, woodworking shop, stamp collecting, etc. . . . Whatever *your* pleasure or leisure-time activity is, you should not engage in it on the Sabbath.[10]

Not engaging in such pleasures means, as well, not thinking or talking about them. On the contrary, we are to concentrate our minds and thoughts on "God's pleasure and

God's ways on the Sabbath." This is accomplished by devoting "Sabbath time to *extra* Bible study, *extra* prayer and especially *extra* meditation!"[11] To avoid conflicts, members are urged to keep a checklist of things to be done in preparation for the Sabbath.

Armstrong has written a 95-page booklet proclaiming the Sabbath doctrine in no uncertain terms:

> *If* Jesus Christ is *in you* (and you are not a truly converted Christian unless He is!) will He, *in you*, profane His Holy Day, and observe a pagan day? *Impossible!* . . . And *if* you, having read the truth in this booklet, now make excuse, or rebel, and refuse to *keep* holy Christ's Holy Day, then on his infallible authority, I say to you that He is not in you![12]

Those who disobey will "pay the death penalty—for eternity!"[13] For those who may still miss the point Armstrong reproduces a photograph of a freight car filled with corpses of victims of Nazi savagery at Dachau, captioned with the grim warning, "Americans, Britons, Australians and other Israelites will again suffer these hideous atrocities (Deut. 28:49, 50) because of disobedience to God's Law."[14]

In his zeal to establish the seventh-day Sabbath, Armstrong rejects a considerable body of evidence from Scripture and the early church fathers which testifies that Christians from apostolic days have observed the first day of the week for "breaking bread" and Christian worship (Acts 20:7; I Cor. 16:2). Ignatius, Justin Martyr, Irenaeus, and Eusebius, among the early fathers, all testify that the Christian day of worship had shifted to that on which the Lord arose.

(2) Passover

Passover is the one and only day in the year when the sacrament of the Lord's Supper is to be observed. From Luke's comment that Jesus and the Twelve sat down to partake of the first Lord's Supper "when the hour had come" (22:14), Armstrong deduces that "there was a definite time—a definite hour—when He held this supper, setting us an example."[15] What if the Israelites in Egypt had observed this ordinance at the wrong time? "They would not have been saved when the death angel passed by that night! God does things on time. He has given us an exact time for this ordinance."[16] We are cautioned by Paul of the dire consequences for those who eat and drink unworthily (I Cor. 11:27, 29): "Surely if we, once we see and know the truth, partake of this most sacred ordinance at any other time than that set apart in the Scripture, we would do it unworthily, and to our damnation."[17]

Explicit instructions are given for fixing the date according to the Jewish calendar as used by Jews today. As in the Upper Room, the service is preceded by footwashing, and unleavened bread and wine are used in the memorial ritual.

Armstrong denies that New Testament references to "breaking of bread" refer to the Communion sacrament, and maintains that the Lord's Supper was observed annually from the beginning. This diverges from the overwhelming majority opinion of biblical scholars.

> Originally the apostolic church celebrated communion at every meeting for worship. . . . Very soon, however, if we may judge from the Acts and the Pauline Epistles, its administration was confined to the meeting on the first day of the week. . . . In the post-apostolic church the Eucharist continued to be celebrated every Lord's day.[18]

References in the church fathers dating to the earliest centuries confirm this partice.

(3) Days of Unleavened Bread

Seven days of Unleavened Bread follow immediately after Passover. This feast shows "our complete deliverance (seven denoting completeness) from our natural tendency to commit sin."[19] The "Wave Sheaf offering" occurs on Sunday, following the weekly Sabbath of the "seven days," and depicts

> Christ, the first of the firstfruits from the dead, being accepted by the Father before the early harvest (the Christians of these last 2000 years) could be reaped. The resurrection of Christ had

> occurred the previous day—the Sabbath—near sunset but the acceptance of His sacrifice by the Father did not occur till that "Sunday."[20]

The scriptural background of this strange sequence is not provided.

(4) Pentecost

In Judaism Pentecost is an agricultural feast celebrating the first fruits of the spring harvest. Armstrong agrees with the traditional view that this day symbolizes the coming of the Holy Spirit and the consequent beginning of the New Testament church. He also sees in it a future significance. "In a larger sense it depicts the entire time of this New Testament church from the arrival of the Holy Spirit till the soon-to-occur second coming of Christ when the reaping of the first harvest of souls will occur."[21] This interpretation, which is without scriptural foundation, is based upon the Armstrong assumption that no one can be saved—i.e., no souls will be harvested—until the "first resurrection" occurs at the time of the Second Advent.

(5) Feast of Trumpets

To ancient Hebrews and modern Jews, the Feast of Trumpets marks the beginning of the civil new year and occurs on the first day of the seventh month (Tishri), usually in September. According to Armstrong symbolism, this feast "points forward to that day when the last trumpet will sound and the dead in Christ rise to meet Him at His second coming. Christ will then put down the Devil's rule and set up His Kingdom, the Kingdom of God, at Jerusalem, to spread progressively over all the peoples of the earth."[22]

(6) Day of Atonement

The Day of Atonement (Yom Kippur) is the holiest day in the Jewish calendar. As described in Leviticus 16, the ritual involved the symbolic laying of the sins of the people on the head of a scapegoat, which was then driven into the wilderness to represent the banishment of sin from the camp of Israel. A second goat was slain and its blood splashed on the mercy seat atop the ark of the covenant in atonement for the sins of the people, who stood in reverent silence at the doors of their tents while the symbolic act was performed by the high priest.

In the Worldwide Church of God, the Day of Atonement pictures "that day in the future when the responsibility for sin will be placed justly upon the head of the Instigator of it, Satan the Devil. Mankind will then become 'at one' with God or in complete accord, all sins having been forgiven and forgotten. The 10th of Tishri is observed as a day of fasting, a day in which we afflict our souls by abstinence from food and drink."[23] This is the only day of the year, other than the weekly Sabbath, on which no work is to be done. With the Seventh-day Adventists, Herbert W. Armstrong identifies Satan—not Christ—as the scapegoat upon whose head "the responsibility for sin will be placed."

(7) The Feast of Tabernacles

To the Children of Israel the Feast of Tabernacles (Lev. 23:39-43) was a thanksgiving festival in gratitude for the fall harvest. The Israelites lived for eight days in temporary shelters as a reminder of their wilderness sojourn when they had no permanent dwellings.

Tabernacles is the biggest feast on the Armstrong calendar. It "begins Tishri 15 at sundown and continues seven days through Tishri 21, the first day being an Annual Sabbath. These seven days picture the millennium when the resurrected Christians, then immortal, rule the earth under Christ."[24] Attendance by members is required, a "second tithe" being assessed to defray travel expenses. In 1973 celebrations were held at 34 sites in 18 countries, with 96,000 (including children) participating. A description of the feast in a recent year is typical:

For eight joyous, exhilarating days, God's people dwelled together in unity and love and experienced a foretaste—a kind of pre-

> view—of the wonderful World Tomorrow. It was an inspiring, encouraging, spiritually rejuvenating, *spiritual* Feast, as well as a time of physical abundance and fine food.[25]

The Feast is seen as "helping us prepare for *our* part in the soon-coming rule of God on a breathtakingly beautiful, bountiful earth," and as providing "a powerful *witness* to the thousands of people in the local communities near our Feast sites around the world." Plush vacation spots form many of the sites, including Squaw Valley in California, Jeckyll Island State Park in Georgia, Wisconsin Dells, and similar facilities in Alaska, Hawaii, the Philippines, Australia, India, South Africa, Europe, and South America.

(8) The Last Great Day

The day following the Feast of Tabernacles is called the Last Great Day. On this occasion Jesus taught in the temple about "living water" (John 7:37). It is supposed by Armstrong to prefigure the "second resurrection."

Prior to 1961 the Feast of Tabernacles and the subsequent celebration of the Last Great Day were held in Big Sandy, ten miles west of Gladewater, Texas. An article in the August 1959 issue of the members-only magazine *The Good News* repeated time and again that the site of the celebration was hardly a matter of chance:

> There is authority for observing the Feast of Tabernacles at Gladewater, Texas! It is time you understood it. . . . God sets the *time* for the annual festivals. In like manner God sets the place! . . . It became evident to Mr. Armstrong together with the ministry and many of the members at the Headquarters Church, that the only place available where we could meet was the very place God had placed His name—on the property near Gladewater, Texas. . . . Since God placed His name at the grounds near Gladewater, Texas, and had led His Church to assemble there, *no* other place in the United States can be chosen for *the Feast of Tabernacles—not even Pasadena*. . . . There can be only *one* place in the United States and Canada. . . ![26]

The exaggerated concern for the divinely appointed place of the festival, so evident in 1959, was later to disappear under a cloud of expediency. To meet the demands of a burgeoning membership a second site, Squaw Valley, had to be added in 1961; and additional meeting centers were opened during subsequent years until by 1973 the number had grown to 34 (13 in the US and Canada).

Omitted from the Worldwide Church of God sacred calendar is the Feast of Dedication or Hanukkah, which commemorates the purification of the temple by Judas Maccabeus in 165 B.C. after its defilement by the Syrian tyrant Antiochus Epiphanes. This was not an Old Testament feast—yet it was observed by Jesus (John 10:22). Armstrong's appeal to Jesus' example as his authority for celebrating the Old Testament feasts would seem inconsistently applied here. A number of Jewish converts to the Worldwide Church of God apparently continue to celebrate the feasts, however.

But Christ's blood swept away both the ceremonial law of Moses and its later appendages. From the orthodox Christian point of view, Armstrong's error is the same as that of the Judaizers in the early church. In the first years after Pentecost, Jewish Christians adhered to the seventh-day Sabbath and kept the annual holy days and festivals. Jews who became Christians did not all of a sudden cease to be Jews. But when the Jewish Christians failed to convince the majority of their fellow Jews that Jesus was indeed the promised Messiah, and after the Jerusalem Council of Acts 15 ruled that Gentile converts did not have to submit to circumcision and in effect become Jews first in order to become Christians, the church entered on a new era. Mainstream Christianity took its cue from Paul and the Jerusalem Council and rejected the old wineskins of Jewish legalism in favor of new wineskins appropriate to the new dispensation of grace.

B. The Ten Commandments

Keeping the Ten Commandments, according to Armstrong's unique interpretation, is more than something the Christian does as a consequence of being saved, to express his love, gratitude, and commitment. Obedience is a condition that must be met in order to achieve salvation, as Roderick C. Meredith makes clear:

> For if you make any claim to being a Christian, remember that Jesus Christ, the *founder* of Christianity, said that you shall live by every word of God (Mat. 4:4). And certainly—through God's help—you must walk according to the *commandments* of Almighty God if you would enter into eternal life (Mat. 19:17).[27]

(1) *Thou shalt have no other gods before me.* Exalting the one true God—and rejecting false gods—is prerequisite to *becoming* God. "God the Father is *reproducing Himself!* He plans that those who overcome human nature in this life and learn—through the help of His indwelling Holy Spirit—to keep His perfect laws, shall be made *like Him*—born into His very family and kingdom!"[28]

(2) *Thou shalt not make unto thee any graven image.* The Worldwide Church of God does not go to the extreme of ruling out all forms of artistic representation, merely "the use of art or sculpture as a *form of worship* or 'aid' to worship. . . . Certainly, since Jesus Christ is God (Heb. 1:8), this would *directly prohibit* any picture or likeness of His person!"[29]

Also under the ban are "idolatrous Church festivals." Traditional facets of the Easter celebration are "symbols of idolatrous sex worship." Christmas is "a pagan, idolatrous festival borrowed directly from heathenism . . . a pagan religious orgy dedicated to the sun-god." Santa Claus was "originally a vile and sinful man." Also strictly forbidden is observance of New Year's Day, Lent, Halloween, and birthdays. Memorial Day, Independence Day, and Thanksgiving, however, are approved, since they are national holidays, not "rooted in paganism."

(3) *Thou shalt not take the name of the Lord thy God in vain.* In the light of Armstrong's disbelief in hell and eternal puishment, people are warned against "asking God to 'damn' someone," for this is "asking Him to do something which He has never intended to do."[30] Oaths are likewise forbidden, and members enjoined to "affirm" rather than "swear" in court. Another blasphemous infraction of the third commandment is the use of the terms "Father" and "Reverend" for priests and clergymen. The

most common violation is "prayer without obedience." "The hypocrisy of religious denominations and religious people is infinitely *worse* than the profanity of the street."

(4) *Remember the Sabbath day to keep it holy.* The repeated Armstrong emphasis on the seventh day as the particular day of the week which God "blessed" and "sanctified" has already been discussed above. In addition to forbidding certain activities, the fourth commandment positively enjoins prayer, Bible study, meditation, visiting the sick, and following Jesus' example of "doing good," as well as assembling "with other *true Christians*" for worship in a spirit of gratitude and joy. But all such exercises and attitudes are unavailing unless practiced on the divinely ordained seventh day.

(5) *Honor thy father and thy mother.* "Just as will be expected of him in the adult world, *a child must be disciplined to do things he does not necessarily want to do.* From babyhood, a child must be taught to respect and obey his parents."[31] Parental discipline in the Worldwide Church of God is harsh, as it seems to inculcate unquestioning obedience. Ex-elder John Judy of Akron has stated that "severe punishment of children is taken as a sign of loyalty to the church." Judy "recalls seeing one father spanking his child at a church meeting as if he were 'whipping a horse.' "[32] But a young mother, formerly a member of the Worldwide Church, denies that this is typical. In a personal letter to the author, she wrote,

> The emphasis is on discipline in much of the literature; but again, I think it is a reaction to our permissive society. I've known only two or three cases in which I thought the parents spanked too much or too hard. In general, the parents are producing respectful, obedient, well-balanced children, who really stand out as examples to the rest of us. I'll always be thankful for the course I had at Ambassador on teaching a child from birth to six years old.

(6) *Thou shalt not murder.* The sixth commandment is rendered thus in the Jewish version (also followed by the New English Bible). It is not seen as forbidding capital punishment. It does prohibit murder, war, euthanasia, and abortion. God alone "who gave life has the right to take

life. Therefore, only God has the right to wage war! And, as Jesus taught, God does not choose to have His children wage war for Him during this age. Jesus said that His servants would fight if His kingdom were of this world. But it is not. And wars fought by and for the governments or kingdoms of this world are in *defiance* of the higher government and rule of Almighty God from whom all real authority proceeds."[33] The Worldwide Church of God instructs its young men to register as conscientious objectors and to refrain from participating in war and in all other aspects of "corrupt human government." When the devastation of World War III reaches its climax, "God *alone*"—unaided by his people—"will wage war to punish rebellious nations in perfect wisdom and justice." This intervention will bring to an end the world's tragic history of repeated wars of killing and destruction.

(7) *Thou shalt not commit adultery.* The seventh commandment was given "to safeguard the *highest earthly relationship.* For marriage and the home is the basis of all decent society."[34] Roderick C. Meredith inquires rhetorically, "Why is the sin of adultery so great as to merit *death*, and, in God's judgment, *eternal death* in the lake of fire? The answer is this: The reason adultery is such a terrible sin in God's sight is that marriage is such a precious, righteous, holy thing that must not be defiled!"[35] The role of women as sober and obedient wives and homemakers is stressed. Divorce, for whatever reason, is considered sinful, and only a first marriage is considered valid. In one instance a Seattle woman's second marriage was broken up after twenty-four years because the sect does not recognize civil divorce.[36] And Earl Hansen tells of "a 79-year-old woman who sits alone in a wheelchair, left because a minister said her husband could not live with his second wife."[37]

(8) *Thou shalt not steal.* This law extends beyond its literal meaning to forbid gambling, false advertising, and "corrupt unionism"—all cases of trying to get something that one does not deserve. But Meredith warns that there are also less obvious ways of stealing. The eighth commandment is broken by

> refusal to let the land lie completely idle every seven years [Lev. 25:3f.] . . . and through the use of water soluble chemical fertilizers [by which] many farmers are *robbing* the soil of the nutrients which would bring forth health-producing food. . . . In effect, the people forced to eat these foods are *robbed* of health, vitality, and in some cases of life itself! The same *condemnation* is due the processors of food who through greed for "filthy lucre" remove the health-giving elements from the foods we eat . . . or add chemical preservatives to foods which are absolutely *dangerous* to the health of those who eat them.[38]

(9) *Thou shalt not bear false witness against thy neighbor.* " 'Respectable' church and civic leaders are often ready and willing to support gambling, prostitution and narcotics if it is to their financial advantage to do so. . . . In plain language, they are *living a lie!*" The person "whose word is no good, who is in the habit of lying to others and to himself—*that man's very character and mental processes are so twisted and perverted that he can never come to understand even the truth of God until his mind is literally 'cleaned up'!*" The reader is reminded that "there are no 'white' lies in God's sight. They are all black. Half-truths, distortions and deceptions are *condemned* throughout God's Word."[39]

(10) *Thou shalt not covet.* Meredith points out that our "Christian" society is literally founded on greed for material things. That is the source of most financial problems and of much physical and mental illness, broken homes, frustrated lives. "Keeping up with the Joneses" and installment-buying are common violations of the tenth commandment.[40]

"Jesus Christ *kept* and *obeyed* every one of the Ten Commandments in the letter and in the Spirit."[41] In doing so he set an example that his disciples then and now are obligated to follow. Failure to comply, as the Armstrong literature repeatedly reminds, will result in "eternal death" in the "lake of fire."

C. Diet and Health

Everything Herbert W. Armstrong undertakes he does with intensity. In 1930, while living in Portland, Oregon, he worked as a salesman of aluminum cookware. The method by which his company promoted sales was inviting people to demonstration dinners, at which health lectures were given along with instructions on how to prepare meals by the use of the aluminum utensils. Armstrong welcomed the opportunity afforded by this job "to make an intensive study of the causes of sickness and disease, and of nutrition and the part diet plays in health or illness." He learned that "the average American meal is . . . a diatetic horror" and that "from 85% to 95% of all sickness and disease which is not of mental origin is caused by faulty diet. . . ."[42] The sales job was short-lived; but concern for health and proper diet has remained an obsession with Armstrong.

God's "physical laws," which govern our bodies, include the dietary regulations in Leviticus 11 and Deuteronomy 14, which define clean and unclean meat. These distinctions were made for man's good, and have nothing to do with outmoded ceremonial or ritualistic requirements. Since men and other forms of life have not changed, neither have God's health rules concerning the eating of unclean creatures. "Swine flesh—pork, ham, bacon, sausage, etc.—is simply not fit for human consumption. The same is true with oysters, lobsters, clams, crabs, shrimp, crawfish, dogs, snakes, rats, and skunks."[43] Also binding are the decisions of the Jerusalem Council (Acts 15), which "*forbade the use of meat from strangled animals and meats with the blood in it.*" "God condemns, also, the eating of animal fat, or blood (Leviticus 3:17, 7:23, etc.)." Animal fat should be cut off; "cheaper hamburger is not good because it is mixed with much fat"; and "Lard should never be used. These things will wreck any stomach in time."

Armstrong refers his readers to articles in the *Jewish Encyclopedia* for further clarification. "It may not be spiritual sin to eat unclean meats," he concludes. "Yet, if one deliberately does it out of lust of appetite, that breaks the tenth commandment and becomes sin. But in all events wrong food injures the body which is the temple of the Holy Spirit. It defiles the body if not the *man*, and if we defile our bodies God will destroy us (I Corinthians 3:17)."[44]

But the dietary laws of ancient Israel constitute only one aspect of man's responsibility toward his body. Roderick C. Meredith details seven "laws of radiant health," which set forth as Christian obligations a balanced diet of properly prepared natural food along with periodic fasting, cleanliness, fresh air, exercise, sleep and rest, avoidance of bodily injury (including that caused by smoking and drinking), and development of a positive mental attitude.[45]

Few Christians would disagree that they owe their bodies, as temples of the Holy Spirit, the kind of respect Meredith's commonsense rules enjoin. But few would agree that Jewish kosher dietary laws still apply under the new dispensation.

TEN:

"This Is Ambassador College"

Few college campuses in the world surpass the three of Ambassador College in aesthetic appeal, opulence, and excellence of equipment. In a day when private and church-sponsored educational institutions are struggling to keep alive, Ambassador appears to be prospering. As *Time* quips: "Ambassador College . . . [is] where the buildings are expensive and the tuition cheap, the boys' sideburns high and the girls' skirts low."[1] Already equipped with impressive facilities, the three-in-one college is expanding to even greater splendor. A $7 million improvement program is underway on the Big Sandy (Texas) campus. And at Pasadena a $22 million expansion campaign includes a $10 million "auditorium-concert hall" of polished Brazilian granite exterior, surrounded by a colonnade of 72-foot white quartz columns. The lobby, with its "bronze glass and onyx walls," is adorned by a 15 x 25-foot triple-tiered chandelier of 1375 imported crystals. The interior of the 1250-seat auditorium is graced by paneled walls of Brazilian rosewood and a bronze and gold leaf ceiling. According to architect Arthur E. Mann, "of all the buildings of North America, there are none that exceed its magnificence in quality and materials, patient craftsmanship and felicitous design."[2]

To members of the Worldwide Church of God this magnificent structure is much more than an auditorium-concert hall. In a letter addressed to the "Brethren of God's Church" in October 1972, Herbert W. Armstrong identifies it as "God's house at His present Headquarters of His Church and His Work." The magnificent structure was launched April 5-7, 1974, with three concerts by the

Vienna Symphony orchestra, flown to Pasadena following a Russian tour at a reported cost of $500,000.

With only twelve hundred students distributed among its three campuses, and with a remarkable 1-to-10 faculty-to-student ratio, requiring a $6 million payroll in Pasadena alone, the per-student cost of maintaining the three facilities must be enormous. Yet tuition and fees are kept amazingly low. Armstrong himself claims that the school has to turn away—in order to maintain the college as it is—six potential students for every one it accepts. Students are charged $22.50 per month for room; $14.00 per week for meals. Tuition, a mere $16 per semester hour, totals less than $550 per year, according to the 1971-1973 catalog. The 1974 issue of *The Worldwide News* lists inclusive annual costs of $1800 for Big Sandy and $2200 for Pasadena—well below figures advertised by comparable institutions. Apparently the annual cost of attending Ambassador College is approximately $1400—or less than half the tariff at comparable institutions. The student's financial picture is even more attractive because of the numerous opportunities for employment in Ambassador's vast publishing, correspondence, and radio-TV operations, which can earn the full-time student about $1750 during the school year alone.

The Ambassador success story is more remarkable when one recalls that this multi-million-dollar enterprise began scarcely a quarter of a century ago with eight faculty members and four students. The plush California campus was augmented by a similarly palatial establishment on the outskirts of London in 1960; and by another lovely facility near Big Sandy, Texas, in 1964. Pasadena boasts a $2.5 million computer, "a modern television studio . . . larger and better equipped than most television stations," and a modern printing plant said to be "one of the largest on the west coast."[2a] Visitors are impressed with the "magnificent landscaping: green-carpeted, contoured, immaculately maintained lawns; beautiful gardens, fountains, streams, pools; outstanding works of art and sculpture"—as well as by the "proud old multi-millionaire mansions restored to original stateliness, skillfully blended with award-winning new buildings of classical-modern design."[3] The beautiful 45-acre campus encompasses a 12-square-block area "in the heart of Pasadena's finest residential district." The setting for the British campus is an exquisite 180-acre estate, its centerpiece being an elegant Tudor mansion. The Texas campus—though not as lavish as the other two—sprawls over an area of 4000 acres and features experimental farms, a nearly mile-long lake (Lake Loma, named after the late Mrs. Herbert W. Armstrong), and its own lighted air strip.[4]

A. Ambassador's Unique Philosophy and Program

More than in physical facilities, Ambassador College's uniqueness consists in its unusual philosophy and program. Evident to any visitor is

> the noticeable absence of hippie-type students. No student or faculty revolt, no protest marches, no riots or violence. These students give evidence of having a purpose, and knowing where they are going.[5]

The explanation is that Ambassador College "has dared to recapture the true values . . . teaching students not only how to earn a living but how to live."[6] Most education is materialistic and emphasizes the intellect alone, Armstrong charges. A permissive system, that leaves students to form their own moral codes, results in rebellion against all authority.

This Is Ambassador College devotes six pages to a discussion of the sociology of minority groups in the United States. Status and recognition have come to American-born Japanese and Chinese and to Jews "not by police and military enforcement of laws, not by marches, demonstrations, threats and violence, but by self-improvement and achievement." The pamphlet credits a strong family system in each of these three groups with their status. Thrift is inculcated, and pride in achievement spurs children on to fulfil their maximum potential.

By contrast, family life in the white majority society is characterized by a high divorce rate and breakdown of family structure. Even worse conditions prevail among American Negroes: illegitimacy, broken homes, low levels of income and education, high rates of crime and delinquency.

> These minority-group studies show two decisive facts: 1) The stronger the family ties, the higher is the rate of education, self-improvement, achievement, and social status. 2) The more broken are the home and family ties, the higher is the crime rate, and the lower the education. . . . The home and family relationship is the basis of a healthy, happy and enduring society. *This must be made a special concern of education.*

Tomorrow's leaders will be tomorrow's parents, "but tomorrow will be too late! The trend of disintegrating family relationship must be checked and reversed today, if society is to be saved alive."[7] Thus Ambassador is literally a "character-building institution." This distinct purpose—and the means of its implementation—attracts approximately half of Ambassador's student body from other colleges and universities.[8]

It may well be that Ambassador stresses learning how to live, but how to earn a living is not neglected.

> More than 99 percent of Ambassador graduates are living successful lives financially—as well as socially, morally, spiritually. When they find the way to enjoy a monetary competence, however, they enjoy knowing how to live, as well. Their marriages are happy and permanent—their home and family life is peaceful and invigorating. Their children are well trained. Yes, life can be worth living![9]

As evidence of the program's success, *The Plain Truth* reports that "of the hundreds of marriages of Ambassador graduates now dating back some 24 years—not more than three have become involved in divorce. And at least two of these were marriages our guidance counselors specifically advised against!"[10]

Of the 120 hours required for graduation, a student must take 24 in the area of religion. Two courses each must be taken in church history, systematic theology, theological research, and comparative religion. The course names differ somewhat from the usual pattern: Church History I is a study of the four Gospels; Church History II a study of Acts plus the Armstrong version of subsequent church history; Systematic Theology deals with the doctrines of God and Man—the latter including "a summary study of Genesis and the Prophets"; Theological Research I treats the doctrine of Scripture (its inspiration and transmission) and biblical archeology; Theological Research II includes "textual and higher criticism" as well as a "survey of the religions of the world"; and "Comparative Religions I & II" cover "a comparative study of doctrine" plus a "discussion of distinct denominations and religious beliefs."[11] Thirty-seven additional course offerings are listed under the headings of "Biblical Studies," "Historical and Theological Studies," and "Professional Studies." The offering of 61 Religion courses contrasts with only six course offerings in behavioral studies, five in biological sciences, seven in physical sciences (including only one course in chemistry and two in physics), four in mathematics, eight in English, and eleven in history. The proportion is rather heavily weighted in favor of religion courses for a liberal arts college, which Armstrong insists Ambassador is. (Nevertheless, all male students are identified to Selective Service boards as "divinity students" eligible for exemption from the draft.)

Launching a college based on his own biblical interpretations and insights was not easy for Armstrong:

> . . . I had to go out into the world of education to find administrators and faculty members. There simply were none who understood and believed the truth as God had opened my eyes to see. I could not fill all the jobs of administration and instruction— I am not *many*, but *only* one man. But two things I could, and did, do. I kept myself as Chairman of the Board of Trustees, appointing as Board members *only* those who believed God's truth, keeping the setting of all policies in the hand of the Board. And second, I made myself the sole instructor in Bible and Theology for the first several years.[12]

As promising students matriculated at the college, Armstrong steered them into positions of leadership after graduation. Nearly the entire Ambassador faculty is Ambassador College trained. The degrees offered include the M.A. in theology and education, Ed.D., Ph.D., and Th.D.

The recruitment of the faculty with more concern for religious commitment than academic credentials signals a lack of conformity to prevailing standards which accounts in part for Ambassador's failure to achieve accreditation. The 1971-1973 catalog lists a faculty of ninety at the Pasadena campus, only six of them women (the librarian, two instructors in music, and three in home economics). The list includes twenty-one holding doctor's degrees (many of them presumably from Ambassador College), thirty-four master's, thirty-one bachelor's, and four (three in music and one in Hebrew) having no degrees. At Big Sandy only half of the faculty (27 of 54) own degrees beyond the baccalaureate. The seven doctorates there include Garner Ted Armstrong (Ph.D. from Ambassador in Child Psychology and Education), who doubles at Pasadena as "Professor of Theology." With his extremely heavy schedule of daily radio and TV broadcasting, writing, speaking tours, and global traveling, Garner Ted would seem to have little time for instructing on either campus. An anti-female bias in faculty hiring policy seems indicated both by practice and this unabashed admission by Armstrong in his autobiography: "Based on experience, after our first year with the college, we adopted a policy of employing only men instructors, except in such courses as music, Home Economics, etc."[13]

According to the catalog, Ambassador's "typical new student will be between 18 and 25, in good health, single and ranking in the upper quarter of his high school graduating class. . . . Married and family men are selected each year but with increased emphasis on outstanding talent plus success in their present occupation to compensate for the loss of those early formative years when college training is most effective." Presumably married women are not acceptable. There is a small enrolment of married black students.[14]

Aubrey B. Haines, in a *Christian Century* article, filed the following commentary on the Ambassador College library (Pasadena campus):

> A tour through the library reveals what reading material the Armstrongs consider the basis of a good liberal arts education. There are books in old bindings, many of them dealing with

> biblical history or archeology. Only three newspapers are to be seen: the *Los Angeles Times*, a Pasadena daily and the *Christian Science Monitor.* More variety is apparent among the magazines, which range from science publications and the *National Geographic* to the *Ladies' Home Journal, Christianity Today, Seventeen* and *True*, the "men's magazine."[15]

A similar report by ex-Ambassador faculty member O. James Ribb about the Big Sandy library indicates that its 23,000 volumes (many purchased in used book stores *en masse*) contain only 40% of the two thousand standard works for college libraries. Nor is there much hope for improvement: the yearly acquisitions budget is only a few thousand dollars (compared to $50,000 for the faculty dining room).

B. The Ambassador College Extension Program

On-campus higher education is supplemented by a four-pronged extension program of media, publishing, a correspondence course, and a program for the blind. The electronic ministry, featuring the mellifluous voice of Garner Ted Armstrong, is carried by more than 300 radio and TV stations worldwide, "seven days a week on most stations."[16] Garner Ted, whose inflections and rapid-fire delivery are so much like those of Herbert W. Armstrong that only listeners of long experience can distinguish between them, began to share the speaking chores with his father in 1956. Gradually assuming more of the microphone responsibilities, he has in recent years become the exclusive proclaimer of the Armstrong gospel. The half-hour programs present well-prepared but extemporaneously delivered comments on a wide range of current topics. Evolution, crime, women's lib, the drug culture, the Jesus movement, pollution, the sexual revolution, the Middle East crisis, and the European Common Market are typical themes. Although the program is billed as an educational service of Ambassador College, offered "in the public interest," it is unmistakably designed to whet the appetite of the listener for more information, so that he will send for *The Plain Truth* or one of the attractive booklets offered free by Ambassador College. Since a primary aim is to turn the listener on so he will turn the program on, potentially offensive Armstrong doctrines like British-Israelism and the seventh-day Sabbath are for the most part played down.

According to a 1974 brochure, *The Plain Truth* magazine "is printed in 5 languages and distributed in over 187 countries worldwide." Circulation of *The Plain Truth* passed the three-million mark with the May 1973 issue, soared to a record high of 3,203,111 in October, slumped to 2,591,988 in January 1974, rose to 2,959,636 in February, then fell to 2,778,721 in April. (A curtailment in free distribution of the magazine at newsstands in certain cities overseas may account for a major portion of the decrease.) With the June 1973 issue the length of the magazine was cut from 52 to 44 pages; a further reduction to 36 pages began in March 1974. *The Good News*, made available to non-members in 1973, reported a circulation of 247,000 (only 33,000 to members) in its February 1974 issue. And *The Worldwide News*, launched in 1973, reports church news fortnightly to 29,000 subscribers.

Like the broadcasts, the typical *Plain Truth* article is aimed at the general public rather than the church's constituency. But in early 1972 both the broadcasts and *The Plain Truth* began to move more in the direction of doctrinal persuasion—and in February 1972 the magazine abandoned its "nondenominational" posture for the first time and declared openly in its masthead, "Ambassador College, as a separate corporation, is associated with the Worldwide Church of God, and a portion of the financial needs of the work is supplied by that Church."

To gather what Armstrong calls "the facts behind the news," *The Plain Truth* uses three sources: the wire services (AP, UPI, Reuters); leading newspapers and news magazines throughout the world, checked by the Ambassador Headquarters news bureau; and trained and accredited press correspondents of its own, stationed around the world.[17]

English editions of *The Plain Truth* are published in Pasadena; Radlett, England; and North Sydney, Australia.

French, Dutch, and German editions are published in England and the Spanish edition at Big Sandy, Texas. According to a January 1973 letter to the "Inner Family of Co-Workers in the very Work of the Living God," *Plain Truth* circulation in the United Kingdom outstrips *Time* by 193,900 to 81,400; in South Africa, the margin is 75,000 to 44,200; in Germany (German language), 58,200 to 36,000; Holland (Dutch language), 29,600 to 24,800; and Belgium (French language), 19,700 to 15,500.[18]

The Plain Truth is distributed free of charge, like all publications of the Worldwide Church of God, "as a public service in the public interest." Each issue carries the following statement: "Your already-paid subscription is made possible by the contributions of those who, voluntarily, have become co-workers in support of this worldwide work. . . . The publishers have nothing to sell, and although contributions are gratefully welcomed, no solicitation is ever made to the public for financial support." More than a dozen new booklets are published annually plus revisions of several old ones and numerous article reprints. The *gratis* offer includes books as well as pamphlets and reprints. Nearly half a million copies of the 324-page volume *God Speaks Out on "The New Morality"* were distributed free of charge and postpaid within five years of its 1964 publication. *The United States and British Commonwealth in Prophecy* (226 pages, 1967), *Modern Dating* (127 pages, 1969) and *The Ten Commandments* (144 pages, 1960)—and of course Volume I of Herbert W. Armstrong's *Autobiography* (510 pages, 1957)—are further examples of major Ambassador publications, several hundred thousand copies of each being mailed postage-paid and without charge all over the world. More than a million copies of the 77-page booklet on *Crime* (1968) have been distributed to date.[19] In 1973 more than four million pieces of literature were mailed from Pasadena alone (and that figure does not include *The Plain Truth* and *The Good News*), more than double the 1972 output.[20]

For several years Ambassador College has penetrated millions of homes via advertising in large-circulation magazines. Space was purchased in *Life*, *Look*, *TV Guide*, and *Reader's Digest* (including German, French, Spanish, and Dutch editions as well as English). Full-page ads were also run in the London Sunday *Times* "and other media in England, besides the largest-circulated magazine in German, and other countries."[21] The advertisements offered an Armstrong booklet and a free, three-month trial subscription to *The Plain Truth*. At the end of the trial subscription, subscribers were offered a year's already-paid subscription. From India alone came twenty thousand new subscribers in response to two double-page ads in the English-language edition of *Reader's Digest* in that country.

More recently a renewed advertising campaign was launched when the Worldwide Church of God contracted double- and triple-page space in "the two largest circulation media in the United States"—*Reader's Digest* and *TV Guide*. A letter to co-workers dated January 28, 1973, reported that over 64,500 subscribers were added in response to a single ad in *TV Guide*.

According to the rate schedule effective in January 1973, a split-run double-page full-color spread in *Reader's Digest*, which the Worldwide Church of God apparently purchased, costs $118,370 to reach a ten-region circulation of 17,130,000. Protests from ex-members of the church, however, led to an intensive investigation of Armstrong beliefs and practices by the *Digest* and termination of all Ambassador College advertising beyond 1973.

Another device by which the church is expanding its outreach is placing *Plain Truth* magazines on newsstands in Britain and certain countries in Europe, Africa, and Asia. Through the cooperation of dealers, the slick-paper four-color magazine is displayed with a paper band around it stating, "This is your copy—already paid—no price to you. Look it over. If you like it, take it with you!"

The extensive Armstrong promotional efforts pay off not only in subscriptions but in mail response. In the January 28, 1973, letter to "co-workers" Armstrong announced that mail from the US alone poured into Pasadena at the rate of 41,000 pieces per week during the first ten months of 1972. "But it began to go up in October, and in the last months, the weekly average leaped to 58,000 letters. And the first four weeks of this month [January 1973] the weekly average jumped to 66,500." The February 22, 1973, issue of the *Portfolio*, the college student paper, published figures even more astounding: "In the first 16 days of February, a total of 241,619 letters were received . . . a 106.1% increase in mail over the same period in 1972!" During the twelve months preceding October 1973, total mail receipts were 4,584,534; "new people added to file" totaled 910,788. When it is considered that one respondent in ten sends in a contribution, it may be surmised that the advertising campaign has more than paid for itself.

Getting *The Plain Truth* into the hands of new readers is designed ultimately to win new converts. The *Plain Truth* reader, it is hoped, will progress to ever deeper involvement, at some point beginning to send in contributions and thus becoming a "co-worker." If he continues, of course, he will eventually ask a minister to call, be inspected as to his attitudes, motives, and receptivity, and be invited to services. Finally, if he continues to pass muster, he will become a baptized, tithe-paying, Sabbath-keeping, feast-attending member of the Worldwide Church of God.

How many who make the initial response go all the way? Relatively speaking, not very many. Over the first thirty-five years of its history, "the Work" grew at the rate of thirty per cent per year.[22] By 1969 the rate of annual expansion had dropped to twenty per cent, though the reduction, deplored in fund-raising letters to members, was publicly glossed over by a claimed growth rate of "40 per cent in two years." More recent statistics indicate that the rate has slowed further to about eight per cent. Even that figure is respectable when compared to the alarming membership losses being suffered by many mainline denominations.

The November 1, 1973, *Worldwide News* reported average US church attendance at 73,500 (including 43,056 baptized members); worldwide attendance, 89,205

(54,574 baptized). There are 259 US churches, 356 worldwide; 518 US ministers; 604 worldwide. In a letter to the author, Garner Ted Armstrong revealed that "current baptized membership [September 4, 1973] is 51,369 in the US and 4,197 in Canada, with tens of thousands of others attending church services." Updated figures from the office of Dr. Robert L. Kuhn, personal aide to Garner Ted Armstrong, list US baptized membership as 45,747 (March 1974); non-US, 12,497 (Jan. 1974), including "approximately 4,200 in Canada." The total of 58,244 falls considerably below the 85,000 figure cited in numerous news stories. The April 11 letter to the author reports worldwide attendance at Sabbath services as 89,421 (72,581 US, 16,840 elsewhere). Nonbaptized "co-workers" may swell the number of financially involved individuals to 140,000 or 150,000.[23] It has been estimated that two-thirds of the members have come from other denominations, and that sixty per cent are women.[24]

Another phase of Ambassador's extension outreach is the correspondence course. A 1969 article mentioned that more than 130,000 students around the world were enrolled.[25] Lessons are available in English, French, German, and Spanish. The increase over the 33,000 enrollees reported in the September 1961 issue of *The Plain Truth* is remarkable. In 1970 it was announced that the course would end with Lesson 61, and then be " 'trimmed down' and condensed into 24 jam-packed, succinct, in-depth lessons!" In 1973 the series was further reduced to twelve lessons, supplemented by 56 optional booklets and reprints. A January 1974 *Good News* article reported that more than six hundred thousand students had enrolled since the first lesson was published in 1954. Though billed as nondenominational, the lessons are credited with bringing "*many thousands* . . . to repentance" through their presentation of "God's truth."[26]

A personal correspondence service provides private instruction by mail for students enrolled in the correspondence course. Requests for literature were handled efficiently and promptly by an all-male staff of 180, according to a 1969 publication.[27] However, since the inauguration of toll-free telephone service in 1973, women as well as men respond to inquiries. Doctrinal questions are usually answered by form letters, since a number of questions are doubtless repeated in thousands of letters. On rare occasions, a personalized reply will be made to an inquirer. But if the questions are too pointed, they go unanswered.

C. The Ambassador College Research Program

In addition to the extension services, Ambassador administers a research program in the areas of archeology, agriculture, and ecology.[28]

The location selected by Ambassador College for archaeological research is the temple wall area in Jerusalem, not far from the Wailing Wall. It has long been Armstrong's belief that the rebuilding of the Jewish temple on the original site will presage the return of the Messiah. That doctrine has been soft-pedaled, however, since an August 1969 arson attempt on the El Aqsa Mosque in Jerusalem by an Australian shepherd named Denis Rohan. Rohan, who had a copy of the April 1969 *Plain Truth* when captured, stated that his intent was to remove the mosque from the temple site in order to prepare the way for rebuilding the temple and for Christ's second advent. The fire caused nearly $100,000 damage to the eighth-century Moslem shrine. Following his trial, Rohan was committed to a mental hospital in Israel. The court said he "was suffering from paranoid schizophrenia and was not punishable for his deed because he had acted under an uncontrollable pathological impulse."[29]

An article in the copy of *The Plain Truth* which Rohan carried featured color photographs and an artist's sketch of the temple mount excavation, with text by Herbert W. Armstrong:

> The messianic future world ruler . . . is to reign on the throne of David! . . . The exact spot of that throne lies buried beneath, *at the very site of our present project!* . . . If the spot of the original throne of David is, in fact, to be the coming seat of world government, then all that accumulated debris of century after

> century must be cleared off before that event can occur! Exciting? Beyond words to describe, it is![30]

Evidently one reader who caught the excitement was Denis Rohan. The spark may well have been ignited by previous Armstrong prophecies, such as that recorded in the January 1969 *Plain Truth:* "Whatever the cause, 1969 could be the year when more and more is heard about a temple in Jerusalem." Richard A. Marson, in researching the Rohan incident, discovered several specific predictions in the Armstrong literature that a Third Temple would indeed be erected on the site of the earlier Jewish temples in Jerusalem "in the near future":

> This cannot be some *other* "temple" in some other area—it must be a temple in Jerusalem—or the prophecies of your Bible fail! . . . But time is fast running out for some of these most shocking events to begin developing! . . . But the stage is being set. When the temple is built—and it most certainly will be built—soon—then watch, as you have never watched before, developments in the Mideast, and in Europe!—Garner Ted Armstrong in *The Plain Truth*, Aug. 1968[31]

Little wonder that the El Aqsa fire was embarrassing to the Worldwide Church of God. Armstrong lost no time in declaring publicly that "Denis M. Rohan, or as given in press dispatches, Michael Dennis William Rohen," although admittedly a *Plain Truth* subscriber and enrolled in the *Ambassador College Correspondence Course*, "*has never* been baptized by any of the Church of God ministers, been accepted as a member of the Church of God, attended a church service, had his name entered on our records as a member. . . ."[32] And Garner Ted told a Worldwide Church of God congregation in Pasadena on November 23, 1969, "You know I didn't say anything about a temple being built or an actual building. It could just be a group of people standing around in that place preaching or something."[33]

The temple mount excavations began in February 1968. The following year the director of the dig, Dr. Binyamin Mazar (former president of Hebrew University) visited the Pasadena campus and lectured on the project. That summer (1969), fifty Ambassador students—plus college and church officials—participated in the excavations.[34] In 1972 the number of Ambassador students involved rose to ninety.[35] But despite major investments of personnel and funds ($100,000 per year), the identifying sign at the excavation site assigns credit only to the Hebrew University, and makes no mention of Ambassador College and its participation.

The second phase of Ambassador's "Scientific Research and Exploration" program is to be conducted in Indonesia jointly with the Belgian Foundation, headed by former King Leopold III, "for the exploration of land inhabited by Aboriginal peoples, the study of these peoples, and other activities in the field of anthropology."[36]

D. The Ambassador College Life-Style

The life of the Ambassador student is hedged about with numerous and restrictive rules. With regard to dress, the *Student Handbook* (1969-70) specifies,

> Men are encouraged to wear dress slacks and sport shirts for campus activities. Blue jeans and Bermuda shorts are not acceptable. . . . Women should wear modest, feminine attire at all times. Slacks, jeans, and shorts are not appropriate dress for street or campus. Skirts and dresses are to be neither too short nor too tight. Anything above the knee is absolutely too short!

Such regulations for women's dress are seen as conforming "strictly to the ways of God, as revealed in the Bible."

Dating regulations are even more severe:

> Dating should be conducted on a brother-sister relationship. All forms of romantic expression should be avoided. As students soon learn in Mr. Herbert Armstrong's Principles of Living class, the selfish practice called "necking" is in direct violation of God's commandment "Thou shalt not commit adultery." Necking is a serious sin! Almighty God condemns such a practice when it is carried on outside of marriage. Any student engaging in such a practice is subject to expulsion from Ambassador College.[37]

Full-time undergraduate students live on campus, unless they are married. During the regular college term, all students are required to be in their dormitories by 10:30

on week nights, 12:00 Fridays and Saturdays. A midnight curfew is enforced for summer school students.

Social life at Ambassador aims at "full participation of the entire student body in each social activity. The evils of fraternity and sorority life . . . are avoided. The social occasions are important in the development of true culture, poise, charm, and personality."[38] To insure that "full participation" does not involve interracial dating, only married blacks are admitted—this despite the catalog's statement guaranteeing open admission "without discrimination because of race, color, or religion." Undergraduate marriages are discouraged. "No underclass girl should be considering marriage. Therefore, no man is permitted to date any underclass girl pursuant to marriage."[39]

Until recent years a rather stringent racial policy was in force at Ambassador. Lester Kinsolving reported in his column for March 11, 1972, that

> an investigation of Ambassador College by the Pasadena City Attorney in 1963 disclosed that according to the institution's constitution and by-laws as adopted in 1951, the student body is "restricted to the race of Israel, whom we believe now to be the white, English-speaking Anglo Saxon and the Celtic people, and the democratic peoples of Northwestern Europe, in addition to the Jews descended from the Kingdom of Judah."
>
> When apprised of this report, Garner Ted appeared surprised and replied rapidly: "That must have been while I was in the Navy. It's been altered dramatically. We have no such restrictions now."

In a 1970 interview, Garner Ted told Alan Bestic, "There is no discrimination here. . . . We have Negro students and one Negro on the faculty. We have almost every race you can think of, including an Arab. There are about twenty-five Negro students."[40]

Women's liberation has not made a dent in the Ambassador institutions. "Ambassador Clubs" for training in public speaking are open "to all *men* students," for the Apostle Paul's admonition that women should maintain silence in church (I Cor. 14:34) is taken literally. There were prophetesses in the Old and New Testaments, but Armstrong believes that these women exercised their gift privately. The prophetic office among women "carried no administrative authority" and was employed "*never* in the capacity of preaching."[41] The theology behind this position is that woman was created to "provide a *help* for the man." In persuading Adam to eat the forbidden fruit, Eve sinned—not only in enticing her husband, but in taking "the *initiative.* She had tried to *lead* the man . . . and as a *result* the whole *human family was cut off from God until* Christ came to *obey* God and make reconciliation."[42]

According to Meredith,

> With the attitude of deep *respect* for her husband, a truly feminine woman will not be arguing, bickering or nagging at her husband. She will anticipate his wishes and his directions. Because of its altered meaning in modern terminology, she may not literally call her husband "lord," but she can and should respond to him: "Yes, *sir!*" when he is addressing her in an "official" capacity as her husband! If she would do this for her boss, then *why not her own husband?*[43]

Women at Ambassador may join the Ambassador Women's Club, whose purpose is "to recapture the true values of womanhood and to prepare the whole woman to fulfill her God-intended role of wife, mother, and a leader among women." According to former minister Barry Chase, makeup has long been forbidden to women of the Worldwide Church of God. "But when a lot of dignitaries began visiting the Ambassador campuses, Mr. Armstrong decided it was all right to spruce up the girls with makeup just so long as they don't wear it to church."[44]

Dormitory life is carefully supervised. The *Student Handbook* specifies that rooms are to be cleaned thoroughly on Sunday, Wednesday, and Friday (before the Sabbath). Radios and tape recorders must not be played after 8 p.m. on school nights, and must never play "rock and roll, go-go music, psychedelic sound effects, and other weird, base programs [which] are not conducive to sound character development [and] do not promote good study habits."

The stand on the use of tobacco is unequivocally and tersely announced in the four-word caption of an article by Garner Ted Armstrong, himself an ex-smoker: "Smoking Is a Sin!"[45] Not only does it harm the body, it also is undertaken only for self-gratification. "A smoker can hardly claim he smokes to satisfy *others*!"[46]

The Worldwide Church of God does not apply similar logic to drinking alcoholic beverages. The difference is Jesus' example. Jesus drank wine, and "Jesus has not changed! He would still be living the *same* kind of life if He were to come in the flesh today as He did live 1900 years ago."[47] Since he drank wine in the first century, it follows that he would also drink wine in the twentieth. Alcoholic beverages are thus served at certain Ambassador social functions—and, within limits, permitted in moderation for students of legal age. Violations of the state law as it applies to minors can result in a student offender's being "campused," according to the *Student Handbook.* But pilgrims attending the Feast of Tabernacles are urged to make the most of the opportunity to enjoy the finer things of life, including "the better wines."[48]

Long hair, for men, is also forbidden for biblical reasons. Paul says that "women should have longer hair, for a 'covering,' and men should not" (I Cor. 11:14). Obviously, then, Jesus did not have long hair, and his disciples, who are obligated to walk "in his steps" (I Pet. 2:21), may not wear their hair long either.[49]

The Worldwide Church of God endorses the laying on of hands and anointing with oil for healing, but renounces speaking in tongues, though both are clearly taught in the New Testament, and Armstrong and his followers repeatedly affirm Scripture to be their norm for faith and practice. It is not necessary to "pray down another Pentecost," because the Holy Spirit, after descending from heaven to earth on the *first* Pentecost, "has been here ever since! All we have to do now is to open up our hearts, and to let the blessed Holy Spirit in!"[50] Tongues-speaking is denounced as "Satan's counterfeit" and as "gibberish"—not the sign, nor even a sign, of being baptized in the Holy Spirit. The "true manifestation of tongues . . . is the ability to speak in real languages"—as on Pentecost, when people of fifteen nationality groups heard the Spirit-baptized Christians proclaim the gospel in their own languages.

But although the gift of tongues is disdained, the gift of

healing is extolled. It will be recalled that Mrs. Loma Armstrong experienced a supernatural healing in 1927 after being anointed with oil and prayed for by a stranger and his wife. This healing enabled her again to bear children. With other healings and amazing answers to prayer, Armstrong became thoroughly convinced of the power of God to supply human needs in response to earnest prayer. Reliance on the Lord instead of medical science to effect healing is considered a measure of spiritual maturity. Drugs are considered "not only worthless, but dangerous!" The use of medicines is described as "witchcraft." And "those who don't repent of trusting in the false god of medical science—falsely so called—are going to suffer the excruciating agonies of the seven last plagues" and are doomed to experience "the second death in the lake of fire."[51]

The *Student Handbook* is less adamant:

> We at Ambassador know by experience that God does keep His promise to heal those who believe. . . . This does not mean [however] that we never seek medical advice or aid. For those who do not understand or have faith in Divine healing through prayer, complete medical service is available. Even for those who know that God is the only Healer, the advice of a physician is often helpful in avoiding further transgression of physical laws.

Setting bones, cleaning and dressing wounds, and similar ministrations "in no way [replace] God as Healer."

Correspondence columns in the various Ambassador College publications carry numerous testimonies of divine healing. The following are typical:

> The doctors told me I had an incurable heart ailment, and said I had only a very few months to live. So I asked you to pray for me, and I also prayed . . . now I am healed. The doctor said . . . it was a miracle. —Alabama

> We are most grateful, because the boy with multiple allergies and tuberous sclerosis for whom we requested a prayer cloth some time ago is able to eat almost everything, and seems to be getting better otherwise each day. . . . —Washington[52]

These tributes are offset partially by reports of inconsistency in the application of the faith principle. It is charged by ex-members that some ministers, including those in the higher echelons in Pasadena, seek medical aid for themselves which they deny to their members. In at least some instances fatal or near fatal consequences have accrued from failure to provide professional help for those suffering from serious injury or illness.

No cries of "Student Power!" are heard on the Ambassador campuses. The trend toward growing student involvement in college administration is unknown. Student officers are appointed, not elected. "This assures the selection of men and women best qualified for the position they hold."[53]

The school yearbook, the *Envoy*, is second to none among college and university annuals in binding, paper, color photographs, printing, and attractive layout. No expense is spared to make it the finest publication of its kind. A journalism class publishes the college newspaper *The Portfolio.* Described as "a limited circulation publication," the *Handbook* emphatically instructs students that it "*may not be sent home to relatives or friends.*"

Physical development is serious business at Ambassador College. Men students are "required to be on the athletic field at 6:00 a.m. every school day morning for physical culture exercises. . . . After the men have left the field, at 6:30, the girls are required to appear for morning exercises."[54] Until 1974, athletic contests were limited to intramural rivalry. Undergraduate class and faculty teams play doubleheader basketball games on Saturday or Sunday nights. No admission is charged, the college band performs, and uniformed officials are provided. Though competition is keen, basketball, Ambassador's main sport, is described as "a character-building activity."[55]

An important adjunct to the three Ambassador Colleges is the elementary and secondary education program provided at the Imperial Schools operated by the Worldwide Church of God. Little has been said or written publicly about these full-time day schools, but they are highly regarded by former Ambassador students, who attest to the quality of the parochial education provided there. Enrolment is composed principally of children of Ambassador College staff members and married students.

This, then, is Ambassador College: unexcelled in physical facilities, narrow in purpose and program, rigid in rules circumscribing the lives of its students, and global in its outreach. The college promotional book describes it aptly as "something never done before—a huge, major-scale operation, worldwide, seemingly incredible, yet in fast-accelerating operation today."[56] How does this undeniably unique institution measure up academically?

O. James Ribb is well qualified to answer that question. Ribb was the first student accepted when the Big Sandy campus opened in 1964; and for eight of the next nine years he was associated with the college as a student and faculty member until he broke with the Worldwide Church of God in early June 1973. One of the few Ambassador faculty members to have an outside degree, he received an M.A. in German from Stephen F. Austin State University in Texas. Shortly after his departure he prepared a nine-page typewritten critique of Ambassador's educational deficiencies.

Ambassador is, Ribb notes, dropping its pretensions of being a "liberal arts institution," and coming to admit that it is a Bible school. But in spite of the ample number of courses in theology that are offered, a student receives very little exposure to the key issues in contemporary religious thought or to the intellectual tools for independent theological study. "Very little use is made of any theological sources outside the Church's publications. . . . Not a single Bible teacher in Big Sandy has a working knowledge of the biblical languages. Greek is not taught; there is a course in modern conversational Hebrew. Interest in biblical languages is not encouraged. . . . Such names as C. S. Lewis or Francis Schaeffer, not to mention those of Paul Tillich or Rudolf Bultmann, are simply never heard on campus. . . . Students are *warned* about the dangers of using their own minds, about philosophy and other religious teachings, about being 'critical.' The pressure to conform is all-pervasive."

Ribb suggests that only Herbert W. Armstrong among college officials still entertains such delusions of grandeur as would compare Ambassador academically with Oxford, Harvard, or the Sorbonne. Those few faculty members with outside degrees are cynical about the Ambassador education, recognizing that Ambassador degrees are often awarded on the basis of service to "the Work," rather than scholastic attainments. Those who seek to defend the institution's in-breeding and setting of its own academic standards are often heard complaining of the "materialism" and "vanity" of the "world's" educational system.

Whether to seek accreditation seems to be a continuing question at the school. Ribb notes that

> many college officials have had serious misgivings about even seeking accreditation, which is understandable in view of the Church's exclusivist theological perspective. The old attitude still persists among some that "We're *God's* college. Why should we seek accreditation from 'the world'?" I've even heard expressed by high officials that accreditation would force the College to lower its standards.

A common belief among faculty members perceptive enough to realize the academic shortcomings of Ambassador is that it is not so much the education as the "way of life" that students learn which is really important.

> The word "balance" is most often used to describe the desired product, best exemplified by leading Church ministers such as Garner Ted Armstrong and by the Church's view of the "real Jesus": robust, articulate, clean-cut. . . . Much of the College's program . . . is directed to instilling this "balance." Quiet, introspective, intellectual students have a difficult time fitting into the Ambassador program. . . .
>
> The faculty themselves do not convey the image of "intellectuals" or "evangelists." They exemplify this ideal of "balance" which includes beautiful lakeside homes, fine cars, golf, and handball.

Perhaps most damaging to Ambassador's claims to merit the name college is this remark of Ribb's: "In nearly nine years of experience in Ambassador College I have never once heard open disagreement with the thought of Herbert W. Armstrong. His ideas on everything from sex and dating to the recommended type of cookware prevail throughout the organization. In any disagreement he can be quoted as an authority in the confident belief that only the irreverent might wish to argue the point."

ELEVEN: "This Is the Worldwide Church of God"

A. Scope

Though its membership of fewer than sixty thousand[1] would earn it a rather modest ranking on a list of American church groups, the Worldwide Church of God, as preceding chapters have shown, is an amazing phenomenon on the contemporary religious scene. Neither the ambiguities in the numbers that measure this success nor the recent slowing of growth invalidates the description of the Armstrong movement's rise as meteoric.

From its hundred-watt beginnings in Eugene, Oregon, forty years ago, the "World Tomorrow" broadcast has become a worldwide electronic ministry, going out in February 1972 over (take your pick) "some 500 stations around the world"[2] or "some 400 radio and TV stations worldwide."[3] A sharp downward turn dropped the number of stations to 263 in mid-1973, but that trend was reversed by the addition of 46 new outlets by the end of the year. The Armstrongs' claim of 100 million listeners for the broadcast,[4] or talk of reaching 150 million people[5] or 150 million homes[6] with "the inspired message of the Way of Life that is the cause of all good" is surely extravagant. Nonetheless, the Armstrong empire merits the title "worldwide."

The annual income of the operation, begun on a shoestring, approaches \$56 million;[7] total assets, \$60 million;[8] and the weekly budget, according to Garner Ted Armstrong, about \$750,000. The far-flung outposts of the empire are scattered from Vancouver to Auckland, from Mexico City to Manila, from Bricket Wood (England) to Johannesburg, from Düsseldorf to Bombay. Priority is given to "modern Israel" (the Anglo-Saxon nations) over the "Gentile peoples" in locating these world offices.

In 1927 Herbert and Loma Armstrong first celebrated the Feast of Tabernacles, alone. Twenty-five years later, 450 people from twenty states assembled for the Feast at Seigler Springs, California.[9] By 1965, 31,000 people met at eight locations for the Feast; in 1973, 96,000 attended at 34 sites (13 in North America, 21 overseas).[10] The church anticipates a rise in North American attendance alone to 150,000 by 1976 and more than 260,000 by 1980.[11]

Expansion is planned on other fronts as well. Contemplated for the future are two new Ambassador College operations in India and Japan. These plans have grown out of Herbert W. Armstrong's contacts with high-ranking government officials in these countries. Just how the contacts are arranged is a mystery. Armstrong himself attributes them to "an unusual series of 'coincidences,' which started about six years ago."[12] Be that as it may, he has gained access to heads of state in at least a dozen world capitals. Prime Ministers Indira Gandhi of India and Golda Meir of Israel, Emperor Haile Selassie of Ethiopia and Prime Minister Kittikachorn of Thailand, Presidents Suharto of Indonesia and Marcos of the Philippines, Prime Minister Tanaka of Japan, and ex-King Leopold III of Belgium are among the international celebrities who have taken time from busy schedules to confer with the Chancellor of Ambassador College. Photographs of Armstrong and his legal counsel Stanley R. Rader (a nonmember but constant companion and confidant of Mr. Armstrong), shown presenting expensive gifts of exquisite Steuben crystal to the foreign dignitaries, have become a trademark of *Plain Truth* issues in which these visits are reported. The peripatetic octogenarian arranged a February 1973 meeting with President Thieu of South Vietnam within weeks of the truce agreement ending the Indochina war. He had interviewed Ambassador Ellsworth C. Bunker during an earlier visit to Saigon and hoped to confer with him again. Also planned was a second meeting with Prince Mikasa, brother of Japanese Emperor Hirohito, "to discuss details of the Ambassador Institute of Biblical Research" to be established in Japan.[13]

The organization recently announced an eight-point expansion program aimed at still greater attainments in the near future.[14] (It is considered futile to plan for the distant future, as the close of history is imminent.) The plans include an all-out, four-color advertising campaign in mass-circulation magazines such as *TV Guide;* continued free newsstand distribution of *The Plain Truth* in foreign countries; daily television, with an effort to reach prime-time audiences; a campaign to reach the Arab nations, enlisting the aid of Mr. Adli Mahtadi, a former Jordanian government official; expanded personal appearances both at home and abroad; and continued publication of at least one new booklet a month.

B. Strategy

In his pastoral letter of January 28, 1973, the eighty-year-old Mr. Armstrong made the surprising announcement, "I am now personally taking over active chief editorship of *The Plain Truth.*" Just what this move signifies is not clear. From the beginning, *The Plain Truth* had carried his name on its masthead as editor. But 1972 was a year of transition for *The Plain Truth,* as it was for other aspects of the Worldwide Church of God. Suddenly, in February, the name of Garner Ted Armstrong disappeared from the magazine's masthead. Dr. Herman L. Hoeh replaced Garner Ted as executive editor, and he continues to serve in that capacity.

Also in 1972, acknowledgment of the magazine's religious identity was added to the masthead. *The Plain Truth* had always been identified as a publication "by Ambassador College." In the statement explaining how subscriptions were paid, no mention was made of the magazine's religious auspices. A brief historical sketch traced the work back to "a series of lectures in Eugene, Oregon in 1933, on the laws of success in life," based on the principle of *giving* instead of *getting.* Response to these "lectures" led to voluntary contributions, which in turn enabled Armstrong to get the message out to the public through radio and the printed page. Armstrong's *Autobiography* tells that story differently, of course. The "lectures" were sermons delivered at religious meetings in a country schoolhouse. The radio broadcasts began as a condensed version of a regular Sunday morning church service. Early *Plain Truth* articles treated theological subjects in the context of current news events. Only in the course of time did the strategy change. *The Plain Truth* became more secular in its content in order to make it more appealing to the general public. Doctrine was disseminated—by pamphlets and the correspondence course—only to readers who wrote for additional free literature. Baptized members were given further indoctrination through the members-only magazine *The Good News* (made available to the general public in 1973).

In June 1969 Armstrong started, with an initial run of 125,000 copies, a journal closely resembling *The Plain Truth* in format: *Tomorrow's World*, "a magazine of Biblical understanding," aimed at the in-between clientele—ready for doctrinal exposure but not quite ripe for conversion and baptism. In three years circulation zoomed to 875,000. Suddenly in March 1972 Armstrong decided to "combine" *Tomorrow's World* and *The Plain Truth.* The merger came shortly after Garner Ted dropped out of sight, which reportedly caused income to fall off sharply. But the announcement released to the public gave no hint that economic rather than strategic considerations were involved:

> Years ago, *The Plain Truth* was primarily a magazine of Biblical understanding, much as *Tomorrow's World* is today. But a few years ago circumstances had developed in which the more religious appearance pretty much limited the readership of *The Plain Truth* to that minority of the population *who were already interested in the Bible and its truths.*
>
> Our commission is to reach not only that small minority of the world's population which was already interested in the Bible and the true Gospel Message—but the whole population, or as much of it as possible. . . .

> To do this . . . we felt it desirable that *The Plain Truth* become less religious-sounding. . . .
>
> This policy immediately began to expand the readership of *The Plain Truth* remarkably. And thus we have been able to get much of God's Biblical truth before a fast-increasing number of subscribers *whom we could not reach before.* Not in religious-sounding or Bible language, but in *their kind of language!* . . .
>
> *Now* the situation has become such that we may begin putting, more and more, the same kind of articles into *The Plain Truth* as you have been reading in *Tomorrow's World!*
>
> Therefore we plan now to combine the two magazines. . . .
>
> You need to realize that today *The Plain Truth* is read by many important people—business executives, professional people, and also many who are high in governments of many nations around the world—and that includes the U. S. Government at Washington, D. C. A number of copies go into the White House every month. I believe this new merger, by which world problems will be *explained* by actual Biblically-oriented articles, will be an important means of getting the message for this very hour directly into the hands of leaders in governments of many important nations around the world!

A comparison of the January 1972 and January 1973 issues of *The Plain Truth* illustrates the change in policy:

January 1972	*January 1973*
Personal from Herbert W. Armstrong: Mr. Armstrong's report of discussions with Adam Malik, President of the United Nations General Assembly, and C. V. Narasimhan, first-ranking Under Secretary-General of the U.N.	*Personal from Herbert W. Armstrong:* "Blueprint for Survival." Review of article in the *Ecologist* urging conservation of natural resources—followed by Mr. Armstrong's blueprint: "the *Gospel* . . . for 18½ centuries . . . not proclaimed to the world."
Why the Vast Differences between Animal Brain and Human Mind? An article refuting "the dogma of Materialism."	*Peace at Last?* The thawing of the Cold War in the light of Bible prophecy.
Advance News in the wake of today's world events. A two-page feature providing concise analysis of five items of world news.	*Advance News in the wake of today's world events.* The feature is reduced to one page and two items.

Leaders on the Move in Search for Peace. A backward look at "the 1971 international chess game."

Public Housing Projects: Why Some Become High Rise Slums. Excellent discussion by competent authorities.

The Silent Epidemic. VD: "the disease no one wants to talk about." Seven pages of informative discussion of America's VD crisis.

As the Paris Peace Talks Go on . . . and on . . . and on. . . . A rehearsal of the "frustrations and failures" of the Paris talks.

What You Can Do. . . . Two pages of "timely tips and helpful suggestions for you and your family." Common-sense safety precautions and anti-drug warnings.

The Eritrean Conflict. Scope and implications of guerrilla warfare in Eritrea—"Ethiopia's fourteenth province."

Iran Today: Nation with a Mission. Capably reported presentation of Iran's contemporary political, social, and economic life.

The Four Horsemen of the Apocalypse. The famous vision as interpreted by Herbert W. Armstrong, with invitation to write for free booklets "unveiling" the Book of Revelation.

Happiness Is. . . . Armstrong's Biblical definition of happiness: living by the Ten Commandments.

Ambassador College Is Unique. The virtues of Ambassador College are extolled.

Sex Begins at Home—for Teenagers with Careless Parents. An indictment of permissive parents, with offer of free booklet *Modern Dating* as a corrective.

What You Can Do. . . . The "timely tips" feature reduced to one page.

Who's That Polluting My World? Eleven pages on environmental pollution problems, with story of "How One Town Solves Pollution and Saves Water."

Why Must Men Suffer? A five-page discussion of the age-old problem, based on Job and New Testament passages.

Who Pays When Everybody Quits? Cover story on the economic problems which will result if "everybody" quits smoking. Prediction that the tobacco "evil" will be eradicated in the "World Tomorrow."

A full page of letters, "What Our Readers Say," and a four-page Radio-TV Log are included in each issue.

The January 1972 number contains no biblical quotations or references and advertises only one of the Armstrong booklets—the secular-sounding *Missing Dimension in Sex*. However, *Tomorrow's World*, "a sparkling nonsectarian magazine of Biblical understanding," is offered free of charge to interested readers "as an educational service in the public interest." By contrast, the January 1973 *Plain Truth* contains 76 Bible quotations and direct references (plus many indirect) scattered through three major articles and the lead editorial by Herbert W. Armstrong. Nine free booklets, including the Ambassador College *Bulletin*, are promoted.

The more direct approach has also been reflected in the television and radio broadcasts. During Ted's exile in early 1972, ten-year-old tapes by the elder Armstrong (also occasional new ones) were replayed for the daily radio broadcasts, while the television programs were suspended. After Garner Ted's restoration to the good graces of his father and to his role as voice of "The World Tomorrow," Herbert W. Armstrong explained the new philosophy in a letter dated May 31, 1972. He announced

> a wholly new format for the television program. It will no longer be just a documentary—it will get the real meaning of events and world conditions across to viewers, tied in with prophecy, and a dynamic calling of viewers to repentance and turning to the living Christ! There will be no pussyfooting. . . .

In a companion letter under the same date, Garner Ted Armstrong added his concurrence with the new policy—really, as he noted, a reversion to the *old* policy "of the broadcasts my father was doing when I was but a boy."

A *Good News* report confides to members of the Worldwide Church of God the philosophy behind another facet of the Armstrong strategy—globe-trotting to the world's capitals:

> God has commissioned His end-time Work to proclaim His truth to a world heading toward self-destruction. . . .
>
> How is this great commission being accomplished? Obviously, it is being done primarily through the doors of radio, television, and the printing press which God has flung open. But this is not all. God has also begun *opening* doors of personal contact with leading world statesmen!
>
> The recent contacts with world leaders were not solicited by Mr. Herbert Armstrong. Yet, this Work is beginning to be recognized by leaders worldwide, and God's leading servant is being brought into intimate contact with important world rulers![15]

The suggestion that heads of state have taken the initiative to seek out the founder of a tiny religious sect to confer with him about matters of global significance is difficult to believe. That such interviews have been arranged is nevertheless true. The international celebrities are apparently quite unaware that the members of Armstrong's organization are being privately informed that their leader is fulfilling the typology of Noah, Abraham, Moses, Christ, and the Apostles in opening doors through which he can proclaim his prophetic message of doom to the world. If they were aware, it is doubtful that any of their doors would be open to him.

Armstrong learned early in his ministry the futility of trying to cram religion down people's throats. High pressure salesmanship, he found, "only aroused hostility." In his autobiography he reflected,

> I am glad I learned that lesson early. I have had to maintain certain business connections with many people, since being plunged into God's Work. I must maintain contacts with radio men, publishers, professional men. I get along splendidly with them. A big reason is that I never talk religion to them.[16]

On a 1970 world tour he was reported to be a smash hit lecturing to 150 Singapore Rotarians on the laws of success. The Minister of Education in Singapore requested that his daughter attend Ambassador College in Pasadena.

Also visited on that tour were President V. V. Giri of India, President Marcos and some high government officials of the Philippines, Prince Mikasa and leading educators in Japan, and the top media people in Australia. While in Manila, Armstrong received a phone call from President

Suharto of Indonesia apologizing for not having been able to see him the previous day in Djakarta and inviting him to return to Indonesia at a later date. The tour concluded, the Armstrong entourage boarded the Ambassador College G-2 jet (one of four aircraft owned or leased by the college) and flew back to Pasadena.

Armstrong's success orientation means going first class all the way and staying at the finest hotels. Conrad Comeau, a former Armstrong jet pilot, further details an affluent life-style for the Armstrongs and other top Worldwide Church of God officials. These leaders drive the finest automobiles and live in splendid homes tastefully decorated with top-quality materials. Armstrong confided to his pilot that one of the Work's leaders has paintings in his home worth more than $70,000—all paid for by tithe contributions of constituents.

To keep the luster on the image of the Armstrong empire, the pilot was told to buy expensive suits (for which the church paid—though his salary of over $20,000 was adequate to buy his own clothes). "I found out later," he says, "that all the ministers receive the same type of gift to purchase their tailor-made suits—even with their relatively large salaries."[17] To impress Israeli officials on a Jerusalem visit, Armstrong ordered a $2000 diamond-studded Star of David cuff link set for his own use. On one occasion he had his Rolls-Royce shipped from the English campus to Brussels so that he could be chauffeured in style to King Leopold's residence. This, Armstrong claims, opens doors that would remain closed to anyone driving up in a taxicab.[18]

In a long letter to the Work's ministers in 1969, Superintendent Roderick C. Meredith cautioned about circulating Worldwide Church of God publications on controversial subjects. Withdrawn from all circulation were publications on medical science, healing, voting, and the race question. Limited to members and prospective members, and available only on a minister's recommendation, was the booklet on divorce and remarriage.

The letter reflects the policy of restricting "inside" doctrines and information. A notice in *The Good News*

(January 1968) illustrates the point:

> We ask you to help us keep *The Good News* exclusively a paper for real members only. Do not leave a copy of *The Good News* on a table or stand where non-members or even relatives might see and start to ask about it or read it. . . .
>
> In *The Good News* we wish to be free to say things to you, as our inner family of God's children, which we cannot say to the world. We wish to be free to feed you, through the columns of *The Good News*, the truly "strong meat" of spiritual food which might choke the carnal minded or prove a stumbling block to the unconverted, and those not wholly yielded to obedience to God.

As noted above, a policy change in 1973 made *The Good News* available to nonmembers.

Locations, times of services, and phone numbers and addresses of ministers are not available to the public. Secrecy is even extended to student newspapers published at the three campuses of Ambassador College. The *Student Handbook* instructs, "*The Portfolio* is free to students of Ambassador College. However, it is a limited circulation publication and *may not be sent home to relatives or friends.*"[19] Consistently a boxed warning enjoins students not to share their *Correspondence Course* lessons with others.

> Should you loan your lessons? Absolutely not! . . . Jesus Christ forbids you to do it *indiscriminately.* Notice! "Give not that which is holy unto the dogs, neither cast ye your pearls before swine, lest they trample *them under their feet,* and turn again and rend you"! (Mat. 7:6).
>
> These lessons are *your pearls! God,* who made the human mind, is saying that most people—until they are really called by God—are going to appreciate this truth no more than dogs or swine would appreciate beautiful pearls![20]

The strict discouragement of doctrinal contact with outsiders, ultimately founded on Armstrong's self-image as the only true apostle of God living today, is also enjoined against fellow-members who disagree with the minister. The flock are instructed not to listen to other religious broadcasts. And what if no Worldwide Church of God is available in an area? May a member attend, say, Seventh-day Adventist services? Absolutely not, Armstrong says.

The Adventists do worship on the proper day, but they do not keep the other festivals and they violate the second commandment with their idolatrous pictures of a long-haired person they call Christ.[21] Baptists, Methodists, the Church of Christ—those who are not modernist in these fellowships are disqualified because they believe in the immortality of the soul. Jehovah's Witnesses are deceivers: "Their deeds are evil. . . . You cannot change them! . . . Any further conversation with one of these people are idle words, for which you shall have to give account in judgment."[22]

Criticism is suppressed by the rule that doctrinal questions may only be discussed with ministers and headquarters. If a member confides in another member that he has a problem with this or that teaching, the second member is obliged to "report him to Headquarters."[23] Not surprisingly, there are defections; and splinter groups—some say as many as sixteen—have broken off from the church. The Fountain of Life Fellowship in Valley Center, Kansas, has a doctrinal position much like the Armstrongs'. Director James Porter was "disfellowshipped back in 1958 over the matter of calling on Jesus' Name in prayer."[24] A group called simply "The Church of God" is headquartered in Cleveland, Ohio, and is directed by Armstrong ex-minister Carl O'Beirn. In 1969 and 1970 O'Beirn was unable to get through to headquarters with his reservations about the lack of proper observance of the new moon and about the use of plush motels instead of literal tents during the Feast of Tabernacles. Finally, when he threatened to proclaim his own beliefs on the subject, he was persuaded to fly to Pasadena to talk in person with the hierarchy. In an hour-and-a-half session that included Herbert W. and Garner Ted Armstrong, Herman Hoeh, and Roderick Meredith, O'Beirn received no biblical satisfaction. At the conclusion, he was told that he had put himself out of the church.[25]

More than three hundred former members have affiliated with the Assemblies of Yahweh, of Bethel, Pennsylvania. Bishop Jacob O. Meyer counts fewer than 750 members in the local congregations of this group, though he claims an outreach extending to Canada, Asia, South America and the Caribbean, and Europe. Like the Worldwide Church of God, the organization offers free literature, including *The Sacred Name Broadcaster* and a correspondence course, and sponsors a radio broadcast. Both groups, Meyer claims,

> originated from one source, the old Church of God, 7th Day, of Stanberry, Missouri. . . . Mr. Armstrong and Elder C. O. Dodd (one of the founders of the Sacred Name revival) were once associated in a loose arrangement in the latter 1930s. . . . All the way down through the four decades of Mr. Armstrong's ministry there has existed a smaller group who sought to correct the errors which Mr. Armstrong was teaching.[26]

Meyer himself was never a member of the Worldwide Church of God.

In February 1974 occurred the largest exodus from the Worldwide Church of God in its forty-year history. The upheaval began when six ministers, led by Alfred E. Carrozzo, pastor of the non-student Headquarters Church in Pasadena and former director of approximately two hundred ministers in the western half of the United States, issued a resignation statement listing moral (alleged sexual misconduct by Garner Ted Armstrong prior to his 1972 eclipse), financial, doctrinal, and administrative complaints. When the dust had settled, about three dozen ministers (23 of "pastoral" rank) were out of the church—through resignation or disfellowshipment. Their number included vice presidents David L. Antion and Albert J. Portune (who "repented" two days later and returned to the fold) and three of the church's eight regional directors: Kenneth Westby, Washington, D.C.; Walter Sharp, Big Sandy, Texas; and George Kemnitz, Chicago. Early in March thirty-five of the ex-ministers met in Washington to form the Associated Churches of God, with offices in the nation's capital. Chairman and vice-chairman of the body's fifteen-member (8 ministers, 7 laymen) board of trustees are Westby and Sharp. An estimated 15 to 20 churches and two to three thousand members were said to be involved. The loosely structured organization will grant local autonomy to its congregations; there will be no tithing requirement; and persons who divorce and remarry will not be deprived of membership. The church's doctrinal committee is headed by Dr. Ernest L. Martin, former head of the theology department at Ambassador's Pasadena campus. Other dissidents were said to be turning to the 5000-member Denver-based Church of God (Seventh Day).[27]

A January 1973 strategy meeting suggested that the Armstrong movement might be ready to begin competing on the evangelistic market as a church, abandoning its secular front.[27a] Members were to be encouraged to begin inviting others to services; listing of churches and ministers in newspapers and telephone directories was to be initiated (but as of July 1974 this innovation had not been effected); a complete return to biblical format was projected for the media outreach.

C. Finances

To meet its huge budget the Armstrong organization has adopted, with notable success, a soft-sell approach that contrasts starkly with most religious programs in America. A typical offer, made to *Plain Truth* subscribers:

> I do not want to send anything unwanted, so I will hold your copy [of *This Is Ambassador College*] ready for mailing as soon as you let me know it will be welcome. We never resort to any of the schemes and gimmicks so prevalent today. I suppose you, like myself, have been pestered with such tricks. . . .
>
> There are so many of these "come-on" schemes to get your money that I know it seems hard to realize that when we offer you something of real value without any charge—and tell you we have nothing to sell—you are not going to be asked to buy anything, or join anything—it is the truth, and there are no tricks or deceptions or gimmicks!
>
> You have never heard of any operation like ours! It is utterly unique. And isn't it, after all, a refreshing experience to find something of vital value, with no such come-ons—something 100% aboveboard, honest and sincere?

The letter also offered at "no cost or obligation" a year's subscription to *Tomorrow's World*, described as "not a sectarian or denominational magazine—entirely non-sectarian, . . . without any denominational bias . . . Like

The Plain Truth, you can't pay for your own—it's already paid."

What soft sell could be softer? The addressee is often totally unaware that the goal of the Pasadena organization is to draw him into full membership of a religious sect that will make enormous demands on his time, his life-style, and—most of all—his money. A typical response to the Armstrong approach is this printed letter from a Texas girl named Deborah:

> I just got your letter this morning telling me that I am now a Co-Worker. I was reading your letter out loud to my mother, and when I got to the part that said my name had been placed on your special Co-Worker mailing list, I couldn't go on any further. I was shedding tears of joy because I guess I want this more than I've ever wanted anything in my life—to help spread the gospel of the Kingdom of God.[28]

They had not asked for her money. But they were getting it—probably more willingly and liberally than if they had. And now that Deborah was a Co-Worker in God's only True Church, she would soon recognize that the church she had been attending, like all other churches, was one of "Satan's counterfeits."[29] The logical outcome would be a request for a minister to call, an invitation to services, and finally submission to baptism.

Then the tune would change. Giving would suddenly become compulsory, not voluntary. Deborah would quickly discover the meaning of the first tithe, the second tithe, the excess second tithe, the "tithe of the tithe," the third tithe, Holy Day offerings, building funds, "free-will" offerings, and the "Emergency Fund." The crunch would be on.

In leading adherents into a fully committed financial stewardship, the first step is to establish that God requires of his people "tithes *and* freewill offerings" (Num. 18:8-32; II Chron. 31:14). Next, it is stated that only one church must receive this money.[30] This is, naturally, the Worldwide Church of God. "*We do not ask the public for contributions, but we are commanded by God to tell the people His laws. It is up to them whether they wish to obey God!*"[31]

1. *The First Tithe.* Based on net income "after expenses you incurred in producing your profit are paid,"[32] the first tithe is sent directly to headquarters in Pasadena.

2. *The Second Tithe.* "Being a *loving* God (I John 4:8), He has not only provided a tithe (tenth) for His ministry to do His Work on earth, but He has also provided a tithe for you that you may grow spiritually and rejoice before Him."[33] The second tithe covers expenses incurred by members attending the Feast of Tabernacles—travel, motel accommodations, meals, and special automobile, clothing, and equipment costs specifically related to the Festival. Members are encouraged to "*eat* in good restaurants and *stay* in nice motels. . . . to enjoy and appreciate the finer things which [they] may not be able to afford at other times of the year"—including "the better wines and the more expensive cuts of meat."[34]

3. *Excess Second Tithe.* "It isn't right to squander and throw away second tithe just to get rid of it." Like the Levites of ancient Israel, the ministers are not required to pay the second tithe, and the members' excess second tithe helps pay their way to the Feast "so that they might teach and make clear the plan of salvation to you." Other excess contributions go to help indigent elderly and widows to attend. Members are instructed, "Once you see how much you need in order to rejoice before God and return home again, you can turn any *extra* which is *over and above* what you need into the business office at the Feast. God will bless you for giving someone else the chance to share in your abundance."[35]

4. *The Tithe of the Tithe.* Ten per cent of the second tithe is to be set aside and sent to Festival headquarters in Big Sandy, Texas, to finance operating costs of the Feast.[36] Again, those in a position to do so are encouraged to send in excess funds to Headquarters.

5. *The Third Tithe.* Twice every seven years a third tithe is collected, designated for the relief of widows and orphans. In 1969 "the church claimed to have given $500,000 to 350 widows, which breaks down to about $1,500 a year each."[37] It has been alleged by former members, however, that widows' petitions fall on deaf ears

while Third Tithe funds are siphoned off for other uses, including the operation of the Armstrong jet planes.[38] According to official statistics reported in *The Worldwide News* (Mar. 18, 1974), Third Tithe receipts in 1972 were $3,746,100, while "Widow Support and Emergency Fund Assistance" expenditures were only $1,872,700. Comparable figures for 1973 were $3,589,000 (receipts) and $3,034,800 (expenditures). When Emergency Fund donations are added to Third Tithe income, a surplus of $2,119,200 is indicated for 1972, $801,300 for 1973.

6. *Holy Day Offerings.* At each of the seven annual Holy Days, a special offering is received. In mid-August members of "God's Church" are mailed four "Holy Day" envelopes.

> These are for your use during the *Fall* Holy Days—for your offerings. . . . They are for special Holy Day offerings during a Church service only—and not for mailing! Please turn in any regular tithes and offerings to your minister separately as you normally do on a weekly Sabbath.[39]

"Robbing Peter to pay Paul" is strictly forbidden. It is more important, according to Armstrong, to maintain a constant income at Headquarters than to have a large offering at the Feasts.[40] Holy Day offerings in 1973 totaled $5,883,200, an increase of $1,615,300 over the previous year.[41]

7. *Building Fund.* Writing from Jerusalem in May 1969, Herbert W. Armstrong pleaded with members to do their utmost in financing a magnificent auditorium, "God's House," in Pasadena. Nearly two years later a *Good News* article urged renewed dedication and sacrifice for the project. "We need to be . . . making second, third, fourth and fifth effort—as we are able—to go above and beyond what we put on our 'statement of intention' cards. Unless we do, brethren, we may not be able to complete the building program."[41a] Lagging efforts notwithstanding, Armstrong gave the go-ahead for the new construction on June 1, 1971, and further announced that plans were being drawn up for a new library building. By February 1972 he was able to report to members that the dreams had become a financial obligation, and "we must pay it, even if we have

to take the money from the proclaiming of the Gospel to the world!"

8. *Freewill Offerings.* Undesignated voluntary offerings, over and above required tithes, Holy Day offerings, and contributions to special projects, are encouraged. It is hinted that those who give beyond that which is required by *law* will be especially rewarded. "Those whose hearts—whose *prayers*, whose *tithes* and generous offerings, and whose service is wholly in the Work of God in turning many to righteousness—they shall shine in their *glorified, resurrected* bodies as brilliant stars, forever and ever!"[42]

None of the Armstrong financial appeals provides for contributions to welfare and social service agencies such as CARE, the Salvation Army, the Red Cross, or the American Cancer Society. Nor is similar work undertaken by the Worldwide Church of God. Perusal of the Armstrong literature fails to disclose any reference to the material needs of the poor, the diseased, the afflicted, and the oppressed. There are many articles, of course, dealing with war, crime, poverty, disease, earthquakes, tornadoes, and other disasters—but always in a context of prophecy, these events being seen as signs of the end-time tribulation. An article on foreign work shortly after the Managua earthquake (Christmas 1972) referred only to the fact that there were no members—only subscribers and two persons interested in baptism—in the Nicaraguan capital.[43] No word about the plight of the other thousands of victims.

9. *The Emergency Fund.* Concern for "the brethren" is the basis of an "*Emergency Fund* . . . maintained in each local church area" for the purpose of "helping members in need." It is also "sometimes called the *Poor Fund* or *Love Fund.*" Used clothing and furniture may be donated in lieu of money. This fund is distinguished from the "third tithe" in that the latter "is *reserved* for certain groups, most of whom need assistance on a regular basis—*the Levite, the stranger, the fatherless and the widow* (Deut. 14:28-29)."

> While not forgetting the parable of the Good Samaritan, we do need to realize there are those who would prey on our good intentions. Realize, too, that God's command in Deuteronomy 15

refers only to those "of thy *brethren.*" If a genuine need arises among *unconverted* people, it would often prove wise to obtain the counsel of one of God's ministers before acting.[44]

"Tithing pays off"—in the here as well as the hereafter, Roderick Meredith argues. As evidence he cites a letter from a Wisconsin member: "Since I have been sending my tithes and offerings to God's true Church, I have had very little unemployment even in our severe winter weather (I am a bricklayer). Every winter before these two, I had to borrow money at the bank to pay taxes and winter bills."[45] Delinquency in paying the required tithes is regarded as serious transgression of the law. In a *Good News* article a simple test is proposed to ascertain the reader's attitude toward sin. "Which sin is *worse?* a) To borrow from your second tithe *in an emergency.* b) To embezzle from your employer."[46] The correct answer given is that the two are equally reprehensible in God's sight, even though the second tithe is designated for the member's personal use (to cover his Festival expenses).

Announcing curtailments in the "Work" is a device sometimes used to induce renewed zeal and sacrifice. In a "Co-Workers" letter on December 29, 1969, Armstrong berated those guilty of "exchanging gifts back and forth with friends and relatives, supposing it was for Christ's birthday! But they didn't give their gifts to Christ—but to one another." Consequently, the work came up short, and Armstrong had to cancel several radio stations and large media advertisements. "That means that several million people will not be hearing God's message—until our Co-Workers make it possible." Those not willing to devote self and substance sacrificially are said to be "in *mortal danger*! I say to you candidly, I know that some, if not many of you, are in *real* danger of the lake of fire!"[47] Threats of this sort continue, even though annual income soared from $32 million in 1970 to nearly $56 million in 1973.[48]

The Armstrong eloquence notwithstanding, there remains the lingering question of how the 60,000 members—even with another 80,000 "Co-Workers"—can come up with the staggering sum of $56 million per year, reportedly several times the income of the Billy Graham Evangelistic Association?[49] Garner Ted Armstrong told Alan Bestic, "Seventy per cent of our income comes from tithing."[50] That would leave a balance of $16.8 million to be raised from other sources. There are unconfirmed reports that a number of wealthy celebrities from the entertainment and business worlds are helping to bankroll the Armstrong enterprise. An August 1972 article in *The New York Times* alleges that chess champion Bobby Fischer "has been a member of the strict fundamentalist church for six or seven years"—which the Worldwide Church of God denied during Fischer's temperamental outbursts at Reykjavik.[51] Fischer was said by the *Times* to give 20 per cent of his income to the church. According to an ex-member Herbert W. Armstrong himself revealed in private conversation that Fischer was a member; however, the August 10, 1973, *Christianity Today* disclosed that he "has become disenchanted with Herbert W. Armstrong's Worldwide Church of God, according to some reports." He was said to be "in seclusion in Denver with an ex-member of the church."

With the appearance of a major article and interview on Texas businessman H. Ross Perot (whose "fortune is now roughly $300 to $400 million") in the March 1974 issue of *The Plain Truth*,[52] rumors started flying that he may be a heavy contributor to the Armstrong enterprise. Similar rumors have linked billionaires Howard Hughes and H. L. Hunt with the Worldwide Church of God.

D. Authority

Since it is believed that to Herbert W. Armstrong has been delegated supreme authority over God's church by none other than Christ himself, members are indoctrinated to submit to Mr. Armstrong in all things or face the threat of excommunication. According to Worldwide Church of God theology, "the succession of ministers . . . begun by the hands of Jesus Christ remained unbroken in the True Church through all ages"—the end of that succession being Herbert W. Armstrong.[52a] He is reported to have a chart tracing his genealogy "back into the line of British kings, and therefore has the complete record of his genealogy thru the House of David clear to Adam—believe it or not!"[53] According to the *Standard Jewish Encyclopedia*, "It is improbable that the genealogy of any Jewish family today can be demonstrated authentically beyond the late Middle Ages." The impartial reader can hardly be blamed for viewing Mr. Armstrong's claim with skepticism, but the members believe this allegation—and many similar to it—and take this as evidence for his divine right to rule over them.

Conrad Comeau, Armstrong's former pilot, cited earlier, tells of working with a medical doctor, a new convert to the church, in the shipping/receiving department at Ambassador College. This use of qualified persons is familiar to anyone with military experience: its object is to humble individuals "showing them that they are nothing. Their attitude is: 'We do not care what you have. We do not care what knowledge or background you possess. You will do as we say.' "[54] At the same time there is a gradual effort to appeal to the ego. The member is constantly reminded that he belongs to "a mighty elite group . . . chosen by Christ Himself to serve in His true church."[55]

Comeau claims that the doctrines of Armstrong's apostolic authority and of the individual's role as submissive and self-sacrificing servant are so ingrained that an Armstrong chauffeur once said to him that if Herbert W. or Garner Ted Armstrong told him to drive the Cadillac over a bridge into the water with him aboard, he would do it.[56] Little wonder, then, that some members of very modest means are reported to give over half of their income to the Worldwide Church of God in response to the threats and promises that emanate periodically from Pasadena.

There is also an almost obsessive fear of disloyalty from within the ranks and persecution by "enemies" outside the organization. Co-workers are asked to pray for the safety of the Armstrongs as they risk their lives daily: "Our lives are frequently threatened by some who hate God's truth." Memorandums are circulated among ministers to be on the lookout for disloyal members.

The rigid authoritarianism of the Worldwide Church of God is based on the theocratic concept of the pyramid, "Government *from the top down.*" Raymond F. McNair explains:

> All true law and all governing power and *authority* comes from God Almighty. It is God the Father in heaven who is the Chief Executive over the whole universe. . . . *Jesus Christ* is second-in-command in God's pyramidical chain of governmental authority. Attending directly under Christ are innumerable heavenly beings—angels and other spirit creatures.
>
> In the Kingdom of God, which Jesus Christ alone can—and soon will—establish on this earth, God the Father rules directly through Christ. Christ in turn rules through those whom He will choose or appoint to be directly under Him. Then those directly under Christ rule over others, who in turn rule over others—all the way down to the bottom of the pyramid of God's system of perfect government! . . .
>
> In a few short years the nations of this earth are going to see first-hand what *the wonderful government of God Almighty* is like. . . . His government will not be left in the hands of the ignorant masses of people.[57]

But although Herbert W. Armstrong condemns the evil governments of this world, he courts the favors of those who rule with cordial interviews, costly gifts, and invitations to visit Ambassador College. In compliance with Christ's command to render to Caesar that which is Caesar's, members are to pay their taxes, obey the laws of the land, and otherwise submit to civil government. But they are not to vote, to run for political office, to serve in the armed forces, or in any other way participate in "human" government.

Herman L. Hoeh sees the pyramid symbol of "government from the top down" as prefigured by the Pyramid of Cheops, allegedly built by Job. Cheops, he says, is but an altered pronunciation of "Job." "God's government is also in the form of a pyramid. Christ is the rejected 'capstone' (Ps. 118:22)." Hoeh declares that Job is called by the Arabs the "wizard of Oz," since he came from the land of Uz (Oz).[58]

The global pyramid organization, as of January 1974, follows:

Herbert W. Armstrong
President and Pastor General

Garner Ted Armstrong
Executive Vice President

10 Vice Presidents including
David Antion
Vice President of Church Administration

8 Regions in U.S.A.,
each with its Director

10 Foreign Offices Worldwide—each with its Director

U.S. regional offices are located in Atlanta; Big Sandy, Texas; Chicago; Cincinnati; Kansas City; Pasadena; Portland, Oregon; and Washington, D.C. In addition to world headquarters in Pasadena, other offices are located in Vancouver; Mexico City; Bricket Wood, England; Düsseldorf; Geneva; Johannesburg; Bombay; Manila; Sydney; and Auckland.

When the Worldwide Church of God was thrown into turmoil early in 1974 by numerous resignations and firings of ministers, the pyramid authority structure was short-circuited to eliminate, at least temporarily, the regional directors and two vice-presidents. In return for their two-day resignations, vice-presidents David L. Antion (Garner Ted's brother-in-law) and Albert J. Portune (director of the "personal appearance" campaigns and former business manager) were granted two-month "leaves of absence." Antion, in a letter to Herbert W. Armstrong, pleaded, "Please let me be a part of helping you. . . . If pushing a broom or raking leaves is the best way—that's fine with me. Job title is not important to me. Accomplishment is."[59] But whether the two penitent officials ultimately would be restored to their prestigious posts and salaries (Portune's 1972 salary, according to IRS figures, was $43,842)[59a] was uncertain as this book went to press.

Garner Ted Armstrong, in a February 27 "communique to all U.S. field ministers," wrote:

> I have temporarily disbanded the present organization of the Church Administration Department and the regional directors. As of now, every church pastor reports *directly* to me in line function. And to assist me, I have appointed a staff of evangelists, consisting of Mr. Raymond McNair, Mr. Wayne Cole, Mr. David Jon Hill and Mr. Ronald Dart. These men will be laboring daily over the telephones to *directly assist me* in whatever needs you have. They also will be making church visits.[59b]

E. The Garner Ted Armstrong Mystery

In February 1972 Garner Ted Armstrong, Executive Vice President of the Worldwide Church of God, Vice Chancellor of Ambassador College, Executive Editor of *The Plain Truth* and *Tomorrow's World*, the radio and television voice of "The World Tomorrow," and heir apparent to the leadership of the Worldwide Church of God's $55 million global empire, suddenly went into hiding. Rumors circulated about the reasons behind his mysterious disappearance; for a time the only official explanation issued by Pasadena headquarters was that the younger Armstrong had taken an "extended leave of absence" for reasons of health. Then the truth leaked out that Garner Ted had been stripped of his authority and microphone for an undisclosed offense and was in bad favor with his father and the Church of God hierarchy.

According to the *Pasadena Star-News*, Herbert W. Armstrong issued a letter to ministers "detailing the background of the asserted 'disciplinary action.' "[60] The ministers were instructed to read the communication at services on February 12, after which they were to destroy it. Earl Hansen, religion editor of the *Seattle Post-Intelligencer*, managed to gain entrance to the auditorium where four hundred Seattle members listened in stunned silence as Garner Ted was described as being "in the bonds of Satan."[61] A Pasadena official later "categorically denied any schism between the two Armstrongs, as well as reports that the son had been 'disassociated from the church [because] . . . he is in the bonds of Satan.' "[62] But under date of April 25, 1972, the senior Armstrong, in response to "many false rumors and baseless conjectures" as well as "many letters from . . . Co-Workers asking for an explanation," wrote his "Inner Family of Co-Workers" contradicting the denial. He confessed the announcement to be "the most difficult and painful . . . [he had] ever had to make in a Co-Worker letter."

> Last autumn I was dismayed to learn that my son had been so overcome with personal, emotional problems, that it led to conduct inconsistent with the high standard of the Work of the Church of God and the scriptural qualifications for a minister of Jesus Christ, and rendered him incapable of carrying on the duties of a minister, and of his responsibilities of Executive Vice President.

Church and college officials, therefore, "had no choice but to remove Garner Ted Armstrong from his office and his responsibilities."

> Mr. Albert J. Portune was made acting Executive Vice President of both corporations, and Mr. Garner Ted Armstrong was granted a leave of absence, hoping that full repentance and overcoming of his personal, emotional problems would allow reinstatement without a long delay, and for the protection of the Work, no public announcement was made.

To clarify the situation further, Mr. Armstrong quoted an exchange of letters purporting to show that "rumors or conjectures of personal conflict" between himself and his son, "and also of unfair treatment against Garner Ted," were groundless. The elder Armstrong's letter of October 18, 1971, begins "My *Very* Dear Son Ted," and refers to Garner Ted's "very sore trial," "extenuating circumstances," and "human weaknesses." He told him, "I know you are having to fight a pull in the other way," assured him of his earnest prayers of intercession, and entreated him, "Go to your knees—repent!" Ted wrote later, addressing the letter "To my Dearest Father." The son thanked his father for being "the most completely understanding, patient, considerate, forgiving father on earth" and spoke of himself as deserving "nothing but death." The letter continues,

> I guess no one can ever know how deeply I was bitten; afflicted of the devil through all my wretchedness of these past few months—or just how subtly and cleverly Satan sought to destroy God's Work through me. . . . I have no excuses. I sinned mightily

> against God, against His Church and His Apostle; against the wife God gave me in my youth; against all my closest friends. . . .
>
> It amazes me that I could have acted that way, Dad; me, Garner Ted Armstrong, who has preached over and over again in piercing clarity about all the vagaries and deceit in human nature; who has been able, with God's Holy Spirit, to graphically describe the very course my own rotten nature so recently took. . . . I have acted like a mindless criminal; like an enraged beast; like someone bent on destruction, and on hurting, and tearing down. I must confess I rebelled at first, when meeting you at Penticton. . . .

At this point Herbert inserts editorially, "where I stopped him from further preaching." The *Pasadena Star-News* supplies background details.[63] Apparently, during the previous September Armstrong had announced a leave of absence for Garner Ted following the fall Festival circuit. " 'But after he had spoken at four of the sites,' " his father related in a statement, " 'I was forced to remove him from further speaking.' " The *Star-News* article says that this occurred at Penticton, British Columbia. After speaking to the Festival congregation at Squaw Valley, California, Ted was enroute to a similar gathering at Penticton, but "was intercepted at the airport by his father and did not deplane. The senior Armstrong had flown to British Columbia from Pasadena after receiving complaints from church officials at Squaw Valley." Immediately after their return to Pasadena, church officials acted to " 'remove him [Garner Ted] from the office of executive vice president,' " according to an official statement.

Garner Ted confessed to being a victim of Satanic influence and pleaded for forgiveness. As a result of this letter, the board and his father did receive him back. "But subsequent events, attitude and conduct, to our great dismay, demonstrated to the Board members, ministers and myself that the process of repentance was not yet complete. . . . we had to come to realize, as did my son also, that he must take a considerable period of time to regain his spiritual strength and stability, before he can even contemplate the resumption of his heavy responsibilities . . . in preaching and broadcasting." The April 25 communication concludes, "Co-Workers and Brethren, I want you to realize that when in this Ministry we preach of righteousness, *we mean it*, even though it involves such disciplinary action right at the very top of the Ministry. . . . Satan has planned this as his Master Stroke to try to destroy the Work of the living God. He has not succeeded. . . ."

By mid-June 1972, Garner Ted was back on the air, more dynamic and effective than ever. Companion letters from father and son dated May 31, 1972, joyfully informed the "Brethren of God's Church" of the reconciliation. "My most fervent heart-rending and prevailing prayers of the last ten months, combined with yours, *have been answered!*" wrote Herbert W. Armstrong. "We know God has forgiven, and filled him—and us—with a completely new dedication for the finishing of the Work of this age." Plans for "a wholly new format for the television program" and for "personal appearance" programs featuring Garner Ted were announced. The letter also carried an urgent appeal for funds, lending credence to reports that the church's income suffered seriously during Garner Ted's absence. June 10 was designated as "a day of fasting and prayer for all members worldwide!"

Following the four-month exile, there was widespread speculation about the real truth behind the mystery. Was marital infidelity implied by Garner Ted's confession that he had sinned against the wife of his youth? His father seemed to imply this in response to a question posed by *Time* correspondent Sandra Burton in a May 1972 interview. Armstrong told her, "Look up *I Timothy*, Chapter 2, first five or six verses, and *Titus*, Chapter 1, verse 6." "Both passages make two points in common," *Time* comments, "that a bishop or church elder must be faithful to his wife and rule strictly over believing children." But when asked more directly the implication of the passages, the elder Armstrong "was cryptic: 'The fault was spiritual, not moral.' "[64] In a later article *Time* stated that "even unfriendly sources now doubt that it was some moral transgression like adultery. Some speculate that it was a disagreement with his father on a few of the W.C.G.'s more arcane beliefs. Others suggest that Garner Ted all along wanted to switch his shows from documentary format to more direct preaching and that he has actually won the battle with his father."[65]

Christianity Today suggested that the disciplinary action might have stemmed from "rumors that Garner Ted opposed the lavish spending of his father and other leaders—money for costly suits and jet trips and not enough for 'the widows.' "[66] In a similar vein, Earl Hansen of the *Seattle Post-Intelligencer* cited a remark attributed to Garner Ted, "There's lot of empire building going on in the church."[67] And Betty Medsger, writing in *The Washington Post*, noted possible significance in the report that Garner Ted "no longer could accept the totalitarian fundamentalism of his father's organization," or in the rumor that "the father has been forced to turn against his son to support others who plan to usurp the son's former power in the organization."[68]

But the *Star-News*, close to the action in Pasadena, pointed to Garner Ted's "sermons with 'double meanings' . . . urging alteration in the Holy Days observed by the denomination."[69] During the younger Armstrong's eclipse two former members, with contacts inside the organization, produced a 17-page typewritten manuscript entitled *Herbert W. Armstrong's Holy Day Dilemma.* The photo-copied essay begins,

> Not too long ago, three top officials of Herbert W. Armstrong's Worldwide Church of God met quietly together at a little restaurant in a small east Texas city. One among the three was Garner Ted Armstrong—recently expelled heir-apparent of his father's church.
>
> The purpose of this quiet meeting, conducted over a cup of coffee and a light snack, was a five page, heavily scriptured but lightly detailed paper on the holy days written and endorsed by several members of the organization and by those who felt the holy days should no longer be kept in the Worldwide Church of God. This situation warranted serious attention. Indeed, those among the three had at their disposal good reason to reconsider some of the original concepts of the church in the light of new knowledge and understanding. But there were those who had insisted on the status quo. Some time later, Herbert Armstrong, himself, came to east Texas and remarked before his people that no young personages in his assemblage were going to force him to

change the doctrines. In fact, he virtually shouted about it in adamant certainty.

Yet, the doctrine of the holy days was beginning to create some serious difficulties, especially around the east Texas communities of Ambassador College. Some—even in ranking positions—had dared to speak out on various aspects of the holy day issue. A few even dared to leave and others had been forced to depart over the question.[70]

Certain references in the letters cited above would seem to substantiate the suspicion that the differences were doctrinal. The fact that Garner Ted's removal was effected in a context of preaching was still another clue. Lester Kinsolving, in an exclusive interview on December 28, 1971, questioned Garner Ted Armstrong about the British-Israel belief of the Worldwide Church. "When asked about this," he relates, "Garner Ted smiled and replied: 'It's a likelihood, but it can't be proved. It's an interesting aside. We certainly don't regard this as a required belief, if that's what you're getting at.' "[71] This relaxed view is a distinct departure from the dogmatic certitude with which the elder Armstrong affirms the Anglo-Israel identity to be "the vital key that unlocks prophecy to our understanding."[72] Could the father have been miffed at his son's shrugging indifference to the import of one of his pet teachings? If so, the doctrinal difference—and whatever other differences there might have been—apparently were patched up. At least so states Herbert W. Armstrong in his May 31, 1972, letter announcing the reconciliation and restoration of Garner Ted to the broadcasts: "This ordeal these past ten months has brought my son Ted and me even closer together in father-and-son affection and deep love than ever before. We are together in Christ's Spirit, in *doctrine*, in God's Work completely."[73] Kinsolving is less convinced: "Garner Ted, even though stripped of all pre-satanic period titles, is apparently happy to be home," he remarked in his *Inside Religion* column for September 24, 1972. "For the tithing of the flock keeps him in mansions, jet planes and the national electronic limelight."

But given the pyramid concept of authority, the theory that Garner Ted's doctrinal criticisms were interpreted by his father as rank insubordination (even blasphemy), which could not be overlooked or tolerated, makes considerable sense. It had happened once before—in Paris in 1956. The incident is recorded in the Armstrong autobiography:

> As the family sat together, reading the Bible and talking, something came up . . . that brought sharp disagreement from Garner Ted. Ted was wrong, but to my surprised and greatly pained realization, was refusing to admit it. Accordingly, I persisted on the point—whatever it was. Instead of admitting he was wrong—which was obvious—Ted allowed himself, for the first and only time since his conversion in my presence, to get into a wrong and antagonistic attitude. I did my best to make it plain and restore him to a right spirit. I did not succeed. He became stubborn, resentful.
>
> I suffered, in a way I seldom have in my life. Here was my son, being used by God as an instrument speaking part time on the air with me. Unless he changed his attitude, and repented of it, I knew he would be used no more.

Armstrong tells of going to his room and kneeling in prayer.

> I begged God to do what I had been unable to accomplish—to restore Ted to a right attitude. I hoped Ted would knock at my door, repentant—but he didn't. . . . I walked several blocks around Paris streets. It seemed like one of the most serious and crucial crises that had ever struck the Work of God in our time.
>
> Finally I went back, and quietly entered our bedroom. Again I prayed, and read the Bible. Then finally, there was a knock at the door. It was Ted. His eyes were wet. "Dad," he said, "I couldn't stand it any longer, and finally I had to go into my bedroom and pray. And as soon as I knelt in prayer, I realized how wrong I was. I'm terribly sorry, Dad—*please* forgive me! I've already asked God to forgive me and help me never again to get into a wrong spirit."
>
> And I have never seen Garner Ted Armstrong in a wrong spirit since. Perhaps *that* was when his earnest *daily* prayers to be kept in a respectful and obedient attitude toward both his heavenly Father and his human father began.[74]

It will be noted that this narrative was written several years prior to Garner Ted's exile in 1972.

Garner Ted's status in the Worldwide Church of God continued to be ambivalent for eight months following his restoration. His offices and media responsibilities were not immediately restored. From July through November 1972 his name appeared on the masthead of *The Plain Truth* as one of nine members on the magazine's publishing board. But the board (including the name of Garner Ted Armstrong) was omitted from the December 1972 and subsequent issues. Was this an indication that all was not well in Pasadena—that Garner Ted's "repentance" was incomplete?

Then in January 1973, at a top-level ministerial conference in Pasadena, Garner Ted Armstrong's full authority as second-in-command of the Worldwide Church of God was reestablished.[75] This despite an alleged personality clash with Stanley R. Rader, the organization's legal counsel, and a power struggle involving Albert J. Portune, Sr., Herman L. Hoeh, and Roderick C. Meredith.

It seems unlikely that the momentum powered by the charismatic father for forty years can be maintained apart from the talents of his gifted son. This is a lesson learned painfully and expensively by the Worldwide Church in 1972. Estimates of revenue loss during the period of Garner Ted's absence from the air run as high as 40 per cent.[76]

An article in *The New York Times* of May 6, 1972, ventured the opinion that "Herbert Armstrong, considered by some members to be a prophet, is still solidly in control of the Worldwide Church of God."[77] But even so, the years are already taking their toll on the 82-year-old leader. Even if he attains his mother's 95½ years, it can be reasonably assumed that Armstrong, blind in one eye and his hearing impaired, is nearing the end of his more-than-two 19-year time-cycles of active leadership in directing the "end-time Work of God." What then?

Lester Kinsolving has described Garner Ted Armstrong as "one of the most effective of all conservative religious broadcasters. Instead of holy ranting or endless Scripture-spouting, Garner Ted, as he does in his magazine, focuses primarily on contemporary concerns, often with good sense, logic and reasoned hope."[78] Even if the public relations figure of 150 million homes is an exaggeration, Garner Ted Armstrong's fluent, conversational, and frequently incisive commentary undeniably reaches untold millions. A man of many and varied talents, Garner Ted ad-libs his way through the half-hour radio and TV programs (save for readings from quoted material and the Bible); and in the summer of 1972 he recorded an unbelievable backlog of 76 programs to free himself for public appearance tours throughout the United States and Canada. At one time he sang on the program and considered making a career of music. A magnificent oil painting from his brush adorns a large section of wall near the snack bar in the student union at Big Sandy. A licensed jet pilot, he maintains his aviation skills at the controls of Ambassador College's jet aircraft.

During the personal appearance tours the 44-year-old son of Herbert W. Armstrong has proven his effectiveness not only as a public lecturer but as a show business personality. One observer likened a New Orleans program to a Broadway show, the entertainment being "absolutely professional from start to finish; no flaws, interruptions, or gaps. It is rapid fire, with nicely spaced changes of pace." Garner Ted Armstrong, the source said, is "a professional emcee."[79] As to message content, the following copy from a newspaper advertisement provides a sample:

> Garner Ted Armstrong . . . with challenging, sincere, straight-from-the-shoulder talk about the dizzying disarray of problems that confronts us all. Some say, "Christ is the answer!" Garner Ted asks, "Which Christ?" . . . and "What was the *question?*" But the real issues are divorce, crime, pollution, pornography, drugs and war. All are an effect of an underlying *cause.* Garner Ted Armstrong knows the causes for these evils—and the only real cure! Here, at last, are the urgently needed answers.[80]

Prime-time hour-long TV specials in August 1973 propelled three of the productions into millions of North American homes. The advertised topics were "Sex and the American Family," "Why Did God Let Little Tommy Die?" and "Is This the End Time?" After an opening musical selection, Garner Ted introduced a "commercial" showing off Ambassador College to its best advantage and presenting pictorially the story of the Worldwide Church of God, including such impressive statistics as "1100 miles of high quality paper roll off the Ambassador College presses each month." All this took no more than ten of the sixty minutes, leaving most of the time to the speaker.

Garner Ted's lectures were amply illustrated, liberally sprinkled with quotations from his well-marked Bible (a camera zoomed in on it once or twice), and expertly delivered with only occasional glances at the notes on the lectern. Absent were references to peculiar Worldwide Church doctrines. The lectures concluded with an appeal to reason, not emotion, and involved no altar call or exhortation to an on-the-spot decision. An off-camera announcer described one of the Armstrong booklets and urged viewers to request it and a trial *Plain Truth* subscription (free) by calling Ambassador's toll-free number.

In July 1973 Herbert W. Armstrong had announced Garner Ted as his successor, likening his action to David's appointing Solomon to the throne of Israel prior to his death. It appeared that the position of heir-designate was firm. Then on February 24, 1974, the front page of the *Los Angeles Times* broke the story that six ministers had quit the church, one of them, Alfred E. Carrozzo, who had served as pastor of a Pasadena congregation and director of some two hundred Western US ministers. In a twelve-page statement the six charged Garner Ted with sexual misconduct over a period of nineteen years. The "last straw," according to ex-minister John Mitchell of Shreveport, was an illicit "relationship with a young stewardess who accompanied Armstrong on college-leased jet planes."[80a] There were other complaints, including suppression of questions raised on doctrinal points, financial extravagance, high salaries and life-style for the hierarchy. But the accusation that rocked the church the most was the disclosure that it was indeed a sex scandal that had resulted in Garner Ted's banishment in 1972. Neither confirming nor denying the allegation, the younger Armstrong told a *Times* reporter that he believed "that when he was later restored he had been fully forgiven by God and the ministers of the church."[81]

Herbert W. Armstrong immediately canceled an early-March personal appearance tour in Manila and flew home. A letter to members advised that all services throughout the US were being canceled for March 2 for the purpose of fasting and prayer. It began to appear doubtful that Garner Ted—perhaps even the Armstrong empire itself—could survive. Garner Ted may well have had second thoughts about the $200,000-a-year job as TV commentator which he says he turned down five years ago in favor of his church position at a salary of $30,000, thirty per cent of which he returns to the church.[82]

TWELVE:
Evaluation

A. By Those Personally Involved

A trademark of person-centered religious movements is that they polarize those exposed to them into two opposite camps—ardent supporters/defenders of the founder and fiercely hostile critics. This polarization was true of the original Jesus movement. It was true of the non-traditional nineteenth-century American religious sects pioneered by Joseph Smith, William Miller, Mary Baker Eddy, and Charles Taze Russell. And it is true of Herbert W. Armstrong's Worldwide Church of God. Most fanatical in their loyalty, of course, are those most deeply involved. And most zealous in their opposition are those once deeply involved who for some reason became disenchanted and broke with the organization—or by daring to voice their criticisms caused the organization to break with them. As John Milton observed, "There is no rage in Heaven like love to hatred turned."

This is not to invalidate the testimony and the judgments of either group nor to overlook the wide range of response between the two extremes. An objective appraisal will recognize that there is much that is good, and will accept as valid the witness of those who personally have observed and experienced that good. At the same time, objectivity requires openness to reasonable testimony concerning the failures and flaws of Armstrong and his "Work." Honest evaluation, therefore, must give dispassionate and equal consideration to opinions good and bad, favorable and unfavorable, positive and negative. A conscientious effort must be made to sift through the data from all sides and to distinguish between rumor and fact, the false and the true, the uncharitable (and therefore possibly distorted) judgment and the fair-minded (and thus more likely to be reliable) criticism.

Sorting through the multitude of reports and opinions, testimonials and accusations, is complicated by the realization that bias, either pro or con, may distort what is said. Normally, the individual with first-hand experience is best qualified to judge, yet often his judgment is most likely to be colored by his emotions. Perhaps the course of wisdom and fairness is to let the testimonies speak for themselves and let the reader decide what allowances, if any, should be made for the evaluator's bias.

If one is interested in perusing dozens of favorable comments from all over the world about the Armstrong religion, he has only to turn to the "What Our Readers Say" columns in *The Plain Truth*, *Tomorrow's World*, the *Correspondence Course*, and *The Good News*. A fair appraisal of the Worldwide Church of God requires an examination of the sincere tributes contained in these letters. Typically they illustrate various levels of involvement on the part of the writers.

Some letters are complimentary, but do not indicate any particular degree of commitment—such as this one from a subscriber in Dawson Springs, Kentucky: "Please keep *The Plain Truth* coming, for it is the best of 41 monthly publications which I receive."[1] Satisfaction at not being exploited is a common theme, expressed in this letter from Mont d'Or, France: "It is the first time in my life that I have found someone who is really interested in me, in my understanding of the Bible, and sends me spiritual nourishment free—without asking a penny!"[2]

Concurrence with the Armstrong interpretation of the Bible is acknowledged with appreciation in many letters. A student from Bayreuth, Germany, wrote in response to the *Correspondence Course*,

> I have to agree with you when you always say that one should open the Bible to every scripture mentioned to prove whether it

> is true. I even used several translations for some scriptures because I could not believe that the Bible said the exact opposite from what I had learned, and come to believe. I also have to admit that I don't know of another correspondence course which covers the Bible so thoroughly.[3]

Many letters indicate a turning away from traditional Christianity as a result of the Armstrong indoctrination—such as this one from a woman in North Highlands, California:

> Thank you so much for the wonderful Bible course. I am on Lesson 2 and want to tell you that I have learned more about the Word of God, in this short time, than I ever learned from going to Sunday School and Church.[4]

Others tell of taking Armstrong material into mainline churches. A man from Norris City, Illinois, related,

> A copy of your magazine, *The Plain Truth*, has been given me by a friend. I have read it from front to back and love it, especially "What Is a Real Christian?" I find I have been believing the wrong way. I would like very much to enroll in your *Ambassador College Correspondence Course.* I will welcome any literature pertaining to the Word of God. Being a Sunday school teacher, I must teach the truth.[5]

Not a few such letters come from the "hundreds of ministers" enrolled in the *Correspondence Course*, such as this one from Escondido, California:

> I am studying Lesson 2 of the Correspondence Course. I am so thrilled with it because it shows me how little I knew. Even after preaching and teaching for over 33 years, the Bible is a new book in my hands. I wish that God would grant me the privilege of going back over my travels and straightening out the things that I taught were the Gospel of Jesus Christ![6]

Many readers feel guilty about accepting the Armstrong literature free and so begin to contribute. A woman from San Mateo, California, is representative: "Recently a friend gave me a copy of your magazine which we have found outstanding in every way. So much so that we would like to subscribe. However, in the magazine we read that there is no subscription rate. Please accept this small contribution to your good work. From time to time we would like to further contribute." An editorial note below the letter states simply, "*We sincerely thank you.*"[7]

The next step is to become a regularly contributing "co-worker." A man from Jamaica, New York, declares this intention: "I should have a part in God's true work, so enclosed is a money order for my tithe and also an offering. I intend to send you my tithes and offerings each month."[8]

Despite disclaimers by the Pasadena publications ("We have nothing to sell, . . . there is nothing to join"), involvement moves inexorably to tithe-paying and baptized membership in the Worldwide Church of God. A man from Hope, Arkansas, writes:

> I wish to receive the Holy Spirit—I would like to be baptized. I have finished reading your article on "Just What Is the Church?" in *Tomorrow's World* magazine. I agree with every word you said. Therefore I would like to live by every scripture of the Holy Bible including Acts 2:38. I would like to follow the example Jesus Christ of Nazareth gave us and be baptized.[9]

To this letter was added the promise that "one of God's ministers (an Ambassador graduate)" in the area would contact the gentleman "as soon as possible."

The writer of the following letter, a *Correspondence Course* student from Colorado, was no doubt ripe for baptism: "Your *Plain Truth*, Bible Course, and program have simply turned my religious beliefs bottom side up. Thanks to you, I am now keeping the Saturday Sabbath. I want to quit my church because I don't believe in their teachings anymore."[10] (The editorial caption above the letter read, "Forsakes 'Mark of the Beast'!") Likewise the husband of the Kingsport, Tennessee, woman who wrote *The Good News*,

> I just have to tell you—my husband (not in the Church) heard about the money crisis in the Work and the lack of increase over May of last year and on his own decided to send back the 7-piece dinette we had ordered and put the monthly payments for it into the Work. It never ceases to amaze me how God is working through my husband. He's Catholic. He also plans on paying third tithe this coming year '69-'70. Isn't it wonderful?[11]

Finally, correspondence from young people may reveal a determination to attend Ambassador College. From Willowdale, Ontario, came this letter to *Tomorrow's World:*

> Thank you very much for your article in October's *Tomorrow's World* entitled "Enjoy Being a Girl." I am nearly seventeen years old, and am planning to apply for Ambassador College this spring. Your article has helped me very much in realizing the purpose of going to Ambassador. You are quite right when you say that if you try to follow the right way, you will be taunted and ridiculed. Many times the other kids have laughed at me and called me a "grannie," but at least I know that I am not alone.[12]

A variety of responses—in many cases (understandably) negative—were engendered by a questionnaire that the writer sent out to persons known to have been affiliated with the Worldwide Church of God. The questionnaire was not designed as a scientific sampling, for the number of returns (25) was far too small to be statistically significant, and the controls required for a scientific poll could not be exercised. For example, a number of the recipients duplicated the questionnaire and sent it on to others, a procedure that tends to increase the number of responses of a specific type: namely, those who agree in essence with the people contacted. The ingrained Armstrong suspicion of "outsiders" with their "prying questions" which are often characterized as "persecution" filters down to the faithful, and makes it difficult to get any response at all from those favorable to the Worldwide Church of God. But a large number of first-hand opinions did result from responses to the questionnaire.

Though it is hazardous (and beside the point) to generalize from so small a sample as this, one interesting fact came to light. Only four of the seventeen respondents who were church members prior to their now-severed affiliation with the Worldwide Church of God belong to a mainline denomination today. Several wrote that they are studying the Bible on their own or in small groups, but they want nothing more to do with religious organizations. Others declined to answer the questionnaire at all because they would prefer to forget entirely their association with the Worldwide Church of God.

The most revealing information gleaned from the questionnaire was that pertaining to what people think to be the strengths and weaknesses of the church. Several answers recurred frequently. Among the perceived strengths were the professionalism of the presentation; the leaders' ability to generate loyalty among members, who see themselves to be involved in the "one true church"; the emphasis on good character and honesty, clean living and healthy eating; the financial soundness of the organization (though some were less sure of that than others); and the stress on biblical teaching as authoritative guidance. On the other side of the ledger, frequent mention was made of the authoritarian structure, with its associated suspiciousness, informing, spying, and threats of retaliation; also, there would seem to be a noticeable belief among ex-members that the hierarchy gives an incomplete or dishonest picture of the way things really operate in Pasadena. The focus of this suspicion is on the glossing over of differences within the headquarters and on the incomplete disclosure of how the vast income received from members is used. With regard to the Work's commitment to $200,000 monthly payments to construct "God's House" in Pasadena, a Cincinnati truck driver commented, "Couldn't $200,000 a month really help spread the Christian gospel to the world?" There were also references to the Armstrongs' teaching about the family and the harmful effects this has had in some cases. Other former members complained about specific doctrinal aberrations.

Several responses were submitted in narrative form. One came from a minister of the Church of God (Seventh Day), now living in Idaho, who was personally acquainted with Herbert W. Armstrong and frequently preached in the church which he served as pastor in Eugene, Oregon, during the early 1940s. Never a member of the Armstrong organization, he nevertheless has the perspective of those years of association from which to assess both the man and the movement. His statement acknowledges the "good done by his ministry"—encouraging personal Bible study, pointing out errors "taught in modern churches," bringing many people not reached otherwise to "accept Jesus as Savior and change their ways."

> But self-exaltation and a strong centralized control have perpetuated certain serious errors that might have been corrected had he remained humble as in his early ministry. Also the manner of teaching lacked Spirit and would more likely make Pharisees than Christians. But no doubt some were truly converted and some are discovering the errors and going on for God.

A 29-year-old social worker from Indiana explains his break with the Worldwide Church of God:

> Armstrong's teaching about the Holy Spirit was the beginning of my questioning. I began to use Bible concordances, dictionaries, exegetical materials, etc., to prove whether or not God is a Trinity. In doing this I also discovered that the Armstrongs are inconsistent in their teaching. . . .
>
> Armstrongism appears to me to be appealing to the self-righteous person. God began to break me apart through this sect, however, because He drew me closer to Jesus. . . .

Another response came from a young Iowa pharmacist:

> Two years ago I would have defended to the death Mr. Armstrong and his teaching. Now I have found that I can objectively look at Mr. Armstrong's ministry, can discuss it with others without becoming emotional, and have been able to look into the encyclopedias and other reference material to see if what Mr. Armstrong says is indeed so. . . . At this point in my research, the only area that I question in Mr. Armstrong's teaching is that of his church being the original church started by Christ. Aside from this one point, I have been unable to disprove any of his other teachings. . . .

Others express themselves less calmly on the basis of their own experiences. Bernard J. A. Desloges, former Las Vegas TV executive, who left in 1969 after sixteen years in the organization, including a year-and-a-half editing the French-language broadcast, claims he was harassed after his departure. Dismissed from his job for having taken time off without pay for religious festivals while still a member of the Worldwide Church of God, he was unable to secure any assistance from the church in litigation to recover his position (which he finally won nonetheless). The Armstrongs, he claims, were afraid of jeopardizing the possible accreditation of Ambassador College, and so failed to support him in taking the consequences of an action they had pressed upon him.

One of the most passionate attacks on the Armstrong movement comes from a West Coast woman who was told by Worldwide Church officers in 1969 that she must leave her second husband, to whom she had been married for 24 years. Since he was an "adulterer" (because of his unscriptural marriage), she was to have no further contact with him—although the church continued willingly to accept his tithe as a "co-worker." She was persuaded to move from Seattle to Pasadena, expecting to serve there as a missionary. "To our bewilderment," she reports, "we were all snatched up as servants . . . wasting our talents and our lives doing the most menial tasks, such as dusting, cleaning toilets, and scrubbing floors." In a fifteen-page single-spaced manuscript, she bitterly describes her "exile" and what it did to her and others like her:

> None of us ever dared to express an opinion because we, as the gullible blind sheep that we had become, due to brainwashing techniques, had been sold a bill of goods. . . . I became concerned for my sanity. I saw little babies and children being beaten in the washrooms constantly. . . . If I admonished a young mother because of her cruelty . . . she would . . . report me to the minister for interfering. . . .
>
> I get upset when I think of those widows and their children in Armstrongism, and of the ministers who turn from gentle men into stern, hard-boiled taskmaster types in a short time after their so-called calling to the Armstrong ministry. . . . Their wives are placed in a terribly subservient position. The husbands . . . become lords and masters instead of lovers. . . .

This charge of Worldwide Church interference in marriage situations is not without parallels. Texas contractor Paul Haecker, an ex-member after ten years in the Armstrong camp, reports that breaking up engagements is a practice not infrequently resorted to by the ministers to test loyalty. His own engagement was broken up twice by a minister's intervention. Family life can be similarly disrupted, according to the testimony of a number of former members and spouses of present members. In the words of *Moody Monthly* writer Roger Campbell, few if any cults have "such a devastating effect upon the lives of [their] adherents and families."[13] Marriages have been broken up with the concurrence—and, according to Haecker, even assistance—of the church.

On June 12, 1973, a jury awarded Paul Haecker custody of his two sons, ages five and six, on the basis that "his former wife believed in witchcraft and belonged to a religious group that did not believe in usual medical care." According to the *Houston Post*,

> During the trial, William C. Martin, a Rice University sociologist, testified that the religious group teaches that modern medicine originated with and is perpetuated by Satan. Martin said they believe that the practice of medicine is witchcraft and that the only kind of medical attention acceptable is in the repair category, such as sewing up cuts or setting broken arms.[14]

According to an eyewitness report, passages from a 1961 issue of *The Good News* were cited in which medicines and vaccines were called the "work of Satan," and the Salk polio vaccine was described as "monkey pus." The article enjoined members to avoid such procedures, as they would cause them "to drift away from God, and could lead to the loss of their Eternal life."

Haecker's first wife had had custody of the children since the couple's divorce in 1969. The former Mrs. Haecker "claimed in her petition that his present wife had been persuaded by Haecker to practice witchcraft, casting spells on her to cause her to die."[15] Later a mistrial was declared, and the mother regained custody.

"Disfellowshipped" families are systematically ostracized as unbelievers with whom one is to have no dealings, although a lengthy account of one such case by Peter Geiger of the *Akron Beacon-Journal* led to categorical denial by Pasadena headquarters and the familiar claim of misunderstanding. Husbands have been known to threaten wives, and wives to complain that family income is being siphoned away to Pasadena for no good reason. One wife suspects that the church has designs on her husband's considerable financial holdings, which it is exploiting not only through tithes and offerings, but also through the sale of luggage, tires, camping equipment, and Bibles useful for Festival-bound pilgrims, a practice since discontinued.

The husband of a former member, now living in Hawaii,

faults the Worldwide Church of God for regimenting the lives of its constituents without regard to their welfare. A case in point: an enlisted man with seven children who was compelled by the church to quit the Navy just two years short of retirement. Thus he had to surrender his pension and other retirement benefits, as well as a five-bedroom house on the Navy base. At last report, the family was living in a federal housing project and the ex-Navy man was eking out a living selling pots and pans and household products.

Those most wounded tend to be most distraught. Others, leaving the Armstrong fold under amicable circumstances, are less critical. One young mother who departed for doctrinal reasons takes particular issue with allegations of cruelty in child-rearing and indignity in the church's treatment of women:

> Never had I seen such feminine, loving, and submissive women. . . . It was obvious that these women were trying their best to be good wives and mothers and follow the biblical teaching. . . . I was impressed with their willingness to stay at home and devote all their time and energy to raising their children. . . .
>
> There is an initial shock . . . when one . . . sees a large room full of women without any make-up, no wigs and fancy hairdos, and their dresses a little longer than the miniskirts we've grown accustomed to. . . . Yet the women [have] an inner beauty, warmth, meekness of spirit, and gentleness that is hard to describe. . . . I've never experienced such hospitality as is shown when you visit their homes. . . .
>
> Another quality is their fervency in seeking the truth in every subject—even in nonreligious areas. . . . This leads to their interest in natural or health foods, natural childbirth, and nursing their babies, etc. . . .

To be sure, every denomination has its disenchanted, its faultfinders, those who abandon it because it has failed to meet their needs. But the charges leveled by those leaving the mainline churches (these days in droves) seem somehow completely different from the ones made against the Armstrong empire. Bureaucracy, hypocrisy, unbelief, irrelevance—these charges against the organized institutional church are indeed serious. But many ex-members of the Worldwide Church of God look back on their experience as one of mental and spiritual bondage—of brainwashing, thought regimentation, financial exploitation, oppressive legalism, and authoritarian tyranny.

A number of books by ex-members of the Worldwide Church of God document in greater detail the circumstances within the Armstrong movement that lead to a feeling of liberation for those leaving it. Presbyterian Charles DeLoach, once an Armstrong "co-worker," broke with the Church of God in 1967. Mr. DeLoach has written a book dealing with the sect's doctrinal deviations called *The Armstrong Error.* In his concluding chapter, "Finding the True Church," he summarizes the motives behind those who join with Armstrong:

> The overwhelming majority of Armstrong's followers are, first of all, people who have a zeal for God; they are also people who are disillusioned with the modern physical church and its hypocrisy; consequently, they seek for the *true* church. The dedication of the Armstrong people to the practice of their religion, the high moral standards they hold to, and their wholesomeness, along with their very interesting Bible study courses, cannot but help attract many sincere *would-be* Christians into their cult. As a result, some of the finest people are being taken from the established *physical* church, where, in these last days, they are sorely needed.
>
> I hold no bitterness or resentment toward the Armstrong people. My personal feeling toward them is one of sorrow, for they have deceived themselves into believing they serve God. But like the dedicated Buddhist, Hindu or Muslim, they serve another. In my own case, my association with them, my study under them, then the lengthy and exhaustive Bible study and library research that was required to free myself from their teachings has given me an understanding of the Holy Scriptures and its true doctrines which I might not have otherwise obtained and which I find priceless.[16]

Richard A. Marson, an electrical engineer from Seattle and an ex-Worldwide Church of God deacon, is the author of *The Marson Report*, largely devoted to refutation of the British-Israel teaching of Herbert W. Armstrong. Marson affiliated with the Armstrong church in 1960. "Many readers of Mr. Armstrong's literature," he explains, "do not fully grasp the fact that every article or book distributed by him is designed as a lure with which to lead its readers into his church."[17] Once in, he was led at last by personal Bible study to the conclusion that the organization was anything but the "one True Church." At informal gatherings of Seattle church members, the local minister made the comment that he "had doubts as to whether or not the Bible could be used in the World Tomorrow because it contained inaccuracies." When questioned on this point he remarked that "whether or not the Bible [is] used in the World Tomorrow [is] not important because Herbert Armstrong's booklets and literature represented an understandable rewriting of the Bible."

> I began to have little incentive for remaining a part of this organization. The time had come to conduct a careful investigation of the group's doctrines. About a month later, I mailed a hasty report expounding on some of the concepts which I had begun to seriously question. The report went to about one hundred of Mr. Armstrong's members. I left the group at this time, whereupon they quickly slammed the door behind me—for sending the report—and forbade any member to see or talk to me.[18]

After publication of *The Marson Report*, Marson learned that a visiting minister from Pasadena had denounced the book before a congregation in Hawaii. The minister accused Marson of writing out of pique at being thrown out of the church for sexual misconduct. Marson demanded a retraction, threatening a lawsuit if it were not forthcoming. The day before the deadline that he specified, four months after the event, Marson learned indirectly that a retraction had at last been made before the Hawaiian congregation. More than a year later, Marson wrote, "To this day, I have never personally received any direct information about it from Pasadena. Mr. Roderick C. Meredith . . . had asked these Hawaiians to see that I heard of the retraction."[19]

Mr. and Mrs. Wayne Leyendecker became involved in the Armstrong religion via the usual route of the "World Tomorrow" broadcast and *The Plain Truth* magazine. They had been members of a Bible Church near Grand Rapids.

> Our decision to follow this new way of life was made near the Christmas season of 1961, and we decided . . . [on] no recogni-

> tion of Christmas. . . . We sent no greeting cards to friends or relatives. We had no Christmas tree. We must have been expecting a great blessing from that "no Christmas" experience, but instead it seemed so barren and empty. We truly missed remembering Christ's birthday that year.[20]

Not satisfied with their Armstrong experience, and driven to intensive Bible study by nagging questions, the Leyendeckers rediscovered the grace of God in Christ and returned to their church. Their feelings on being received back into the fold of evangelical Christianity are related in their chapter written for the book *We Found Our Way Out:*

> We are grateful to God that He guided us out of the errors of Armstrongism into the truth of Christ and His salvation. It was such a relief to find that all the demands of God's law were fulfilled in Jesus Christ, and our hearts' demands for peace and assurance are also fulfilled in him.[21]

B. By Qualified Observers

Much illuminating commentary has been provided by students of religion and theology who have not been personally involved in the Worldwide Church of God.

One of the most competently researched and comprehensive treatments of the Armstrong movement is *Radio Church of God: How Its Teachings Differ from Those of Seventh-Day Adventists*, by Harry W. Lowe. Lowe notes the elusive nature of the Armstrong creed: "a difficulty encountered in studying the teachings of H. W. Armstrong's Radio Church of God is that no compilation of them exists."[22] He explains that Ambassador College has been the primary label by which the Armstrong organization has identified itself to the public in large measure because "education work can enter some countries where religious interests cannot."[23] Lowe's final criticism is at the point of the movement's fruits. Absence of "a consciousness of the peace of Christ in the life and victory of redeeming grace" in day-by-day living, as confessed by "persons who have left the Radio Church of God," is cited as proof that evidential fruit is missing. Lowe elaborates,

> We have gone through about thirty-six copies of *The Plain Truth*, noting the letters under "What Our Readers Say," and we have not found any that speak of the victorious experience through Christ's grace. There may be some that we have not seen, but the main emphasis surely seems to be on blessings received from tithe paying or keeping the law, or a consciousness of knowledge or enlightenment beyond the blindness of those around them. None seems to emphasize a deeper love for Christ as Saviour.[24]

Another carefully documented treatment of the Armstrong sect is Roger R. Chambers' *The Plain Truth About Armstrongism.* The author devoted two years to intensive study of this subject while a master's student at Cincinnati Bible College. He is pastor of the West Side Church of Christ, Hamilton, Ohio. Chambers is concerned that faithful Christians are being "lost to a religious system so bizarre that (church leaders are) totally unprepared to answer the audacious claims . . . and specious arguments of Armstrongism." He is convinced that it is a waste of time to hack away at isolated theological aberrations in the Armstrong creed. Nearly all of those teachings have survived "in other sects, and are not likely to succumb to the onslaught of those who oppose them in Armstrongism." But the taproot of the "Armstrongite heresy," which Armstrong himself describes as the long-lost key to the meaning of the 90 per cent of Bible prophecy that pertains to the present generation, is the identification of the United States, Britain, and the democracies of Western Europe as modern Israel. If that doctrine falls, Chambers contends, "Armstrongism is destroyed."[25] Thus he focuses his attack on this single vulnerable point.

Walter R. Martin, one of the most prolific writers on Christianity-related cults in America today, has dubbed the religion of Herbert W. Armstrong the "New Galatianism" because of its stress on law-keeping.[26] He emphasizes that the sect is eclectic despite its claims to originality and revelation. Armstrong obviously has appropriated doctrines from Seventh-day Adventists (Sabbatarianism, dietary rules, end-time prophecies, conditional immortality, annihilation of the wicked), Jehovah's Witnesses (denial of the Trinity and the resurrection of Christ in the same body in which he was crucified—as well as a number of Adventist doctrines adopted by the Witnesses), the Mormons (the "God-Family" teaching), and British-Israelism. Martin's caustic assessment of Armstrong and his movement concludes:

> Were it not for Armstrong's dynamic presentation and wide radio coverage coupled with the spiritual vacuum which today pervades many quarters of Christendom, his entire system of interpretation would be the object of humor instead of the serious consideration it now demands.[27]

Roger F. Campbell, pastor of the Waterford, Michigan, Community Church, has spent more than a decade researching the Armstrong movement. His initial observation has been confirmed by his long study: "almost nothing he [Armstrong] had to say was original, or new, but it certainly was reorganized. In fact, I began to see that I had found one of the most interesting, and to borrow Mr. Armstrong's own words, 'shocking, incredible,' cases of organized confusion that I had ever run across."[28]

Leslie K. Tarr, president of Central Baptist Seminary in Toronto, views the Worldwide Church of God as one "of the major anti-Christian movements of our time." It is his belief that "the rise and spread of the Worldwide Church of God indicate both the biblical ignorance and the spiritual void of our time."[29] Noel Smith, late editor of the *Baptist Bible Tribune*, who insists that he "tried to handle [Herbert W. Armstrong] as gently as possible," nevertheless excoriates the "Armstrong system" for its implicit racism.

> His system holds the "Jews" alone responsible for the crucifixion. His system inherently holds that all the white Americans and white English are hereditarily innocent. If this attitude doesn't inflate Anglo-Saxon pride and promote anti-Semitism, what could do it? And his system emphasizes that God's blessings in this age are upon white Americans and white English. That puts the Negro, the Japanese, the Chinese and all the rest of them outside the camp. They are to come in at the back door and eat at the second table.[30]

Smith also scores the Armstrong religion for its lack of social concern:

> Genuine Christianity has always had its missions among the wretched and outcasts as well as its churches and cathedrals for the upper classes. But when did you ever see a mission of one of these cults on a Skid Row or a Bowery? When did you ever in your life see a tear of urgent and profound concern trickle down the cheek of one of these cult leaders?[31]

So the evaluations continue, most of them focusing on the heresies Armstrong propounds and the skilful packaging in which they are dispensed to the public. The heresies are, as an *Eternity* editorial puts it, "interlaced with . . . much Scripture, and . . . adherents are . . . adept at arguing from prooftexts."[32] Hence the appeal to conservative Christians.

C. By Religious Sociologists

William C. Martin of Rice University in Houston, writing about Armstrong for a general rather than religious audience in *Harper's* magazine, emphasizes that "what is heard and seen . . . even most of what is read by those who write away for the free literature is the tip of an iceberg." Martin describes the Armstrong movement's hold on its members as "tyrannical in nature and pernicious in its effects."[33] Armstrong is quoted by Martin as saying, "although the designers of the . . . IBM 360 [computer] don't know they designed this fantastic tool for God's work, they did!" Apparently he has no scruples against using computers to store personal data on his members.[34]

Martin believes, on the basis of this and other information, that the Worldwide Church of God is more correctly described as a religious empire than as a sect. Still, it is helpful to examine what a religious sociologist has said about the familiar distinction between "sects" and "denominations" and to apply his insights to the Armstrong movement. What will emerge, we hope, will be some answers to the perplexing question of why persons affiliate with such an organization.

Professor Bryan R. Wilson of All Souls College, Oxford, England, might have had the Worldwide Church of God in mind when he articulated the following contrast between the *sect* and the *denomination:*

> Typically a *sect* may be identified by the following characteristics: it is a voluntary association; membership is by proof to sect authorities of some claim to personal merit—such as knowledge of doctrine, affirmation of a conversion experience, or recommendation of members in good standing; exclusiveness is emphasized, and expulsion exercised against those who contravene doctrinal, moral, or organizational precepts; its self-conception is of an elect, a gathered remnant, possessing special enlightenment; personal perfection is the expected standard of aspiration, in whatever terms this is judged; . . . the sect is hostile or indifferent to the secular society and to the state. . . .
>
> Sects have a totalitarian rather than a segmental hold over their members: they dictate the members' ideological orientation to secular society; or they rigorously specify the necessary standards of moral rectitude; or they compel the member's involvement in group activity. . . . Not only does the sect discipline or expel the member who entertains heretical opinions, or commits a moral misdemeanor, but it regards such defection as betrayal of the cause, unless confession of fault and appeal for forgiveness is forthcoming.[35]

The denomination, on the other hand, is characterized by "traditional" membership. Individuals are born into the organization rather than identifying themselves with it by voluntary decision. Creedal and moral requirements are minimal and discipline lax. The denomination's self-image is that of "one among many," rather than a "gathered remnant." Its stance in relation to the culture is one of accommodation and conformity instead of conflict and rejection. Investment of time, talent, and money is nominal, as opposed to the sectarian's sacrificial commitment.

Wilson identifies four types of sect: (1) the Conversionist sect, whose chief concern is evangelism; (2) the Adventist—or revolutionist—sect, which "focuses attention on the coming overturn of the present world order"; (3) the Introversionist or pietist sect, which stresses withdrawal from the world and inward spiritual experience; and (4) the Gnostic sect, which "emphasizes some special body of teaching of an esoteric kind." Clearly, the Armstrong movement exemplifies the second category, of which Wilson writes,

> . . . It is typified by its emphasis on the Bible, and particularly of its exegesis of the allegorical and prophetic books from which the

> time and circumstances of the second advent of Christ are discerned. The conventional eschatological ideas of heaven and hell are regarded as false, and the resurrection of the dead for judgment is accepted as the principal eschatological event. Christ is regarded as a divine commander, not only as a saviour, and a high moral standard is based on the moral precepts of Jesus. Participation in the new kingdom will be limited and only those who have maintained doctrinal and moral rectitude will be eligible; admission to the fellowship is by thorough understanding of necessary doctrine, and not by affirmation of conversion. Evangelism is undertaken by way of preaching the word but quick conversions are not sought and revivalism is despised as emotional and misguided. The established church is regarded as fulfilling the role of the anti-Christ.... The sect is hostile toward the wider society and looks forward to its overthrow.[36]

Wilson notes that "the principal methods of sect emergence are by spontaneous development around a local charismatic leader, by schism, and by organized revival."[37] In the case of the Worldwide Church of God, the first of these methods is applicable. "Some such sects disappear when the leader dies or departs. Others, particularly those in which the leader offers a new gnosis which is consonant with the age, spread and retain their identity. The gnosis may be a new combination of ideas or the retailing of older ideas to a new audience."[38] It would appear that Herbert W. Armstrong has accomplished both of these—and if the equally dynamic and charismatic Garner Ted Armstrong succeeds in weathering the storms of conflict presently raging within the organization, prolongation of the sect's life for at least another generation seems assured.

"Sects proliferate in periods of social unrest," Wilson says. When large numbers of people are deprived or oppressed, there is more receptivity to offers of deliverance such as those held out by the Armstrong doctrines. And the origin of this movement during the depression years of the 1930s bears out Wilson's analysis. Another observation is the fact that sects, more than long-established denominations, tend toward schism. This tendency to fragment "usually centers on the question of purity of doctrine, and successful schism usually finds its leader in the very inner elite of the movement."[39] Absence of "elite" leadership in the dozen or more offshoots of the Worldwide Church of

God may not augur well for the future of these splinter groups—the newly formed Associated Churches of God excepted.

Eric Hoffer, in *The True Believer*, suggests another twist to the motivation behind sect involvement. He states that some mass movements appeal "not to those intent on bolstering and advancing a cherished self, but to those who crave to be rid of an unwanted self. A mass movement attracts and holds a following not because it can satisfy the desire for self-advancement, but because it can satisfy the passion for self-renunciation."[40] Which may explain the willingness of the Worldwide Church of God member to accept a "God's-eye view" of himself as "a self-centered, hostile, shriveled-up, rotten, vile, filthy, sinning hulk of rotting human flesh" and to be able to say—and "*really mean it*"—" 'I'm carnal, I'm selfish, I hate myself.' "[41]

In a similar vein, Hoffer quotes H. G. Wells to the effect that "at the time of the Reformation people 'objected not to the church's power, but to its weaknesses. . . . Their movements against the church, within it and without, were movements not for release from a religious control, but for a fuller and more abundant religious control.' "[42] Later Hoffer remarks, "Those who fail in everyday affairs show a tendency to reach out for the impossible. It is a device to camouflage their shortcomings. For when we fail in attempting the possible, the blame is solely ours; but when we fail in attempting the impossible, we are justified in attributing it to the magnitude of the task."[43] Thus the success of the Armstrong appeal to exchange poverty and ignominy in this life for riches and preferment in the "World Tomorrow."

The foregoing may account, at least in part, for the mystery of how intelligent, educated, and ostensibly balanced individuals can become drawn into total commitment to a religious system that is so oppressive and totalitarian in its demands. But there are other factors:

1. *Disillusionment with the Religious Establishment.* It is probable that the Worldwide Church's most productive mission field is the ranks of uncommitted or disenchanted church members. The Armstrong religion's chief appeal is

to solidly conservative persons who deplore what they see as the drift of the historic churches toward left-wing radical political philosophy, social activism, and liberal theology. The Armstrong emphasis on infallible Bible truth (instead of Bultmannian "demythologizing"), old-fashioned Christian morality (as opposed to "situationism"), family loyalty and firm discipline (against women's liberation and permissiveness), neatness and cleanliness (in contrast to the hip generation's image of unkemptness)—all of these and other reactions to contemporary changes in the society play into the hand of Herbert W. Armstrong and his organization.

J. K. Van Baalen quotes "an old saying to the effect that 'the cults are the unpaid bills of the church.' "[44] His point is that the failures and defects of the churches have caused many people to turn elsewhere for identification and fulfilment. In another connection Van Baalen uses the phrase "infidelity parading under the guise of an advanced Christianity."[45] He thinks it descriptive of liberalism's "attacks upon the fundamentals of the Christian faith." But it is also descriptive of the Armstrong movement.

2. *The Offense of the Cross.* But well-known cult authority John H. Gerstner believes Van Baalen to be only partially correct in his analysis. In an interview Gerstner, Professor of Church History at Pittsburgh Theological Seminary, suggested a theological reason for the exodus from mainline churches into the cults—the offense of the Cross. Many people, he believes, simply cannot comprehend or accept a way of salvation predicated upon nothing more than a simple faith-response to the free gift of God's grace in Christ. They are persuaded that salvation must be earned, worked for, deserved. The religious system of Herbert W. Armstrong is a "natural" for those who are so-minded; for it provides an opportunity for man to couple faith (by which past sins are forgiven through Christ's atoning work on the Cross) with works (by which status can be gained and maintained through law-keeping and obedience).

3. *Despair over World Conditions.* Not only have the

Armstrongs exploited the churches' failures, but they have capitalized on the prevailing mood of pessimism and frustration in the world of the late twentieth century. To banish the clouds of gloom that hover over humanity, the Armstrong version of the gospel offers a simplistic solution: the dawn of "a bright new beautiful 'World Tomorrow', from which all the evils of contemporary society will be eradicated and in which utopian conditions of peace, prosperity, and complete happiness will prevail."[46] "Wars and rumors of wars," the sharpening focus upon Israel as a potential arena of international conflict, the gravitation of the Common Market nations toward Armstrong's oft-predicted United States of Europe, intensified poverty and hunger, multiplied floods and earthquakes, accelerated moral decay and secularism—all of these "signs of the times" have increasingly bolstered the prophetic role of Herbert W. Armstrong, despite numerous "false prophecies" that would tend to downgrade his credibility.

But the Armstrong faith provides not only an escape hatch into eternity, but sure-fire remedies for many of the complex problems that plague us here and now. Professor William C. Martin has written,

> If the world seems out of control, what could be more reassuring than to discover the road map of human destiny? This is part of the appeal of Garner Ted Armstrong, who declares to listeners, in a tone that does not encourage doubt, foolproof solutions for the problems of child-rearing, pollution, and crime in the streets, plus a definitive answer to the question, "Why Are You Here?"[47]

4. *The Promise of Power.* One of the principal reasons for the success of the Armstrong religion is its appeal to vanity, pride, and ambition. Those baptized into the Worldwide Church of God have been "called by God." They have been "put into" an exclusive organization which no man, of himself, can join. They are now members of Christ's "Little Flock," commissioned to warn (not convert) the world, to be transformed into spirit-beings and to rule over mortals—even over angels—in the "World Tomorrow." More than that, they are destined to become not merely like God but actually God—members of the

God-Family, enjoying equal status, privilege, power, and glory to those of the Father and the Son.

5. *Skilful Use of Promotional Techniques.* Fredrick Trautmann, assistant professor of speech at Temple University, has written that "the Armstrongs are the world's foremost God-Hucksters of Broadcasting."[48] He might have added "and of the printed page." Certainly there are few more skilfully conceived or professionally executed propaganda campaigns bidding for human attention today. The radio and television broadcasts are arresting, swift-moving, dynamic, persuasive. *The Plain Truth* is one of the most attractively printed, illustrated, written and edited magazines being produced anywhere. Millions of copies of free, slick-paper, four-color booklets, including the cleverly written correspondence course lessons, have gone out around the world. A personal correspondence department provides almost instant response to 250,000 letters per month. And so on. . . .

Trautmann has analyzed the Armstrong "power of persuasion" into ten components:[49]

a. Proven sales techniques.

b. The notion of prophecy. Trautmann quotes Chaucer: "Trust in the future tense makes men part with every single thing they ever had."

c. An appeal to unseen but omnipotent forces that control world events. "Herbert Armstrong cites miracles to prove his place in 'the purpose being worked out here below.' "

d. Sincere and firm assertion of the "truth," without regard for contradictory ideas.

e. Endless repetition of the same theme, varied only by differences in the events around us.

f. The immediacy and familiarity of the news, as opposed to abstract discussion of God or complicated biblical exegesis.

g. The power of the "transfer device." Presentation of accurate news probably casts a halo of truth over the entire message. The Armstrongs explain what is only reported elsewhere.

h. Emphasis on rationality. Trautmann catalogs the familiar rational phrases to which the listener is exposed:

> Let's use our minds . . . Proof . . . Does that seem reasonable? . . . Clear proof . . . Let's think about this . . . Scientific proof . . . This stands proved . . . Research . . . Anyone in his right mind knows this is true . . . Analysis . . . Who can deny the logic of this? . . . Truth . . . Let's analyze . . . The plain truth . . . You *know* that's wrong . . . The absolute truth . . . Let's talk sense for a change . . . Truth is truth, you can't deny it if you want to or not . . . Documentation . . . I can prove that to you . . . Objectivity . . . Truth exists independently of people . . . Credibility.

i. Belligerence toward all that is not pure, noble, true, just, and American: socialists and Communists, Catholics, hippies, Germans—even bigots.

j. The "power of some of those elements that have been a part of all the noble attempts to win the allegiance, mold the belief, and control the thoughts of millions." The Armstrongs offer the sense of belonging to a group, a charismatic leader, revelation, and an explanation of the chaos of life.

There are those who believe that the Armstrongs—especially Garner Ted—have come to realize that certain of the church's doctrines rest on shaky foundations. But they fear to alter or repudiate these teachings lest their credibility suffer. Admission of error would be tantamount to a confession of fallibility, and widespread disillusionment and defection would be certain to ensue. Thus a major strength would be converted into a critical weakness, and the future of the "Work" jeopardized.

Former member Richard A. Marson, in a letter dated February 23, 1972, during Garner Ted's exile, alerted Herbert W. Armstrong to this danger:

> When, I wonder, are you ever going to let your researchers destroy that fictitious novel called *The United States and British Commonwealth in Prophecy?* There is the source of your error. . . . Quite some time ago, I received a letter from a man once high in your organization. He says concerning your false teaching as follows: "While preparing a new edition of . . . the USBCP some years ago I had my men cover every available work

> on the subject. There is a dismal lack of evidence, but abundant contradictions. . . . What happened to this just man whom I happen to know fears God above all else in his life? He was driven from the church in a manner which fully reminded me of the religious inquisitions of the middle ages! This was not the only man treated in such a manner while trying to seek out and promote truth. . . .
>
> It is nothing less than disgusting to hear of your raging before some in Pasadena and Texas that the young leaders of your organization will never force you to change when all they wanted to do was correct false doctrine from the inside before others forced a change from the outside.

Marson's appraisal of the internal disquiet has been verified by another source with reliable contacts in both Pasadena and Texas. If the reports are accurate, Herbert W. Armstrong is in a precarious position indeed. It remains to be seen whether or not Garner Ted, should he continue in power, will renounce certain of his father's pet doctrines, or maintain the elder Armstrong's position of intransigence.

When the Armstrongs—the father, the son, or both—pass from the scene—what then? The questions will still have to be faced by their successors. For the Worldwide Church of God rests on the foundation of Herbert W. Armstrong's alleged infallibility as God's chosen apostle. If that foundation crumbles, the superstructure will inevitably topple. A temporary and expedient commitment to the Armstrong doctrines, even though the church's leaders know some of them to be false and others in need of drastic correction and revision? Or a frank admission of error and an effort to pull as many of the chestnuts out of the fire as possible, realizing that such a policy may ultimately spell disaster for the organization? The next few years, during which these questions must be confronted by the church's leadership, should prove fateful.

On the other hand, the predictable outcome may not occur at all. For the predictable is based on that which is reasonable, whereas religious commitment involves an emotional response that is nonrational—or even irrational at times. Blind loyalty to Herbert W. Armstrong, his teachings, and his Worldwide Church of God may entirely obscure reason, and thus prevent a rational reaction to doctrinal change (should it occur) or to continued regimentation by strong-armed totalitarian authority. So the Worldwide Church of God may continue to grow.

Whatever happens, the Armstrong Empire has already written one of the most fascinating chapters in the history of American religion.

Postscript

Time was when the Worldwide Church of God pointed to the absence of factions among its tightly knit members, who clung unfailingly to pure doctrine, as a sound indicator that the Pasadena-based denomination was God's "headquarters church" for this age.[1] But this facade of unity—which remained solid during the first stages of the research for this book—began to evidence large cracks in February 1974. The *Los Angeles Times* broke the story: "Six Ministers Resign from Armstrong Religious Sect."[2] Undaunted, Herbert W. Armstrong now argues that this very development of factions within the church is proof that the Worldwide Church of God is the true church, for it "could not be God's true church . . . unless Satan managed to inject some false teachers into it."[3]

Whether indicative of its authenticity or inauthenticity, the strife and schism within the Armstrong empire have antecedents long before the dramatic attacks and counterattacks of early 1974. The full account is one of decisions nullified by reconsiderations, resignations negated by restoration, forgiveness followed by disfellowshipment, and lurid charges met with contradictory responses. The exact number of dissidents involved is difficult to fix precisely; the ultimate resolution impossible to predict. Not surprisingly, in view of the delicacy of some of the issues involved, the recent shakeup in the Worldwide Church of God has produced little calm and detached commentary by participants.

Alfred E. Carrozzo, ex-minister of the Imperial Church at Pasadena and once supervisor of two hundred ministers in the western half of the country, claims to have been disillusioned with things as early as 1965. Together with three evangelists of the church, Carrozzo finally took a decisive step on August 31, 1972. They presented a document entitled "Employee Frustrations at Headquarters" to Herbert W. Armstrong, a bill of particulars citing both doctrinal and practical problems, many of them to be repeated later by others leaving the fold.

There was a credibility gap, Carrozzo alleged, caused by conflicts in the messages delivered by the two Armstrongs, as well as by contradictions of former pronouncements (for example, the denial, after the arson attempt on the El Aqsa Mosque, that the church had predicted the restoration of a literal temple in Jerusalem).[4] Furthermore, members were confused by the failure of the earth-shaking events prophesied for January 1972 (the end of the second 19-year cycle) to materialize. Carrozzo also pointed to a declining interest in Bible studies and Sabbath services, which he attributed to "repetitive use of old outlines" and suppression of doctrinal questions. He charged Armstrong with misrepresentation in asserting that he has never courted contacts with world leaders. He expressed concern over alleged "power conflicts" involving the Armstrongs, Stanley Rader, Roderick C. Meredith, and Albert J. Portune. The document went on to complain that lower echelon employees had to "subject their families to substandard living conditions in order to support the affluent atmosphere of Ambassador College." Policy changes were being made without adequate explanation; there was rapid turnover of administrative personnel; and the influence of Armstrong lawyer Stanley Rader, not a member of the church, was increasing. Consequently, Carrozzo charged, more than five hundred Worldwide Church of God members had left for the Assemblies of Yahweh.

When after a year of waiting Carrozzo had seen no signs of hope for improving these conditions, he resigned on November 14, 1973. At the request of members of his former flock who followed him out of the Worldwide Church of God, he formed an independent church in Pasadena, the 20th Century Church of God.

The scene now shifted east. Less than two weeks after

Carrozzo's resignation John Mitchell shocked his congregation at Shreveport, Louisiana, by declaring that Garner Ted Armstrong had disqualified himself to be a minister of Jesus Christ by repeated acts of sexual immorality over a period of years. The next evening David Antion, Vice President of Church Administration, told a specially convened congregation of three hundred that Mitchell's charges were substantially true. Mitchell reported that he had that day discussed the subject with Garner Ted, and that the latter had admitted the charges, arguing that he was exempt from the New Testament standards for ministerial behavior because his adultery had been prophesied (Mal. 2:14); also because "all great men that God uses for great purposes are men of great passions"; furthermore, because he had been miraculously born for this job; and, finally, because his father's decision to restore him in 1972 superseded the biblical directives.[5]

In a November 28 meeting with 315 members of the Shreveport and Texarkana congregations Garner Ted declared that his "past sins were none of their business," and forbade further discussion of the matter. Assuring the gathering that he had the full backing of his father, he announced that "John Mitchell had been fired, disfellowshipped, and marked" (as a heretic), as would happen to anyone who contacted Mitchell. After the meeting, a large number of the audience, nonetheless, pledged support to Mitchell. That night, Bill Sutton, Mitchell's associate minister, telephoned David Antion to tender his resignation. Later about 125 Shreveport and 60 Texarkana members withdrew to form the Church of God—Shreveport Conference.

Tom Fish, an Ambassador graduate and former Mormon, who had served one of the St. Louis congregations for two years, told a hundred members assembled in a rented theater on December 2 that he could no longer continue as a minister in the Worldwide Church in view of Garner Ted's immorality. Fish was flown to Pasadena for a reconciliation meeting with the top brass, briefly restored, then summarily disfellowshipped. A hundred or more of his former congregation have joined him in establishing the Church of God of South St. Louis.

On January 8, 1974, Dallas pastor Barry Chase personally tendered his resignation to Walter L. Sharp, regional director of the Work in five southwestern states. His reasons were the now-familiar ones—Herbert Armstrong's authoritarianism, his son's immorality, and the church's policy regarding divorce and remarriage, which, Chase claimed, sentenced "hundreds of God's people to life without a marriage partner." Chase subsequently became pastor of the Dallas Church of God, composed of former Worldwide Church members.[6]

The dissension growing, Garner Ted flew to Big Sandy, and on Monday, February 25, suspended fifteen officials and ministers, including Walter Sharp. During a two-hour conversation aloft, with Garner Ted at the controls of the Ambassador College jet, the younger Armstrong tried in vain to dissuade Sharp from siding with the dissidents. Sharp told a reporter, "I advised him that the ministers objected to doctrinal matters which were tearing the church apart, and that there was no open forum to be heard. The church is forced to live by the dictates of one man, Herbert W. Armstrong."[7]

As resignations and dismissals increased, so did the list of complaints against the church and its leadership. In an open letter dated February 25, Alfred Carrozzo and a group of former ministers contended that Garner Ted's philandering was known by Pasadena officials as early as the summer of 1971. According to the Carrozzo report, when "Ted was put out of the ministry and disfellowshipped on January 30, 1972 . . . it was confirmed that *the problem had continued over a nineteen year period.*"

Financial extravagances, inequities, and irregularities continue to be charged. Despite soaring income, the faithful are plagued with repeated pleas to dig deeper to avert a financial crisis. Internal Revenue records show income of $32 million in 1970, $35 million in 1971, and $41 million in 1972.[8] Official Worldwide Church figures report even higher income—in excess of $54 million in 1972.[9] In October 1973, when income was on its way to a record high of almost $56 million, Garner Ted told pilgrims at the Feast of Tabernacles at Mt. Pocono, Pennsylvania, that the Work was in "financial crisis," and appealed to them to "help put the Work back on its feet" by giving sacrificially. "Eat hamburger instead of steak," he admonished, "and send the Work the difference."

Lavish spending on the ten-million-dollar "House of God" in Pasadena, including the flying in of the Vienna Symphony, at a reported cost of $500,000, for its April 1974 opening ceremonies, has also come under critical fire. The plush Ambassador campuses and the affluent life-style of the well-salaried upper-echelon leaders contrast radically with the subsistence-level austerity of many members and ministers. One family, moved to guilt by the financial appeals from Pasadena, wrote that they had decided to give up some new furniture they had purchased and to apply the installment payments to the church instead. The pastor of a congregation of four hundred told the author, without complaint, that 1973 was the first year he had had sufficient income to pay tax on it.

The influence of Stanley R. Rader on the Armstrong leadership is another bone of contention. A New Yorker of Jewish extraction, the 44-year-old attorney and former law professor (University of Southern California) has been in the employ of the Worldwide Church of God since 1956, but has never been baptized. According to the *Los Angeles Times* Rader is "among the college's most highly paid professional persons. As general legal counsel for the church and college, he received $55,000 in [1972] . . . but also shared the $76,000 fee paid to the certified public accounting firm of which he is a partner with Henry F. Cornwall."[10]

Floyce Korsak of the *Dallas Times Herald* interviewed residents of Big Sandy and learned that Ambassador College is not without its critics in that small east Texas town. The arrival of Worldwide Church of God personnel in large numbers set the stage for a referendum responsible for the establishment of eight liquor stores in the formerly dry community. A law enforcement official complained of "having a lot of trouble with their own young people drinking, and they're the very ones who voted it in." The reporter was also told the Worldwide Church of God people kept to themselves, not mingling with the community. A retired nurse wished "they would either change their beliefs about medicine or move out." She told of working for a doctor who was not permitted by parents to administer anesthetics to children brought in for suturing open wounds or setting broken bones.[11]

Following the dismissal on February 25 of fifteen ministers, Garner Ted officially canceled Sabbath services on March 2, "in order that every one of God's people can remain at home and devote themselves to the entire day of *Fasting* and *Prayer* for the health and well being of God's church!" Endeavoring to keep the lid on the boiling controversy, he outlawed all meetings of local church officers and disbanded the Church Administration Department and the regional directors. "As of now," he instructed, "every church pastor reports *directly* to me."[12] An interim "Ministerial Coordinating Team," under the direction of C. Wayne Cole, was established to assist in this area.

The next day another bombshell struck. Two of the eight vice presidents, David L. Antion and Albert J. Portune, resigned. Two weeks earlier Antion had submitted a five-page memorandum on the subject "Problems." He had deplored the lack of confidence "in the field ministry toward Headquarters in Pasadena," which was "now intensifying to an explosive condition." Doubts had been raised about the church's position on healing, prophecy, divorce and remarriage, church eras.

In the fall of 1972 Antion and Portune had urged Herbert Armstrong to convene meetings of the church's evangelists to consider such questions. But when the meetings began in November 1972, only minor issues (tithing, inviting people to church, hair length and sideburns) were discussed. Even this superficial beginning, Antion recalled, "took a lot of prodding and pushing to accomplish." At the January ministerial conference in Pasadena, a new policy of "openness" was announced (admission of "outsiders" to worship services, newspaper advertising of church meetings, listing of ministers' telephone numbers). But "the meetings died after January 1973."

Now, in February 1974, the two urged that immediate attention be given the issue of divorce and remarriage. This should be the subject of free inquiry; else there would be full-scale rebellion. The Antion-Portune memo proposed a "wide scale meeting . . . of all the Regional Directors and of the men in their regions who are the most disturbed by these problems." A "true Christian" and biblical approach to the "long standing problems that have beset the Church" was urged. It was further requested that "those suspended or terminated . . . be restored in position and reputation."

Antion and Portune then laid down an ultimatum that unless their recommendations were adopted by 9 a.m. the following day, "this memo will constitute our resignation from the Work." Stanley Rader announced to the press that the proposal of the two vice presidents was "totally unacceptable."[13] Their resignations were thus forced.

But two days later, both Antion and Portune were back in the fold and promptly given "two months' leave with full pay," their future roles in the Worldwide Church undetermined. Antion assured Garner Ted that he was "100 percent behind God, his Work, and Mr. Armstrong," and wrote Herbert of his eagerness to help in any capacity, even "pushing a broom or raking leaves."[14] *Christianity Today* later reported that Antion, "no longer a top officer, . . . is a teacher at Ambassador College and an evangelist."[15]

Portune, however, resigned a second time on April 28 and cast his lot with the newly formed Associated Churches of God. Once chief financial officer of the Worldwide Church, he had stepped down from that position in September 1973 because he "didn't feel clean" about signing checks for items like multi-million-dollar jets. In his final letter of resignation he charged the church with "neglect, errors, continuing oppression, . . . misrepresentations, corruption, and ungodly methods."[16]

On March 5-8, 1974, thirty-five ex-ministers of the Worldwide Church met in Washington, D.C., and established the Associated Churches of God. Fifteen to twenty congregations and two to three thousand members were claimed. Former regional directors Kenneth Westby and Walter Sharp were named chairman and vice chairman, respectively, of the group's fifteen-member board of trustees. Ernest Martin, former dean of the London branch of Ambassador College and resigned head of the Pasadena theology department, became chairman of biblical doctrine; Albert Portune, it was announced after his second resignation, would become director of evangelism. According to Barry Chase, a member of the doctrinal committee, the national office will function as a "clearinghouse for information and general church related services." He described it as a "means for coordinating a national effort, not to dictate doctrine or policy."

Westby defined three significant differences between the Associated Churches of God and the Worldwide Church. In the first place, the new federation will have no tithing requirement. Secondly, persons remarried after a divorce will be eligible for membership. Finally, the churches will operate with local autonomy and "no rigid central authority."[17]

Congregational government is actually a throwback to the administrative philosophy espoused by Herbert W. Armstrong in the Radio Church of God of the 1930s. In stark contrast to the authoritarian structure of the present Worldwide Church, the Armstrong church of those early years operated on the principle that "all authority and power to rule is limited solely to each local congregation." Herbert W. Armstrong declared in a 1939 *Good News* article that "there is *no Bible authority* for any super-government, or organization with authority over the local congregation!"[18] Later, as the Work grew, Armstrong reversed his position completely and established the very sort of centralized administration he had previously condemned as Satanic. In a vehement, thirty-page letter denouncing "defecting ministers," addressed on May 2, 1974, to "Dear Brethren of God's Church," he now accused dissidents of rebelling "against the *Government of God*." The divine plan, he asserts, is "government *from the top (God) on down.*"

Those who have now left the Worldwide Church of God Armstrong accused of allowing "Satan to subtly inject into their minds an attitude of resentment and rebellion against any authority over them." This has resulted in causing "some to leave God's Church, and perhaps even God's salvation and gift of eternal life!" In an obvious reference to the Associated Churches of God, he stated that "the living Christ does not set up additional churches, on disloyalty, rebellion, false accusation, and character assassination." In an earlier letter, Armstrong had bitterly accused defecting ministers of "greed to try to get God's tithes *mis-appropriated so that it might go into their own pockets.*" He further contended that they wanted to "abolish all authority which Christ as our Head *set* in His Church." They would substitute "*voting*—the 'democratic way' " for "God's way."

Just how extensive are the inroads made on Worldwide Church of God membership by the 1974 exodus is difficult to determine. The Associated Churches of God claim at least two thousand former adherents of the Armstrong organization. *Christianity Today* reports that "some of the dissidents are casting friendly glances at the little denomination from which HWA split in 1930: the 5,000 member Church of God (Seventh Day) headquartered in Denver."[19] And it is likely that some few of the disenchanted have gravitated toward Jacob Meyer's Assemblies of Yahweh and similar sabbatarian groups. C. Wayne Cole announced in the April 2, 1974, ministerial *Bulletin* that "the total defection of membership from the Church appears . . . to be in the neighborhood of 1800 to 2000."

Based on a comparison of figures received by the author from Garner Ted Armstrong's office in September 1973 and again in April 1974, the *Los Angeles Times* quoted this source to the effect that US membership of the Worldwide Church had dropped nearly 11%—from 51,369 to 45,747—between September and March. The publication of these statistics prompted a letter to the author from Robert Kuhn, Garner Ted Armstrong's administrative assistant on June 5, 1974: "Since our baptized membership has in fact *grown* from September 1973 through March, April, and May 1974, we seemed sure that there was some mistake in your figures. Upon checking, however—much to my chagrin—we found the error has been ours!" Corrected membership statistics showed an increase from 42,795 on September 4, 1973, to 46,183 on May 3, 1974, a gain of 12.6 per cent. Non-US membership, according to Kuhn's office, was 12,497 as of January 1974. The worldwide total of 58,860 adult baptized members falls considerably below the 85,000 membership figure given in numerous news reports. It is likely that the larger figure is an outdated worldwide *attendance* figure.

A number of observers had predicted a major split in the Armstrong empire following the initial rash of withdrawals and dismissals. But the statistics cited above indicate that losses were more than absorbed by a sizable influx of new converts. Total income for the period from January 1 through March 22, 1974, was up 10.5 per cent over the previous year; and donation mail for March showed a 19 per cent increase over the average for the preceding six months.[20] Exulted Garner Ted in a headline story on the front page of the March 18 *Worldwide News:* "The Church has never been stronger."

His optimism notwithstanding, Garner Ted confessed to deep trauma in response to the revived accusations of improper conduct on his part. "I've had to vomit a few breakfasts and go without a few meals lately, and have my stomach all churned up," he confided to his ministerial colleagues in the April 2 *Bulletin.* A month earlier he revealed that he had been unable to tape television programs for a period of two weeks. "My health has been seriously affected. My sleep has departed from me, and my wife and I have been put through emotional trauma almost beyond endurance."[21]

On May 6, 1974, the Worldwide Church launched the largest ministerial conference in its history with the dedication of the magnificent new auditorium in Pasadena. Registered were 95 local church elders and 408 full-time ordained ministers, including 103 from overseas.[22] Significantly, deposed vice president David Antion moderated one of the forums. At the opening meeting, Herbert W. Armstrong announced a major doctrinal change. "The new teaching will provide that those coming into the church will be forgiven at baptism of past marital mistakes which were made apart from the knowledge of God's way." No longer were candidates for membership who had remarried after divorce compelled to dissolve the second union before baptism. As reported by *The Worldwide News*, "the announcement, termed 'monumental' by Garner Ted Armstrong, drew several rounds of applause during the course of the explanation." The meeting was taped and was slated to be played in every Church of God congregation the Sabbath of May 11. Thus was laid to rest the most controversial doctrinal issue in the recent history of the Work.

On the final day of the conference, Garner Ted announced another major change. No longer was payment of the "third tithe" (for "widows and orphans") compulsory for all members. "From henceforth, only those who are 'able' should pay third tithe . . . and those who are experiencing severe financial straits in order to pay third tithe should be exempted." The elder Armstrong, however, emphasized that this did not in any sense relax the tithing obligation for those who could pay the third tithe.[23]

Restudy and modification of other teachings were promised. As early as February 1974, Herbert W. Armstrong told members that he had reviewed the controversial healing doctrine "*thoroughly* and in depth" and that a new booklet on this subject was "now ninety-five percent complete."

That Garner Ted Armstrong has chafed under his father's repressive and dogmatic doctrinal pronouncements has become increasingly evident. Coincident with his return to the airwaves in June 1972 was a switch from largely secular to religious subject matter. According to inside sources, the reforms instituted by the January 1973 ministerial conference were largely due to his influence. In a 1973 *Good News* article Garner Ted deplored the church's "shame-fear syndrome" with its paranoid suspicion of "enemies" and "outsiders":

> It has been reinforced by the fact that we meet in rented halls, oftentimes without outside identifying characteristics or signs. . . .
>
> Apparently all of this was to ensure that we did not, under any circumstances, experience any disturbance during a Sabbath service, such as an audible challenge from someone in the crowd. But because of this "syndrome," many people have turned away their own loved ones, their own families and mates. . . .[24]

But now, Garner Ted continued, "all that is changing." The Worldwide Church of God was to be listed in phone directories of those cities where there were churches, giving a toll-free number for information about the Church. Moreover, the policy of admission to services has been relaxed:

> With the Worldwide Church of God now becoming very well known through our own radio-TV programs and personal appearance campaigns, we are getting numerous inquiries from new people wanting to attend church. My father stated at the Headquarters Ministerial conference this last January that we should make all who *want* to attend *welcome*, even if their interest is only *casual.*[25]

Members are now encouraged to witness unobtrusively to neighbors and associates. It is suggested that the latest *Plain Truth* be placed on the automobile seat or carried to work in a lunch pail with the intent of showing it casually to fellow workers. The ministers' calling cards, which once carried the designation "Ambassador College Representative," now bear the legend "Worldwide Church of God Minister."

On July 14, 1973, I wrote the Letter Answering Department at Ambassador College to inquire if the new policy meant that I was free to attend services. In his reply David G. Hunsberger informed me that:

> Local pastors will still have a responsibility in approving or disapproving one's attendance in their services. . . . Because you are a writer, I think the local pastor might naturally feel somewhat wary toward you because most of those who have chosen to write about us have done so from an extremely prejudicial viewpoint.

On August 24, 1973, I wrote Garner Ted Armstrong, soliciting his cooperation with my research. I informed him that I had written his father three times during the previous summer with no reply. With the assistance of an Ambassador College graduate who still maintains contacts in Pasadena, I received a courteous two-page answer from Garner Ted, assuring me of his willingness to arrange a mutually convenient interview. On October 18 I was able to visit him at his motel room on the "Last Great Day" of the Feast of Tabernacles at Mt. Pocono.

Garner Ted was relaxed and not at all defensive in his comments. His manner was winsome and his response to questions forthright. We briefly discussed "signs of the times" in the Middle East, where war had just broken out for the fourth time in 25 years. He asked if I had read *The Preachers* by James Morris, which includes a chapter on the Armstrongs, and remarked that, considering that Morris viewed the movement from the outside, he had been "reasonably fair" in his assessment, as had William C. Martin in his July 1973 *Harper's* article.

Looking pensively he reflected, "The church has made many mistakes."

"But isn't this inevitable for an organization which has mushroomed so rapidly?"

"Yes, but that doesn't *excuse* the errors. The Church should *admit* its faults and not cling to them dogmatically."

I told him I was glad to note the softening of his position toward some of the Worldwide Church doctrines, adding, "But perhaps you don't like the term 'soften.' "

"I don't take issue with it. What I'm saying is that we should *admit* our errors."

"Such as British-Israelism?" I inquired.

"It's not essential to salvation. It hasn't been *proven* to my satisfaction that the Ten Lost Tribes relocated in specific places in northern Europe. It certainly is not a *necessary* doctrine. And it is manifestly ridiculous to think of the United States being Manasseh in a literal sense, because the US is a melting pot. *Some* things, however, seem odd coincidences. For example, the queen of England being crowned on a crude throne beneath which is a rough stone—although it can't be *proved* that this stone is the *liafail*, Jacob's pillar stone."

Recalling his father's emphasis on Anglo-Israel identity as the master key which unlocks the meaning of ninety per cent of those biblical prophecies which apply to the last days, I observed, "You appear to have modified your father's position on this subject."

Ted shrugged. "Well, I think we have to let it be known that this is not a doctrine essential to salvation."

"One of your doctrines which makes me feel very much an outsider is that which assigns the mark of the beast—and the lake of fire—to those who worship on Sunday."

"I don't believe that," Ted retorted. "We're not sure what the mark of the beast is and what it signifies. On such non-crucial doctrines I don't pretend to be dogmatic. But I think we should be dogmatic regarding such doctrines as the deity of Christ, the atonement, the bodily ascension of Christ, and those teachings having to do with the whole scheme of redemption." Admitting that the Sunday-mark-of-the-beast doctrine had been taught in the early history of the Worldwide Church, he declared, "*I* haven't taught this for at least twenty years. In fact, as long as I have been in the Work this doctrine hasn't appeared in the literature."

I refrained from contradicting, but later checked my files and verified that Sunday worship was identified with the mark of the beast as recently as 1967: "Satan . . . will enforce, by military *might*, the branding of the people of the world with *Sunday* observance—the 'mark of the beast'! . . . For those observing it can ultimately suffer *eternal* death!"[26]

"What about your father's 'one True Church' dogma?" I asked.

"I don't believe that, either," he replied, "except for the invisible church, the Body of Christ. But it is definitely not necessary to belong to the Worldwide Church of God in order to be saved. There are people who have never heard the broadcast, seen our literature, or even heard of the Worldwide Church of God. Nevertheless, they will be saved if they meet the conditions set forth in the Scriptures."

From my fifty-minute conversation with Garner Ted Armstrong I received the strong impression that he was the real power in the Armstrong empire and his father a mere figurehead. Subsequent events were to prove me wrong. For it would be unlikely that Garner Ted would have wired Herbert W. Armstrong to cancel the triumphant Manila campaign and return to Pasadena to handle the February 1974 crisis had his father been nothing more than a figurehead. It was to the elder Armstrong that Carrozzo had gone with the request for doctrinal study and modification. It is Herbert, not Ted, whose consent must be gained before doctrinal or tactical changes can be effected. And it is Herbert, not Ted, who has emerged as the executive in dealing with complaints, resignations, dismissals, and other top-level administrative problems. Barry Chase and other ex-ministers have verified this judgment: Herbert W. Armstrong, far from being senile, as sometimes rumored, is still firmly in control.

At press time ferment continues in the Worldwide Church of God. Personal appearance tours are on the increase. Herbert W. Armstrong's overseas crusades, interrupted in February by the ministerial revolt, resumed in Manila May 17-19, 1974. Garner Ted planned a tour of his own for on-the-spot radio and television broadcasts.[27]

History was made in the Worldwide Church in the spring of 1974 when Garner Ted's wife Shirley became the first woman to be named a trustee of Ambassador College and of the Church.[28] The low-key publicity given the appointment, coincident with the revival of talk about scandal concerning her husband, led some to speculate that strategic considerations were involved.

The absence of a comprehensive doctrinal statement has occasioned confusion, contradiction, and dissension in the Worldwide Church of God throughout its history. At last that omission is being rectified. A "Theological Research Project" has been established for the twofold purpose of framing a brief ("one page, if possible") statement of faith and a detailed "exegetical handbook"—the latter to be "a project of seven to ten years."[29] Director of the study is Charles Dorothy, editor of the Spanish edition of *The Plain Truth* and professor of Spanish at Big Sandy.

Not only have there been defections and internal strife, but the ramparts of the Armstrong empire have been bombarded by lawsuits. In addition to child-study cases, involving member and non-member parents, a man in the Seattle area is seeking $100,000 damages for loss of eyesight due to the church's medical policy; a Fort Worth man is asking $10 million because the church persuaded his wife to forsake him and become involved in "adulterous relationships," and "mentally intimidated and harassed his son and caused him to have a mental breakdown";[30] and a California ex-member filed suit for $11 million against Herbert W. Armstrong, charging that he "revealed confidential facts about [his] private life" (including sexual sins confessed during counseling) before a church audience of 1500 people.[31]

* * *

On February 23, 1974, I attended my first Worldwide Church of God service in the auditorium of Chaney High School in Youngstown, Ohio. The two monitors at the door (one of whom was disfellowshipped a few weeks later and joined the Associated Churches of God) were cordial and admitted me without question. Inside I found a congregation of four hundred, all but two of them white. I was impressed with the extreme friendliness of everyone, including the pastor, Eugene Noel. The following Tuesday I returned for Bible study, shared by a group of 150, and again received a cordial reception. On March 16, with the minister's permission, I took a group of college students to the Sabbath service.

April 13 was the last day of the Feast of Unleavened Bread, and presumably the anniversary of Christ's resurrection. There was a two-hour service that morning, followed by a break for lunch. I arrived in time for the afternoon service, two-and-a-half hours long, of which the sermon took up 75 minutes. During the announcements Eugene Noel said he had learned that Barry Chase, a former minister of the congregation, had been in town calling on members in an effort to divide the flock—a report which later proved to be false. Noel warned against "participating in the unfruitful works of darkness" (Eph. 5:11), and instructed the members not to communicate with heretics who have been disfellowshipped.

Noel devoted most of his address to a comparison between the Israelites in the wilderness and God's people today. The two thousand defectors were said to have forsaken God's church and "gone back to Egypt." As the children of Israel had grumbled and complained against Moses, so these modern Israelites had rebelled against Mr. Armstrong. In purging these dissidents, God had cleansed his church of leaven.

Not surprisingly, the Bible texts which Noel quoted,

while the faithful followed along, were mostly from the Old Testament. The Worldwide Church of God may be changing to meet the crises its leadership and policies have brought upon it, but the general impression remains that the New Testament message of freedom in Christ still remains obscured behind the screen of Armstrong legalism. Whether the dissidents who have learned that works righteousness is a dead end will meet with enough success to force a basic rethinking on this score by the Worldwide Church hierarchy is, one would suppose, doubtful.

Appendix A

Chronological Outline

1892	Herbert W. Armstrong born in Des Moines, July 31.
1917	HWA marries Loma Dillon in Chicago.
1924	The Armstrongs motor to HWA's parents' home in Salem, Oregon, and remain in the Pacific Northwest.
1925	HWA, "goaded" into Bible study by Loma's "fanaticism" in espousing Sabbath (seventh-day) observance, is persuaded she is right.
1927	HWA is converted and baptized by a Baptist minister, but refrains from joining any church.
1928	HWA offers his first audible prayer—table grace in an Oregon farmhouse—and preaches his first sermon.
1930	Garner Ted Armstrong born in Portland, February 9.
1931	HWA ordained by the Oregon Conference of the Church of God, which he had helped to organize the previous year.
1933	HWA breaks with Oregon Conference; begins independent ministry with meetings near Eugene, Oregon. Some 20 converts agree to establish "a new Sabbath-keeping Church of God."
1934	"Radio Church of God" launched over KORE, Eugene. First issue of *The Plain Truth* mimeographed and mailed to 106 listeners.
1938	*The Plain Truth,* after a lapse of 2½ years, resumes publication in January with circulation of 1050.
1940	Broadcast is extended to Seattle. Printing press replaces mimeograph; *The Plain Truth* circulation climbs to 3000. Mail response now ranges between 200 and 300 letters per week.
1941	Time purchased on Hollywood radio station and broadcast renamed "The World Tomorrow." Transcriptions are made for multiple distribution and daily broadcasting begun.

1942	Nationwide radio coverage achieved with addition of 50,000-watt WHO, Des Moines. *The Plain Truth* now mailed to 35,000 subscribers in all states and provinces of the US and Canada.
1946	Broadcast now on "early prime time" six nights per week, coast to coast. First baptizing tour.
1947	Ambassador College opens its doors with 4 students and 8 instructors.
1951	*The Plain Truth* circulation over 50,000. *The Good News* magazine issued to members.
1952	Others assist in writing articles for *The Plain Truth.* Five young Ambassador graduates are ordained by HWA to become ministerial assistants.
1953	January *Plain Truth* lists eleven radio stations—up four since April 1951. The Work "leaps" to Europe via Radio Luxembourg, as second "19-year time-cycle" begins.
1956	*The Plain Truth* expands to 24 pages. GTA joins Pasadena faculty.
1957	GTA, 27, now carries "a good share" of the broadcasting; appointed vice president of college and church, executive editor of *The Plain Truth* (now in two colors).
1958	Death of HWA's elder son Richard David, following an automobile accident. "The World Tomorrow" now worldwide. *The Plain Truth* enlarged to 32 pages; circulation 175,000.
1959	Spanish-language broadcasts begun over Radio Tangier International. Weekly wattage increased to 5 million.
1960	German-language broadcast begins. Ambassador campus at Bricket Wood, England, opened.
1964	French-language broadcast begins. Third Ambassador campus opens at Big Sandy, Texas. *Plain Truth* circulation 500,000.
1965	*The Plain Truth* gets full color cover; circulation 600,000.
1966	*The Plain Truth* goes to full color throughout; circulation 775,000.
1967	*The Plain Truth* reaches 1,000,000 circulation. "The World Tomorrow" expands to television. Death of Mrs. Herbert W. Armstrong.
1968	The telecast becomes full color. "The Radio Church of God" is renamed "The Worldwide Church of God."
1969	*The Plain Truth* passes the 2,000,000 mark. Church now has 125,000 "co-workers," 200 churches, 56 "outlying Bible studies." Ambassador College joins the Hebrew University in excavation near Temple wall in Jerusalem. Enrolment now 1400 on three campuses. Feast of Tabernacles held at 22 sites in 12 countries; attendance: 54,000 in US and Canada, 9,000 abroad. New doctrine-

oriented magazine *Tomorrow's World* begun in June with 125,000 circulation.

1970 HWA makes two around-the-world tours and is received in foreign capitals by heads of state and other dignitaries. "The World Tomorrow" attains 50 million watts of power per week.

1972 Long-predicted removal of "God's Church" to "place of safety" in January, at conclusion of second 19-year time-cycle of Armstrong Work, fails to materialize. Disappearance of GTA produces nationwide publicity and widespread speculation. His return to the broadcast after four months brings revival. GTA launches North American personal appearance campaign in major cities. "The World Tomorrow" begins daily telecasting; is carried by 382 radio and 75 TV stations worldwide. *Tomorrow's World* (875,000 circulation) retired with April issue.

1973 GTA restored to full authority, named by HWA as his successor. Regional reorganization and new policy of openness announced. *The Plain Truth* circulation tops 3,000,000 with May issue. *The Good News* is offered to non-members for the first time; circulation climbs to 247,000, including 33,000 members. *The Worldwide News* is mailed to 29,000 subscribers. Ambassador College enrolment slumps to 1131. Festival attendance increases to 96,000 at 34 sites around the world. Church attendance averages 89,205 worldwide (up 8 per cent); US attendance, 73,500. Churches and ministers number 356 and 604 worldwide; 259 and 518 in US. Financial income $55,988,500. Average weekly mail receipts, 88,164; new names added to file in twelve-month period, 910,788.

1974 Worldwide Church of God rocked by scandal as ministers resign charging GTA with "monumental immorality" prior to his 1972 exile; doctrinal, financial, and administrative complaints also filed. The "Associated Churches of God," with headquarters in Washington, D.C., is established by 35 ex-ministers; 2000 members claimed. The *Ambassador College Correspondence Course* marks 25th anniversary: more than 600,000 students reported; current enrolment over 200,000. HWA begins personal appearance campaign in foreign capitals. Baptized membership: 58,244 worldwide (including 45,747 in US and approximately 4200 in Canada).

Appendix B

Summary of Teachings and Practices

Many of the distinctive teachings and practices of the Worldwide Church of God, listed below in summary form, are discussed at greater length in the body of the book. Basic work on this summary was done by a graduate of Ambassador College. Titles of articles (in quotation marks) and books (italicized) published by Ambassador College Press are also supplied.

1. *The Church.* The only true church is the Worldwide Church of God, which is not a denomination or a sect. Its leadership, under the president and pastor general Herbert W. Armstrong, is appointed rather than elected. The mission of the church is not to convert but to warn people of impending disaster. All other church organizations are of the devil and will be rooted up.

Ambassador College Publications: *A True History of the True Church; The Autobiography of Herbert W. Armstrong; This Is Ambassador College; This Is the Worldwide Church of God; Where Is God's True Church Today?;* "A Crusade for Sanity"; "False Conversion—A Mortal Danger"; "Preach Door to Door?"; "Should We Listen to Others?"; "Why So Many Denominations?"

2. *Science and Faith.* Irrefutable evidence that God exists and that the Bible is his inspired and perfect word can be found. To Herbert W. Armstrong alone has been given the key to interpret the Bible correctly. Scientific theories of organic evolution are flatly contradicted by the Bible.

Ambassador College Publications: *A Theory for the Birds; A Whale of a Tale; Answers from Genesis; Does God Exist?; Our Awesome Universe; The Proof of the Bible; Some Fishy Stories;* "Did Jesus' Miracles Really Happen?"; "Seven Proofs God Exists"; "How Long Were the Days of Creation?"

3. *The World Before Man.* Long before man existed the earth was ruled by the angel Lucifer, who rebelled against God, taking about

one-third of the angels with him. The utter desolation on the moon and other planets reflects the great battle that took place. Thereafter, God re-created the world in six literal days. During a gap of time of indeterminate length, between Genesis 1 and 2, the dinosaurs and other prehistoric life existed.

Ambassador College Publications: *Did God Create a Devil?*; "Dinosaurs"; "Satan's Fate."

4. *The Godhead.* There are two separate individuals now in the God-family—the Father and his Son, Jesus Christ. The Yahweh of the Old Testament was Jesus, who created the world, called Abraham and Moses. He is also Melchizedek. The Holy Spirit is not a person but a force.

Ambassador College Publications: *The Real Jesus*; "Did Jesus Have Long Hair?"; "Is It Wrong to Have Pictures of Jesus?"; "Is Jesus God?"; "Is Michael Christ (Dan. 10:21)?"; "Why Were You Born?"

5. *Man.* Man did not "fall" but was created with fallible human nature, so that he could learn to fight evil and go the right way. God thus intended that man should rebel and subsequently return to him. Salvation is the process by which God reproduces himself, creating other human beings who then become members of the God-family. Man literally *becomes God.*

Ambassador College Publications: "Are People Lost Because of Adam's Sin?"; "Human Nature Is Violent."

6. *Salvation.* Salvation has six stages—(1) repentance; (2) faith; (3) baptism by a minister of the Worldwide Church of God; (4) reception of the Holy Spirit; (5) overcoming of sin; (6) resurrection and change into Spirit beings—i.e., becoming God.

Ambassador College Publications: *All About Water Baptism*; *Just What Do You Mean—Born Again?*; *Just What Do You Mean—Conversion?*; *What Do You Mean—Salvation?*; *What Is a Real Christian?*; *What Is Faith?*; "Are Babies Saved If They Die?"; "How Can You Be Imbued with the Power of God?"; "What Is Real Repentance?"

7. *The End of the Present World Order.* God has permitted Satan to rule and man to sin for six thousand years. The time is almost up: the signs of the times as Jesus listed them in Matthew 24 are evident, not only in violent convulsions, but in the outreach of the gospel to all nations through the ministry of the Worldwide Church of God.

Ambassador College Publications: *How To Understand Prophecy*; *Is This the End Time?*; *The Key to the Book of Revelation*; *1975 in Prophecy*; *The Truth About Earthquakes*; "6000 Years for Man's Rule"; "Volcanic Disaster—A Prophetic Reality"; "What is Armageddon?"

8. *The World Tomorrow.* After 2½ years of tribulation and one year of the outpouring of God's wrath, Jesus Christ will return. The

dead in Christ will be resurrected and changed into divine beings and will, with the then living members of the "one True Church," rule the earth for a thousand years. Christ will rule with a rod of iron.

Ambassador College Publications: *Just What Do You Mean—The Kingdom of God?; The Wonderful World Tomorrow—What Will It Be Like?; What Is the Reward of the Saved?; Who Will Rule Space?;* "Is Heaven the Reward of the Saved?"; "The Coming Utopia—the Wonderful World of Tomorrow"; "What Is the Place Jesus Is Preparing?"

9. *Predestination.* Predestination has to do with being called, not with being saved or lost. Some are called now; most will receive the call later, after a future resurrection. How they respond will determine whether they will be saved (reborn as spirit beings) or lost (annihilated in the lake of fire).

Ambassador College Publication: *Predestination Does the Bible Teach It?*

10. *The Three Resurrections.* The first resurrection at the second coming of Christ will include all who have overcome sin and are ready to enter the Godhead. After the millennium, there will be a resurrection of the vast bulk of mankind who never had a real chance for salvation. They will be restored to physical life for a hundred years during which they will be taught God's truth and given the chance to repent. At the end of this century, all who have persisted in rejecting God will be resurrected and cast into the lake of fire and annihilated. Then God will re-create the earth, and populate it by the now-immortal members of the God-family, who will rule the universe forever in peace and harmony.

Ambassador College Publications: "If You Die—Will You Live Again?"; "The Secret Rapture—Fact or Fiction?"; "What Is the Purpose of the Resurrection?"

11. *Death.* Man does not have an immortal soul. Those who die simply return to the dust and cease to exist until God restores them in a future resurrection.

Ambassador College Publications: *After Death—Then What?; Lazarus and the Rich Man; Where Are Enoch and Elijah?;* "Did the Thief on the Cross Enter Paradise Immediately?"; "Do You Have an Immortal Soul?"; "Practice of Cremation Wrong?"

12. *Jesus' Death and Resurrection.* The crucifixion occurred on Wednesday, April 25, AD 31; the resurrection three days and three nights (72 hours) later. The notion that Jesus died on Good Friday and arose on Sunday was inspired by the devil to trick Christians into substituting Sunday for the Sabbath as the day of worship. When Jesus died, he ceased to exist until the resurrection. The corrupt body laid in Joseph's tomb was not the same body which was raised.

Ambassador College Publications: *The Crucifixion Was Not on Friday; The Resurrection Was Not on Sunday;* "Did Christ Die of a Broken Heart?"

13. *Hell Fire.* The lake of fire is a literal burning that will consume the wicked at the end of this present age. Prior to the establishment of the new heavens and earth, it will engulf the earth's surface and purify it. Rebellious human beings will be instantaneously annihilated. The devil and his angels, who will be cast into it following the millennium, will not be destroyed by the flames, since they are spirit beings. Their suffering will be mental and will continue for all eternity.

Ambassador College Publications: *Did God Create a Devil?;* "There Is a Real Hell Fire"; "Worms Never Die in Hell?"

14. *The US and Britain.* The peoples of these two nations are the descendants of the lost ten tribes of Israel. Germany, heading a ten-nation United States of Europe, will destroy and take into captivity the peoples of the US and Britain. Eventually, the few survivors of the "Israelite" nations will be taken to Palestine to rule with Christ in the World Tomorrow.

Ambassador College Publications: *The Mark of the Beast; The Modern Romans; The US and the British Commonwealth in Prophecy; Who Is the Beast?;* "Are Christians Again to be Martyred?"; "How Sound Is the Rock of Gibraltar?"; "Middle East in Prophecy"; "USA Riding to Total Collapse in 20 Short Years"; "Will Russia Attack America?"

15. *Special Days.* The seventh day, Saturday, is the only true Sabbath, reckoned from sundown Friday to sundown Saturday. Sunday worship makes the worshiper liable to the lake of fire. The seven annual festivals of Leviticus 23—Passover, Unleavened Bread, Pentecost, Trumpets, Atonement, Tabernacles, and The Last Great Day—are to be observed on the correct day as calculated on the religious calendar. Pagan holidays are an abomination and not to be observed; this includes Christmas, Easter, New Year's Day, Lent, Halloween, and Valentine's Day, but does not include Thanksgiving and Mother's and Father's Days. Birthdays are not to be celebrated.

Ambassador College Publications: *Which Day Is the Christian Sabbath?;* "What Should a Person Do About Sabbath Visitors?"; *God's Sacred Calendar; How Often Should We Partake of the Lord's Supper?; Pagan Holidays or God's Holidays—Which?;* "How to Observe God's Festivals"; *Easter Is Pagan; The Plain Truth About Christmas;* "The Truth About New Year's!"; "Where Did God Command You to Observe Lent?"; "Should a Christian Celebrate Birthdays?"

16. *Tithing.* A tithe is computed as one-tenth of net income. There are three tithes: the first given directly to the church for general administration; the second used to pay the expenses of family

attendance at the annual festivals (and a tithe of this tithe is sent to headquarters to finance festival operating expenses); the third, collected every three-and-a-half years, is used for widows and orphans. The tithes are supplemented by freewill offerings.

Ambassador College Publications: *The Seven Laws of Success;* "How to Get Out of Debt"; "Is Money the Root of Evil?"; "What You Should Know About Tithing."

17. *Physical Health.* True Christians look to God rather than men and medicine for healing. The elders should be summoned to anoint with oil and pray for a sick person. Doctors may be employed for "repair work" (setting broken bones, etc.); professional care for teeth and eyes is approved. Natural childbirth at home is recommended. Unclean foods (Leviticus 11) should not be eaten; natural foods and raw milk are recommended. Smoking is destructive of the body; Christians are enjoined not to use tobacco in any form. Since Jesus drank wine, moderate drinking is permissible, though drunkenness is forbidden.

Ambassador College Publications: *Does God Heal Today?; The Seven Laws of Radiant Health;* "Eat Right to Be Healthy"; "How to Cook Vegetables"; "What To Do About Overweight"; *You Can Quit Smoking;* "Should a Christian Raise Tobacco?"; "Alcoholism—a Worldwide Curse"; "Is Drinking a Sin?"

18. *Family Life and Morality.* Divorce is not recognized for any reason, even adultery. All remarried divorced persons are living in a constant state of adultery. Divorced couples are not accepted for baptism until they agree to separate and either return to their former mates or remain single (whether or not children are involved). Normal sexual practice in marriage is approved; adultery, premarital sex, homosexuality, and all kinds of perversion and pornography are condemned. Mechanical means of birth control are advocated; use of the pill is discouraged. Reasonable family planning is urged. Spanking should be administered to children beginning at a few months of age. Spanking must be done with love and firmness; children must be taught to obey instantly and without question. Children should not be permitted to participate in public school sports or group activities. Church-sponsored dances are encouraged, but sexually suggestive dancing is forbidden. Similarly, rock music is condemned as unconducive to character development. "Good" music, including the hymns of Herbert W. Armstrong's brother Dwight, is encouraged. Women are not to wear makeup or wigs, and their dresses should come to the middle of the knee. Men are not to have long hair, sideburns, or beards.

(The divorce and remarriage policy was relaxed in May 1974. See Postscript.)

Ambassador College Publications: *Divorce and Remarriage; How to Have a Happy Marriage; Marriage—Soon Obsolete?; God Speaks*

Out on the New Morality; Is Sex Sin?; Modern Dating; "The Shocking Truth About Queer Men"; *The Plain Truth About Child Rearing;* "What Is Worldliness?"

19. *Women.* Women are not permitted to preach or to be ordained as ministers. They may serve as deaconesses. Mothers are not to work outside the home except in unusual circumstances.

Ambassador College Publications: *The New Feminism; True Womanhood;* "Should Women Preach?"; "True Womanhood—Is It a Lost Cause?"

20. *Wealth.* It is not a sin to be rich; wealth is often a reward to those faithful to God. God is a God of quality and beauty; Christians should strive to obtain the best they can afford, but not at the expense of their financial obligations to the church.

Ambassador College Publication: "Does God Hate the Rich?"

21. *Race.* According to the Ambassador College constitution and by-laws (Art. 9, 2), "God Almighty by His own will segregated the races at ancient Babel and decreed that they should remain physically segregated." Intermarriage is a sin. Segregation will be strictly enforced in the World Tomorrow.

Ambassador College Publications: *The Origins of the Nations; The Wonderful World Tomorrow—What Will It Be Like?;* "The Development of the Races"; "The Race Question."

22. *Civil Government.* Christians should not vote, hold political office, serve on juries or in the armed forces. They should pay taxes, respect governmental authority, and be "good citizens."

Ambassador College Publications: "Respect Government Authority"; "Should a Christian Fight?"

23. *Pentecostalism.* Although faith healing is practiced by the Worldwide Church of God, the healings of the Pentecostal movement generally are believed to be Satanic deceptions. Speaking in tongues is strictly forbidden.

Ambassador College Publications: "The Truth About Healing Revivals"; *The Tongues Question.*

Appendix C

Non-traditional Doctrines Shared by the Worldwide Church of God and Other Religious Groups

I. *Seventh-day Adventists*

1. The seventh-day Sabbath is the only acceptable, God-ordained day for rest and worship.
2. Sunday worship is the "mark of the beast" (Rev. 14:9). Those who persist in this practice after being enlightened concerning the "true" Sabbath will be destroyed in the lake of fire.
3. Man does not possess a soul which survives physical death, but is like animals, birds, and insects in his mortality. His identity, however, is preserved in a divine "memory bank" against the day of his future resurrection—a doctrine known as "conditional immortality" or "soul sleep."
4. There is no eternal hell, or place of eternal punishing. The fate of the wicked is annihilation in the "lake of fire."
5. Jesus Christ was endowed with fallible human nature—the nature of Adam after the Fall—but nevertheless remained sinless.
6. Satan, not Christ, is the scapegoat of Leviticus 16 upon whose head "the responsibility for sin will be placed."
7. The Pope (as a symbol of the Roman Catholic Church) is the "great whore" of Rev. 17, the "false prophet" of Rev. 19:20, and the "man of sin" of II Thess. 2:3-4—a doctrine formerly taught but no longer officially proclaimed by Seventh-day Adventists.

8. The Old Testament dietary laws (Lev. 11) are in force today.

II. *Jehovah's Witnesses*

1. Jesus *became* the Son of God when he was conceived in Mary's womb.

2. Jesus was not resurrected in the same body which was crucified and laid in Joseph's tomb.
3. Jesus' death atones only for past sins. Salvation is contingent on rituals and obedience, in addition to faith.
4. Those who die in ignorance will be resurrected for a "first chance" to receive salvation.
5. The Trinity doctrine is denied. The Holy Spirit is not a person but a "divine force."
6. The only valid baptism is by immersion, administered by a minister of the "one true Church."
7. The Roman Catholic Church and her "Protestant daughters" are "Satan's counterfeits."
8. Christians should not involve themselves in "this world's government." Voting and participation in the armed forces are opposed.
9. Theocratic rule "from the top down" is rigorously enforced.
10. Christmas and Easter are of pagan origin and are therefore sinful.
11. The Cross is referred to as a "stake," excommunication as "disfellowshipment."
12. Use of tobacco is forbidden; use of alcoholic beverages in moderation is permitted.
13. Blood transfusions are not advocated.

III. *Mormons*

1. The Trinity is denied. God is a "Family"—and the destiny of every true believer is to become *God* (not merely *like* God), a member of the "God-Family."
2. Adam's Fall fulfilled God's will of *desire* as well as his will of purpose—for only through sinning could Adam and Eve become mortal, propagate the race, and benefit from the divine plan for redemption.
3. Christ's death atones for *past* sins only. Compliance with ritual and moral requirements are added to faith as conditions for salvation.
4. Members of the black race are victims of the curse of Noah.

IV. *British-Israelism*

1. The white Anglo-Saxon peoples of northwestern Europe, Great Britain, and the United States are the true Israel today and heirs of the biblical promises for Israel.
2. Legends from ancient folklore concerning the "lost ten tribes" of Israel are accepted as historical: e.g., the Stone of Scone is Jacob's "pillar stone"; the British monarchs are lineal descendants of King David.

Appendix D

AMBASSADOR COLLEGE-WORLDWIDE CHURCH OF GOD COMPARATIVE STATEMENT OF INCOME AND EXPENSE FOR YEARS ENDED DEC. 31, 1973, 1972

INCOME	**1973**	**1972**
Contributions	$36,934,200	$36,653,700
Holy Day Offerings	5,883,200	4,267,900
Third Tithe	3,589,500	3,746,100
Big Sandy Income – Student and Other	2,925,800	2,660,100
Property Fund	1,711,900	2,037,800
Festival Fund	1,407,800	1,411,200
Second Tithe	1,032,900	1,560,500
Tuition, Room and Board	714,400	563,000
Imperial Schools Income	271,700	270,000
Emergency Fund Donations	246,600	245,800
Other Donations	537,800	367,300
Interest Income	385,900	371,900
Other Income	346,800	117,400
TOTAL INCOME	$55,988,500	$54,262,700
EXPENSES		
Broadcasting and Media (Schedule 1)	$ 7,264,300	$ 6,422,200
Publishing (Schedule 2)	8,951,700	7,404,800
Ministerial and Church (Schedule 3)	10,934,800	8,353,500
Departmental and Administrative (Schedule 4)	14,336,000	12,743,200
Festival Expenses	3,010,400	2,863,300
Ambassador College, United Kingdom	4,570,600	3,867,200
Ambassador College, Big Sandy	4,203,100	4,189,400
Depreciation	2,105,000	2,611,300
Other Noncash Charges	179,200	5,500
TOTAL EXPENSES	$55,555,100	$48,460,400
NET INCOME	$ 433,400	$ 5,802,300

BROADCASTING AND MEDIA	**SCHEDULE 1**	
Salaries	$ 1,850,500	$ 1,116,200
Radio Time	2,552,900	3,013,200

	1973	1972
Television Time	1,732,000	857,400
Magazine Advertising	424,000	784,000
Newsstand Distribution	238,300	213,000
Television Production	194,700	72,300
Supplies	100,800	155,700
Shipping	47,200	58,800
Magazine Ad Production	32,900	25,500
Miscellaneous	91,000	126,100
TOTAL BROADCASTING AND MEDIA EXPENSE	$ 7,264,300	$ 6,422,200
	1973	**1972**
PUBLISHING AND CIRCULATION DIVISION	**SCHEDULE 2**	
Salaries	$ 5,087,200	$ 4,651,600
Paper and Printing Supplies	1,568,900	781,800
Postage	962,600	673,400
Rental Expense – Electronic Data Processing Equipment	908,300	929,900
Repairs and Maintenance	38,100	62,800
Miscellaneous	386,600	305,300
TOTAL PUBLISHING AND CIRCULATION EXPENSE	$ 8,951,700	$ 7,404,800
MINISTERIAL AND CHURCH	**SCHEDULE 3**	
Salaries	$ 5,968,400	$ 4,485,500
Widow Support and Emergency Fund Assistance	3,034,800	1,872,700
Church Hall Rental	842,200	724,600
Ministerial Expense	494,600	479,400
Vehicle Operating Expense	372,900	547,700
Summer Educational Program	162,000	186,700
Miscellaneous Church Expense	59,900	56,900
TOTAL MINISTERIAL AND CHURCH EXPENSE	$10,934,800	$ 8,353,500
DEPARTMENTAL AND ADMINISTRATIVE	**SCHEDULE 4**	
Academic Salaries	$ 1,706,300	$ 1,767,600
Physical Plant Salaries	2,371,300	2,664,300
Administrative Salaries	2,114,000	1,798,200
Taxes, Licenses and Fees	759,000	973,700
Interest	1,332,000	1,263,100
Telephone and Utilities	912,300	713,600
Insurance	532,500	540,700
Departmental Expenses	1,049,200	620,700
Buildings and Grounds	400,800	261,000
Transportation	253,400	210,700
Business Jet Expenses	475,200	367,600
Business Jet Rental	379,200	252,800
Travel and Moving Expense	969,300	327,500
Supplies	215,700	294,900
Miscellaneous	865,800	686,800
TOTAL DEPARTMENTAL AND ADMINISTRATIVE EXPENSE	$14,336,000	$12,743,200

Appendix E

U.S. REGIONS AND CHURCH AREAS OF THE WORLDWIDE CHURCH OF GOD

-JANUARY, 1974

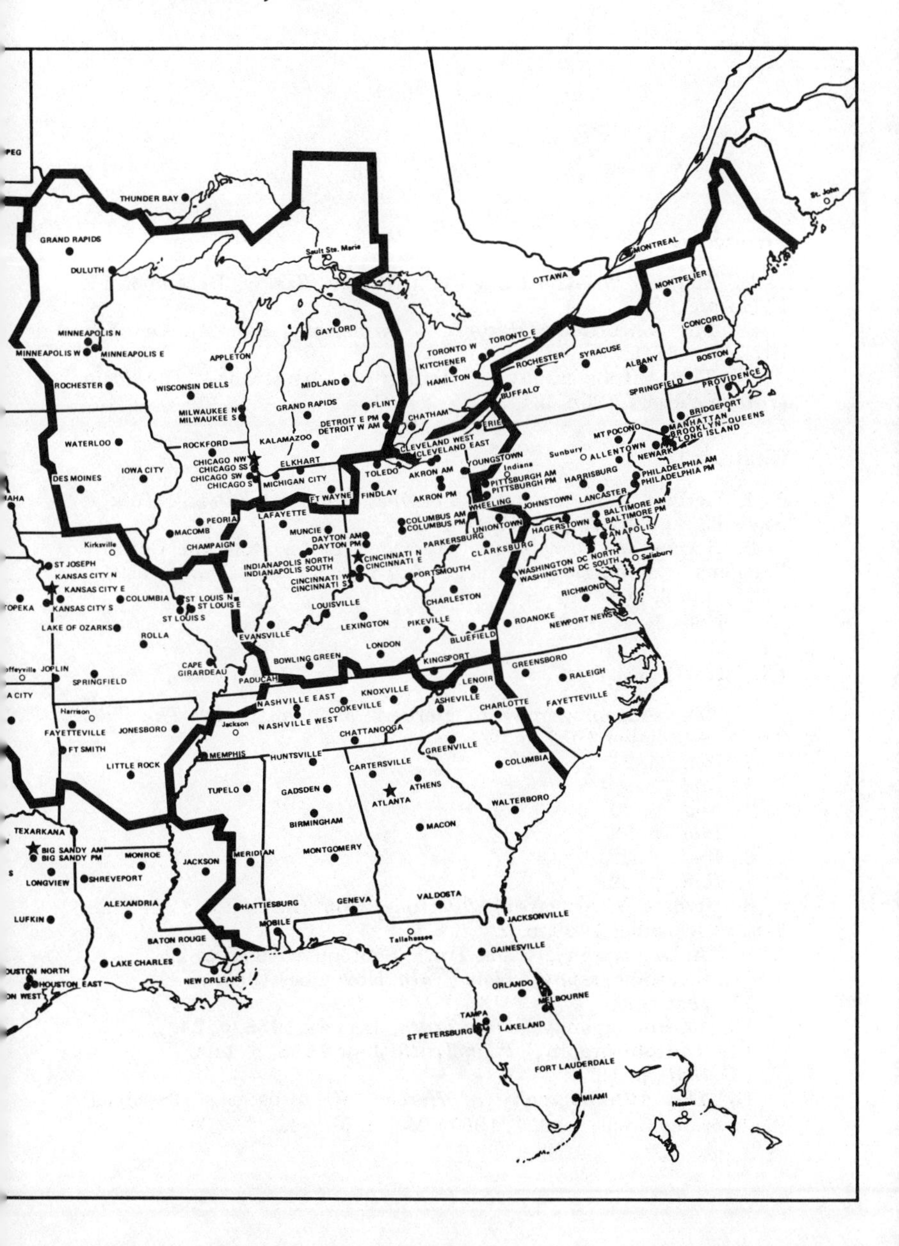

Notes

Foreword

1. "Herbert W. Armstrong," *Christianity Today*, December 17, 1971, pp. 6ff.

2. "Mr. Jones, Meet Herbert W. Armstrong, *Eternity*, October 1972, pp. 19ff.

3. "The Autobiography of Herbert W. Armstrong," *The Plain Truth*, February 1968, p.4.

Chapter I

1. Herbert W. Armstrong, "Personal from the Editor," *Tomorrow's World*, July-August 1970, p. 2.

2. Herbert W. Armstrong, "An Open Letter from the Editor." Pasadena: *Ambassador College Correspondence Course* (1954, 1968), pp. 2, 16.

3. *Ibid.*, p. 7.

Chapter II

1. "The Autobiography of Herbert W. Armstrong," *The Plain Truth*, September 1957, p. 4.

2. *Ibid.*, p. 21.

3. *Ibid.*

4. *Ibid.*, p. 20.

5. *Ibid.*, p. 22.

6. *Ibid.*, p. 20.

7. *Ibid.*, p. 22.

8. Herbert W. Armstrong, "Personal from the Editor," *The Plain Truth*, December 1969, p. 2.

9. "Autobiography," *Plain Truth*, September 1957, p. 22.

10. "Autobiography," *Plain Truth*, November 1957, p. 4.

11. *Ibid.*, p. 17.

12. "Autobiography," *Plain Truth*, January 1958, p. 24.

13. "Autobiography," *Plain Truth*, June 1958, p. 14.

14. *Ibid.*, p. 18.

15. *The Autobiography of Herbert W. Armstrong* (Pasadena: Ambassador College, 1957, 1967), Vol. I, p. 171.

16. *Ibid.*, p. 174.
17. *Ibid.*, p. 187.
18. *Ibid.*, p. 210.
19. *Ibid.*, p. 221.
20. *Ibid.*, p. 223.
21. *Ibid.*, p. 224.
22. *Ibid.*
23. *Ibid.*, p. 240.
24. *Ibid.*, pp. 270f.
25. *Ibid.*, p. 282.
26. *Ibid.*, p. 284.
27. *Ibid.*, p. 288.
28. *Ibid.*, p. 289.
29. *Ibid.*, p. 292.
30. *Ibid.*, p. 295.
31. *Ibid.*, p. 294.
32. *Ibid.*, p. 296.
33. *Ibid.*, p. 297.
34. *Ibid.*, p. 300.
35. Herbert W. Armstrong, "Personal from the Editor," *The Good News*, August 1969, p. 3.
36. *Ibid.*, p. 4.
37. *The Autobiography of Herbert W. Armstrong*, p. 311.
38. *Ibid.*, p. 337.
39. *Ibid.*, p. 342.
40. *Ibid.*, p. 346.
41. *Ibid.*, p. 399.
42. *Ibid.*, pp. 314f.
43. *Ibid.*, p. 319.
44. *Ibid.*, p. 385.
45. *Ibid.*, p. 456.
46. *Ibid.*, p. 450.
47. "Autobiography," *Plain Truth*, April 1960, p. 5.
48. *The Autobiography of Herbert W. Armstrong*, p. 492.

Chapter III

1. *The Autobiography of Herbert W. Armstrong*, Vol. I, pp. 493-495.
2. *Ibid.*, p. 498.
3. *Ibid.*, p. 499.
4. *Ibid.*, p. 501.
5. *Ibid.*, pp. 505-507.
6. *This Is the Worldwide Church of God* (Pasadena: Ambassador College Press, 1971), p. 17.
7. *The Autobiography of Herbert W. Armstrong*, p. 509.
8. "Autobiography," *Plain Truth*, December 1960, p. 10.
9. *The Autobiography of Herbert W. Armstrong*, p. 510.
10. "Autobiography," *Plain Truth*, March 1961, p. 14.
11. *Ibid.*
12. *The Autobiography of Herbert W. Armstrong*, pp. 454, 472.
13. "Autobiography," *Plain Truth*, March 1961, p. 31.
14. *Ibid.*
15. *Ibid.*, p. 12.

16. "Autobiography," *Plain Truth*, November 1961, p. 5.
17. *Ibid.*, p. 23.
18. "Autobiography," *Plain Truth*, December 1961, p. 19.
19. "Autobiography," *Plain Truth*, January 1962, p. 11.
20. "Autobiography," *Plain Truth*, December 1961, p. 25.
21. "Autobiography," *Plain Truth*, January 1962, p. 39.
22. "Autobiography," *Plain Truth*, February 1962, p. 12.
23. *Ibid.*
24. *Ibid.*, p. 16.
25. "Autobiography," *Plain Truth*, June 1962, p. 43.
26. *Ibid.*
27. "Autobiography," *Plain Truth*, November 1962, p. 13.
28. *Ibid.*, p. 44.
29. "Autobiography," *Plain Truth*, December 1962, pp. 30-32.
30. "Autobiography," *Plain Truth*, May 1963, p. 26.
31. "Autobiography," *Plain Truth*, June 1963, pp. 28f.
32. "Autobiography," *Plain Truth*, October 1963, p. 17.
33. "Autobiography," *Plain Truth*, September 1963, p. 17.
34. *Ibid.*
35. *Ibid.*, p. 18.
36. "Autobiography," *Plain Truth*, January 1964, p. 9.
37. *The Autobiography of Herbert W. Armstrong*, pp. 235f.
38. *Ibid.*, p. 400.
39. *Ibid.*
40. Most historians agree on A.D. 29 as the most probable year for the crucifixion and resurrection and Pentecost. See James Hastings, *Dictionary of the Bible*, rev. ed. by F. C. Grant and H. H. Rowley (New York: Scribners, 1963), p. 157.
41. Hastings, *op. cit.*, p. 1051.
42. *The Autobiography of Herbert W. Armstrong*, p. 408.
43. "Autobiography," *Plain Truth*, April 1964, p. 30.
44. "Autobiography," *Plain Truth*, March 1965, p. 24.
45. *Ibid.*, p. 25.
46. Cf. J. D. Douglas, ed., *The New Bible Dictionary* (Grand Rapids: Eerdmans, 1962), p. 505.
47. "Autobiography," *Plain Truth*, August 1967, p. 5.
48. *Ibid.*, p. 22.
49. "Autobiography," *Plain Truth*, September 1967, p. 20.
50. *Ibid.*
51. "Autobiography," *Plain Truth*, February 1968, p. 41.

Chapter IV

1. Herbert W. Armstrong, "Personal from the Editor," *The Good News*, August 1969, p. 3.
2. *Ibid.*, p. 4.
3. *Ibid.*
4. *Ibid.*
5. *The Autobiography of Herbert W. Armstrong*, Vol. I, p. 505.
6. Acts 20:28; I Cor. 1:2; 10:32; 11:16, 22; 15:9; II Cor. 1:1; Gal. 1:13; I Thess. 2:14; II Thess. 1:4; I Tim. 3:5, 15. "The complete number" of passages is reduced to ten in the Revised

Standard Version, which translates "church of the Lord" in Acts 20:28, and "God's church" in I Tim. 3:5.

7. Herman L. Hoeh, *A True History of the True Church* (Pasadena: Ambassador College, 1959), p. 28.
8. *Ibid.*, p. 10.
9. *Ambassador College Bible Correspondence Course*, Lesson 49 (1968), p. 11.
10. *Ibid.*, p. 12.
11. *Ibid.*, p. 3.
12. Hoeh, *op. cit.*, p. 14.
13. *Ibid.*, p. 15.
14. *Ibid.*, p. 16 (italics added).
15. *Ambassador College Bible Correspondence Course*, Lesson 49, p. 14.
16. Hoeh, *op. cit.*, p. 17.
17. *Ambassador College Bible Correspondence Course*, Lesson 49, p. 15.
18. *Ibid.*, Lesson 50 (1968), p. 6.
19. *Ibid.*, p. 9.
20. *Ibid.*, p. 11.
21. *Ibid.*, p. 13.
22. *Ibid.*, p. 15.
23. *Op. cit.*, p. 20.
24. *Ambassador College Bible Correspondence Course*, Lesson 50, p. 6.
25. *Ibid.*, Lesson 52 (1968), p. 4.
26. Hoeh, *op. cit.*, p. 23.
27. *Ambassador College Bible Correspondence Course*, Lesson 52, pp. 6, 7.
28. *Ibid.*, Lesson 53 (1968), p. 6.
29. Hoeh, *op. cit.*, p. 23.
30. *Ibid.*, p. 24.
31. *Ibid.*, p. 25.
32. Frank S. Mead, *Handbook of Denominations in the United States* (Nashville: Abingdon, 1970), p. 75.
33. *Ambassador College Bible Correspondence Course*, Lesson 53, p. 12.
34. *Ibid.*
35. *Ibid.*
36. Hoeh, *op. cit.*, p. 26.
37. Herbert W. Armstrong, "Just what do you mean . . . The Kingdom of God?", *Tomorrow's World*, June 1969, p. 7.
38. *The Autobiography of Herbert W. Armstrong*, p. 504.
39. Herbert W. Armstrong, "Personal from the Editor," *The Plain Truth*, November 1969, p. 44.
40. *Ibid.*, January 1969, p. 32.
41. *Ambassador College Bible Correspondence Course*, Lesson 53, p. 14.
42. Herman L. Hoeh, "If World War III Comes—There is a Way of Escape" (Ambassador College reprint, 1963), p. 6.
43. *Ambassador College Bible Correspondence Course*, Lesson 53, p. 15. (The reference is to the three Ambassador campuses in

California, Texas, and England.) There is no proof that the schools of the prophets at Bethel, Jericho, and Gilgal (II Kings 2:1-5; 4:38) were the *only* such schools in Israel.

44. *Ibid.*

Chapter V

1. For example, Richard A. Marson, *The Marson Report Concerning Herbert W. Armstrong* (Seattle: The Ashley-Calvin Press, 1970); Roger R. Chambers, *The Plain Truth About Armstrongism* (Grand Rapids: Baker, 1972); Walter R. Martin, *The Kingdom of the Cults* (Grand Rapids: Zondervan, 1965), pp. 295-323.
2. Herbert W. Armstrong, *The US and British Commonwealth*, p. 4.
3. *Ibid.*, p. 8.
4. *Op. cit.*, p. 18.
5. Albert M. Hyamson, "Anglo-Israelism," in *The Encyclopedia of Religion and Ethics*, ed. James Hastings (New York: Scribners, 1910), Vol. I, p. 482.
6. Harry W. Lowe, *Radio Church of God* (Mountain View, California: Pacific Press Publishing Association, 1970), p. 78.
7. *The Autobiography of Herbert W. Armstrong*, Vol. I, p. 345.
8. *The US and British Commonwealth*, p. 9.
9. *Ibid.*, p. 10.
10. *Ibid.*, p. 15.
11. *Ibid.*, p. 24.
12. *International Standard Bible Encyclopedia* (Grand Rapids: Eerdmans, 1939), Vol. I, p. 523.
13. Armstrong, *The US and British Commonwealth*, p. 24.
14. *Ibid.*, p. 26.
15. *International Standard Bible Encyclopedia*, Vol. II, p. 1176.
16. Armstrong, *The US and British Commonwealth*, p. 26.
17. *Ibid.*, pp. 34f.
18. *Ibid.*, p. 36.
19. *Ibid.*, p. 56.
20. *Ibid.*, p. 57.
21. *Ibid.*, p. 35.
22. D. Winton Thomas, ed., *Documents from Old Testament Times* (New York: Harper, 1961), p. 67.
23. *International Standard Bible Encyclopedia*, Vol. IV, p. 2673.
24. Armstrong, *The US and British Commonwealth*, p. 89.
25. *Ibid.*, p. 40.
26. *Ibid.*, p. 44.
27. *Ibid.*
28. *International Standard Bible Encyclopedia*, Vol. II, p. 900.
29. *The US and British Commonwealth*, p. 95.
30. *Ibid.*, p. 96.
31. *Ibid.*
32. Matthew Henry, *An Exposition of the Old and New Testament* (New York: Robert Carter & Brothers, 1880), Vol. V, p. 401.
33. *International Standard Bible Encyclopedia*, Vol. III, p. 1589.
34. *The US and British Commonwealth*, p. 121.
35. *Ibid.*, p. 103.

36. *Ibid.*
37. *Ibid.*, p. 108.
38. *Ibid.*, p. 109.
39. *Ibid.*, p. 118.
40. *Ibid.*, pp. 118, 121.
41. *Ibid.*, p. 121.
42. *The New Century Dictionary* (New York: Appleton-Century-Crofts, 1953), Vol. II, p. 2580.
43. William Henry Smith, *The Ten Tribes of Israel Never Lost*, p. 91 (quoted in Harry W. Lowe, *op. cit.*, p. 91).
44. *The US and British Commonwealth*, pp. 115f.
45. *Ibid.*, p. 116.
46. Ernest Klein, *A Comprehensive Etymological Dictionary of the English Language* (Amsterdam, London, New York: Elsevier, 1966), Vol. I, p. 201; Vol. II, p. 1389.
47. *The US and British Commonwealth*, p. 116.
48. *Ibid.*, pp. 116f.
49. *Ibid.*, pp. 117f.
50. *Ibid.*, p. 118.
51. *Ibid.*, p. 106.
52. *Ibid.*, pp. 122f.
53. *Ibid.*, pp. 70f.
54. *Ibid.*, p. 126.
55. *Ibid.*
56. *Ibid.*
57. *Ibid.*, pp. 126-128.
58. *Ibid.*, p. 166.
59. *Ibid.*, p. 150.
60. *Ibid.*, p. 173.
61. *Ibid.*, pp. 181f.
62. *Ibid.*, p. 199.
63. *Ibid.*, p. 198.
64. *Ibid.*
65. *Ibid.*, pp. 199f.
66. *Ibid.*, p. 199.
67. *Ibid.*
68. *Ibid.*, p. 200.
69. *Ibid.*, p. 160.
70. Marson, *op. cit.*, p. 150.
71. *Ibid.*, p. ix.
72. *Ibid.*, p. 210.
73. *Ibid.*, p. 212.

Chapter VI

1. "The Nazi underground is now plotting a war that shall end at Armageddon!" Herbert W. Armstrong, "Middle East in Prophecy" (Ambassador College reprint, 1956), p. 5. It was predicted in this article that the battle of Armageddon would take place "in all probability in less than 16 years"—i.e., 1972.
2. Herbert W. Armstrong and Garner Ted Armstrong, *The Wonderful World Tomorrow* (Pasadena: Ambassador College, 1966), p. 3.

3. *Ibid.*, pp. 4-32.
4. C. Paul Meredith, "An Open Letter from the Director." *Ambassador College Bible Correspondence Course,* Lesson 4 (1955, 1968), p. 2.
5. Herbert W. Armstrong, "What is Armageddon?" (Pasadena: Ambassador College reprint, 1955). See also his *The Book of Revelation Unveiled at Last*! (1959), pp. 19-42.
6. Herbert W. Armstrong, "Will Russia Attack America?" (Ambassador College reprint, 1956), p. 5.
7. *Ibid.*
8. *Ibid.*
9. *Ibid.*
10. *The Wonderful World Tomorrow,* p. 40.
11. C. Paul Meredith, "Is This the *Only* Day of Salvation?" (Ambassador College reprint, 1958), p. 2.
12. *Ibid.*, p. 3.
13. Herman L. Hoeh, "If World War III Comes—There Is a Way of Escape" (Ambassador College reprint, 1963), p. 5.
14. *The Wonderful World Tomorrow,* pp. 41f.
15. *Ambassador College Bible Correspondence Course,* Lesson 3 (1965, 1968), p. 9.
16. *The Wonderful World Tomorrow,* p. 52.
17. *Ibid.*, pp. 52f.
18. *Ibid.*, p. 53.
19. *Ibid.*, p. 54.
20. *Ibid.*
21. *Ibid.*, p. 56.
22. *Ibid.*, pp. 57f.
23. *Ibid.*, pp. 58f.
24. *Ibid.*, p. 59.
25. *Ibid.*, p. 65.
26. *Ibid.*, p. 71.
27. *Ibid.*, p. 39; cf. *Ambassador College Bible Correspondence Course,* Lesson 3 (1955, 1968), p. 9.
28. *Ambassador College Bible Correspondence Course,* Lesson 4, pp. 4f.
29. *Ibid.*, p. 11.
30. *Ibid.*, pp. 11f.
31. *The Wonderful World Tomorrow,* p. 37.
32. *Ibid.*, p. 44.
33. *Ibid.*, p. 45.
34. *Ibid.*, p. 44.
35. *Ibid.*, p. 46.
36. *Ambassador College Bible Correspondence Course,* Lesson 4, p. 5.
37. *Ibid.*
38. *The Wonderful World Tomorrow,* p. 63.
39. *Ibid.*, p. 72.
40. Herbert W. Armstrong, *Lazarus and the Rich Man* (Pasadena: Ambassador College, 1953), p. 8.
41. *Ibid.*, p. 11.

42. Robert Young, *Analytical Concordance to the Bible* (New York: Funk & Wagnalls), p. 1022. The frequencies are: Matthew, 25; Mark, 14; Luke, 7; John, 25.

43. Herbert W. Armstrong, "Where Will the Millennium Be Spent?", *Tomorrow's World*, September 1971, p. 6.

44. Alexander Maclaren, *Expositions of Holy Scripture* (Grand Rapids: Eerdmans, 1938), *St. John*, Vol. II, p. 276.

45. Herman L. Hoeh, *Where Are Enoch and Elijah?* (Ambassador College reprint), pp. 12, 14.

46. Geerhardus Vos has cautioned would-be expositors of the Apocalypse, "In regard to a book so enigmatical, it were presumptuous to speak with any degree of dogmatism" (*International Standard Bible Encyclopedia*, Vol. II, p. 987).

Chapter VII

1. *Does God Exist?* (Pasadena: Ambassador College Press, 1957, 1971), pp. 5f.

2. David Jon Hill, "Why Is God the Father called a Father?" *Tomorrow's World*, September-October 1970, p. 24.

3. *Ibid.*, p. 26.

4. *Ibid.*

5. *Ibid.*

6. *Ambassador College Bible Correspondence Course*, Lesson 9 (1956, 1966), p. 5. (The Correspondence Course has been revised, so that current numbers do not correspond with those previously used.)

7. Herbert W. Armstrong, *Just What Do You Mean—Born Again!* (Pasadena: Ambassador College, 1962), p. 15.

8. Herbert W. Armstrong, *Why Were You Born?* (Pasadena: Ambassador College Press, 1957), p. 21.

9. A. M. Hunter, *The Gospel According to John. The Cambridge Bible Commentary on the New English Bible* (Cambridge: Cambridge University Press, 1965), p. 164.

10. G. Campbell Morgan, *The Gospel According to John* (Westwood, N. J.: Revell, n.d.), p. 274.

11. G. Geis, "The God Family—Open or Closed?", *Tomorrow's World*, September-October 1970, pp. 30f.

12. *Ambassador College Bible Correspondence Course*, Lesson 9, p. 8.

13. *Is Jesus God?*, p. 3.

14. Garner Ted Armstrong, *Who—What—was Jesus before His Human Birth?* (Ambassador College reprint, 1972), p. 2.

15. *Ibid.*, p. 3.

16. *Ambassador College Bible Correspondence Course*, Lesson 3 (1955, 1968), p. 6.

17. *Ambassador College Correspondence Course*, Lesson 9 (1972), p. 10.

18. Herbert W. Armstrong, "Millions Do Not Know What Christ Really Was!", *The Plain Truth*, November 1963, pp. 11f.

19. Garner Ted Armstrong, "Do You Have an Immortal Soul?" (Ambassador College reprint, 1957, 1971), p. 3.

20. *Questions on Doctrine* (Washington: Review and Herald Publishing Association, 1957), p. 22.
21. Herbert W. Armstrong, "Why Christ Died—and Rose Again," *The Plain Truth*, April 1963, p. 10.
22. *Ibid.*, p. 40.
23. A. H. Strong, *Systematic Theology* (Philadelphia: Judson, 1907), p. 1018.
24. Herbert W. Armstrong, *The Resurrection Was Not on Sunday!* (Pasadena: Ambassador College, 1952), p. 4.
25. Cf. Robert W. Funk, *A Greek Grammar of the New Testament* (Chicago: U. of Chicago Press, 1961), p. 746; and W. F. Arndt and F. W. Gingrich, *A Greek-English Lexicon of the New Testament* (Chicago: U. of Chicago Press, 1957), p. 78.
26. Harry W. Lowe, *Radio Church of God* (Mountain View, California: Pacific Press, 1970), p. 99.
27. *Ibid.*, p. 103.
28. *Ibid.*, p. 108.
29. *Ambassador College Correspondence Course*, Lesson 9 (1956, 1966), p. 9.
30. *Ambassador College Correspondence Course*, Lesson 20 (1959, 1967), p. 15.
31. David Jon Hill, *op. cit.*, p. 28.
32. A. H. Strong, *op. cit.*, pp. 315, 323-325.
33. J. D. Douglas, ed., *The New Bible Dictionary* (Grand Rapids: Eerdmans, 1962), pp. 1299f.
34. Herbert W. Armstrong, *Did God Create a Devil?* (Ambassador College reprint, 1959), p. 1.
35. *Ibid.*
36. *Ambassador College Correspondence Course*, Lesson 29 (1963, 1969), pp. 4-6.
37. *Ibid.*, p. 6.
38. *Ibid.*, Lesson 30 (1963, 1967), p. 4.
39. Garner Ted Armstrong, *What Is Satan's Fate?* (Ambassador College reprint), p. 4.
40. *Ibid.*, p. 5.
41. *Ibid.*
42. *Ibid.*
43. *Ibid.*, p. 7.
44. *Ibid.*, pp. 7-8.

Chapter VIII

1. Garner Ted Armstrong, "God Doesn't Need You!", *The Plain Truth*, March 1965, p. 7.
2. *Ibid.*, pp. 43-44.
3. Herbert W. Armstrong, *What Do You Mean—Salvation?* (Pasadena: Ambassador College, 1961), p. 6.
4. Herbert W. Armstrong, *Just What Do You Mean—Born Again?* (Pasadena: Ambassador College, 1962), p. 7.
5. *Ibid.*
6. Walter R. Martin, *The Kingdom of the Cults*, p. 316.

7. Herbert W. Armstrong, *Just What Do You Mean—Born Again?*, p. 11.
8. Floyd V. Filson, *John. The Layman's Bible Commentary*, Vol. 19 (Richmond: John Knox Press, 1963), p. 45.
9. A. E. Carrozzo, "Repent!" *Tomorrow's World*, February 1971, p. 14.
10. Herbert W. Armstrong, *What Do You Mean—Salvation?*, p. 15.
11. *Ibid.*, p. 16.
12. *Ibid.*, p. 5.
13. Herbert W. Armstrong, *The US and British Commonwealth*, p. 37.
14. *Ambassador College Correspondence Course*, Lesson 24 (1961, 1968), p. 3.
15. Garner Ted Armstrong, "Should You Be Baptized?", *Tomorrow's World*, September 1969, p. 10.
16. Herbert W. Armstrong, *What Do You Mean—Salvation?*, pp. 11, 21.
17. David Albert, "In the Name of Jesus," *Tomorrow's World*, February 1971, pp. 18f.
18. Robert L. Kuhn, "Receive the Gift of the Holy Spirit," *Tomorrow's World*, February 1971, p. 23.
19. *Ibid.*
20. Ambassador College Graduate School of Theology, *What is Faith?* (Pasadena: Ambassador College Press, 1952), p. 20.
21. *Ibid.*
22. *Ibid.*, p. 23.
23. *Systematic Theology*, p. 864.
24. Cf. Herbert W. Armstrong, *What Do You Mean—Salvation?*, p. 17.
25. Burton H. Throckmorton, Jr., *Study Guide on Romans* (New York: Presbyterian Distribution Service, 1961), p. 36.
26. Herbert W. Armstrong, *What Do You Mean—Salvation?*, p. 21.
27. Herbert W. Armstrong, *All About Water Baptism* (Pasadena: Ambassador College, 1948), pp. 6-8.
28. Herbert W. Armstrong and Garner Ted Armstrong, *The Wonderful World Tomorrow*, p. 62.
29. *Ibid.*, p. 65.
30. *Ibid.*, p. 66.
31. David Jon Hill, "Twelve Rules for Bible Study," *Tomorrow's World*, July 1969, p. 29.
32. Herbert W. Armstrong, *The Proof of the Bible* (Pasadena: Ambassador College, 1958), p. 40.
33. Herbert W. Armstrong, "The Seven Keys To Understanding The Bible," *Tomorrow's World*, January 1971, p. 3.
34. *Ibid.*
35. *Ibid.*
36. David Jon Hill, "Twelve Rules for Bible Study," *Tomorrow's World*, August 1964, pp. 31ff., September 1964, pp. 12ff.
37. I. C. Peterson, "Reflections from a Head-of-the-Dragon Point

of View." Unpublished 1972 transcript of tape-recorded report by Conrad Comeau, former Armstrong jet pilot, p. 27.

38. *Bulletin of Ambassador College*, 1971-1973, p. 43.

39. L. Leroy Neff, "Should We Repeat the 'Lord's Prayer'?", *The Plain Truth*, January 1963, p. 47.

40. *International Standard Bible Encyclopaedia*, Vol. III, p. 1921.

Chapter IX

1. "The Autobiography of Herbert W. Armstrong," *The Plain Truth*, September 1963, p. 16.

2. Herman L. Hoeh, "It Does Matter Which Days We Observe!", *The Good News*, August 1969, p. 7.

3. *Ibid.*

4. Kenneth C. Herrmann, *God's Sacred Calendar, 1970-1971* (Pasadena: Ambassador College, 1970), p. 1.

5. *Ibid.*, p. 7.

6. *Ibid.*, pp. 2, 11.

7. Hoeh, *op. cit.*, p. 10.

8. *The US and British Commonwealth in Prophecy*, p. 168.

9. Bill McDowell, "Keep God's Sabbath Holy!", *The Good News*, March 1968, p. 17.

10. *Ibid.*

11. *Ibid.*

12. Herbert W. Armstrong, *Which Day Is the Christian Sabbath?* (Pasadena: Ambassador College, 1962), p. 90.

13. *Ibid.*, p. 94.

14. *Ibid.*, p. 81.

15. Herbert W. Armstrong, "How Often Should We Partake of the Lord's Supper?", *Tomorrow's World*, March 1971, pp. 3-4.

16. *Ibid.*, p. 4.

17. *Ibid.*, p. 5.

18. Henry E. Dosker, "Lord's Supper: Historical," *International Standard Bible Encyclopaedia*, Vol. III, p. 1925.

19. Herrmann, *op. cit.*, p. 11.

20. *Ibid.*

21. *Ibid.*

22. *Ibid.*

23. *Ibid.*

24. *Ibid.*

25. "The 1969 Feast of Tabernacles," *The Good News*, November-December 1969, p. 3.

26. *The Good News*, August 1959, pp. 3-6.

27. Roderick C. Meredith, *The Ten Commandments* (Pasadena: Ambassador College, 1960), p. 17.

28. *Ibid.*, p. 22.

29. *Ibid.*, pp. 37f.

30. *Ibid.*, p. 51.

31. *Ibid.*, pp. 71, 73.

32. "Garner Ted Armstrong, Where Are You?", *Time*, May 15, 1972, p. 87.

33. Meredith, *The Ten Commandments*, p. 96.

34. *Ibid.*, p. 102.
35. *Ibid.*
36. *Time, loc. cit.*
37. Earl Hansen, "Garner Ted Armstrong and His Church of God Spiral," *Seattle Post-Intelligencer*, April 22, 1972, p. A15.
38. Meredith, *The Ten Commandments*, p. 116.
39. *Ibid.*, pp. 121f.
40. *Ibid.*, pp. 130f.
41. *Ibid.*, p. 141.
42. *The Autobiography of Herbert W. Armstrong*, Vol. I, pp. 382f.
43. Herbert W. Armstrong, "Is *all Animal Flesh Good Food?*" (Ambassador College reprint, 1958), p. 2.
44. *Ibid.*, p. 6.
45. Roderick C. Meredith, *The Seven Laws of Radiant Health* (Pasadena: Ambassador College Press, 1955, 1973), pp. 9-19.

Chapter X

1. *Time*, May 15, 1972, p. 87.
2. Harold N. Hubbard, "Ambassador Beauty on Display April 7," *Pasadena Star News*, March 31, 1974, p. A-3.
2a. *This Is Ambassador College* (Pasadena: Ambassador College Press, 1969), p. 6.
3. *Ibid.*, pp. 6f.
4. *Bulletin of Ambassador College, 1971-1973*, p. 21.
5. *This Is Ambassador College*, p. 7.
6. *Ibid.*, pp. 13-15.
7. *Bulletin*, p. 26.
8. *This Is Ambassador College*, p. 59. *The Plain Truth* (July 1965) reported that transfers to Ambassador in the early sixties came from more than 160 colleges, including Yale, Harvard, and the University of California.
9. *Bulletin*, p. 38.
10. Roderick C. Meredith, "Ambassador College Is *Unique*," *The Plain Truth*, January 1973, p. 20.
11. *Bulletin*, pp. 87f.
12. "Personal from Herbert W. Armstrong," *Tomorrow's World*, August 1971, p. 48.
13. "Autobiography," *The Plain Truth*, May 1963, p. 26.
14. *Bulletin*, p. 51.
15. "Colleges Re-educate for Christ's Return," *The Christian Century*, February 19, 1969, p. 264.
16. "Personal from Herbert W. Armstrong," *The Plain Truth*, February 1972, p. 49.
17. Undated letter from Herbert W. Armstrong to *Plain Truth* subscribers, received in January 1969.
18. Letter from Herbert W. Armstrong to "Co-Workers," dated January 28, 1973, p. 2.
19. *This Is the Worldwide Church of God* (Pasadena: Ambassador College Press, 1972), p. 200.
20. *The Worldwide News*, January 21, 1974, p. 7.
21. Herbert W. Armstrong, "Personal from the Editor," *The Plain Truth*, April-May 1970, p. 1.

22. Herbert W. Armstrong, Letter to "Dear Family of Co-Workers," October 27, 1972, p. 2.

23. Herbert W. Armstrong reported 125,000 co-workers in 1970 ("Personal from the Editor," *The Plain Truth,* April-May 1970, p. 48). It is assumed that this figure includes members.

24. Stanley E. Anderson, *Armstrongism's 300 Errors Exposed* (Nashville: Church Growth Publications, 1973), p. 181.

25. Richard H. Sedliacik, "Why Study the Bible in the Space Age?", *Tomorrow's World,* June 1969, p. 33.

26. Richard H. Sedliacik, "The New Correspondence Course," *The Good News,* November-December 1970, pp. 15f.

27. *This Is Ambassador College,* p. 33.

28. *Bulletin,* p. 23.

29. "Eschatological Stirrings: Madman at the Mosque?", *Christianity Today,* February 27, 1970, p. 35.

30. Herbert W. Armstrong, "Uncovering 3000 Years of History!", *The Plain Truth,* April 1969, pp. 4f.

31. Richard A. Marson, "The Worldwide Church of God: A Former Member Speaks Out," pp. 125-127.

32. Herbert W. Armstrong, "Personal from the Editor," *The Plain Truth,* October 1969, pp. 1, 47.

33. Marson, *op. cit.,* p. 131. The comment, recalled from memory by an eyewitness, is paraphrased.

34. Herbert W. Armstrong, "Personal from the Editor," *The Plain Truth,* October 1969, p. 47.

35. Herbert W. Armstrong, Letter to "Inner Family of Co-Workers," August 29, 1972, p. 1.

36. "Personal from Herbert W. Armstrong," *The Plain Truth,* November 1972, p. 47.

37. "Girls Were Not in Men's Clothes," *The Plain Truth,* July 1960, p. 25.

38. *Bulletin,* p. 46.

39. *Student Handbook,* p. 25.

40. Alan Bestic, *Praise the Lord and Pass the Contribution* (New York: Taplinger, 1971), p. 27.

41. Roderick C. Meredith, "Should Women *Preach?*", *The Plain Truth,* November 1963, p. 27.

42. *Ibid.,* p. 27.

43. Roderick C. Meredith, *True Womanhood: Is It a Lost Cause?* (Pasadena: Ambassador College Press, 1965), pp. 12f.

44. Jim Brigance, "Storm Rolls Over Church Sect," *Henderson* (Texas) *Daily News,* Feb. 28, 1974, p. 1.

45. Garner Ted Armstrong, "Smoking is a Sin!", *The Plain Truth,* July 1964, pp. 25ff.

46. Garner Ted Armstrong, *Should a Christian Smoke?* (Ambassador College reprint, 1964), pp. 2-4.

47. Roderick C. Meredith, *Is Drinking a Sin?* (Ambassador College reprint, 1961), p. 1.

48. Leslie L. McCullough, "How to Use Your Second Tithe," *The Good News,* September-October 1971, p. 20.

49. Garner Ted Armstrong, *The Real Jesus* (Pasadena: Ambassador College, 1971), p. 7.

50. Ambassador College Graduate School of Theology, *The "Tongues" Question* (Pasadena: Ambassador College, 1957), p. 13.
51. Robert C. Boraker, "The Truth About Drugs and Vaccines," *The Good News*, October 1959, pp. 6-8.
52. *The Good News*, April 1968, p. 2.
53. *Student Handbook*, p. 31.
54. "Girls Were Not in Men's Clothes," *The Plain Truth*, July 1960, p. 28.
55. Herbert W. Armstrong, "Personal from the Editor," *The Plain Truth*, March 1965, p. 2.
56. "Fast-accelerating," perhaps, with respect to physical and fiscal expansion. But the three-campus 1972-73 enrolment of 1131, reported in the 1973 *Envoy*, indicates a sizeable drop from the combined figure of 1600 (700 at Pasadena; 550 at Big Sandy; 350 in England) supplied by *The New York Times* on May 7, 1972 (and confirmed in *Christianity Today*, April 14, 1972). A healthy increase in 1973-74 enrolment figures may signal a reversal of the downward trend.

Chapter XI

1. To this figure may be added another seventy thousand "Co-Workers" whose financial contributions play a decided role in the outreach of the movement.
2. "Personal from Herbert W. Armstrong," *The Plain Truth*, February 1972, p. 49.
3. *This Is the Worldwide Church of God* (1972), pp. 15f. In May 1972 *Time* reported 400 radio and 99 television stations; in September 1972 syndicated religion columnist Lester Kinsolving cited 300 radio and 65 television stations.
4. *This Is the Worldwide Church of God*, p. 16.
5. *Ibid.*, p. 19.
6. *This Is Ambassador College*, p. 60.
7. *The Worldwide News*, Mar. 18, 1974, p. 7. Total income for 1973 was reported as $55,988,500—an increase of $1,725,800 over 1972.
8. Herbert W. Armstrong announced total assets of $58,349,500, at the 1969 Feast of Tabernacles.
9. Thomas Ham, "Hundreds Hear Vital Messages at Feast of Tabernacles," *The Good News*, December 1952, p. 5.
10. *The Worldwide News*, November 1, 1973, p. 1.
11. *The Good News*, January-April 1971, p. 20.
12. " . . . And You Shall Be Brought Before Kings," *The Good News*, March 1974, p. 15.
13. Herbert W. Armstrong, Letter to "Inner Family of Co-Workers in the Very Work of the Living God," January 28, 1973, p. 1.
14. *Ibid.*, pp. 1-3.
15. Raymond F. McNair, "Highlights from the World Tour," *The Good News*, November-December 1970, p. 1.
16. *The Autobiography of Herbert W. Armstrong*, Vol. I, p. 332.
17. Quoted by I. C. Peterson, "Reflections from a Head-of-the-Dragon Point of View," p. 25.

18. *Ibid.*, pp. 35f.
19. *Ambassador College Student Handbook*, p. 16. More recently, it has been reported that the stringent "secrecy" policy is being relaxed.
20. *Ambassador College Correspondence Course*, Lesson 8 (1956, 1966), p. 16.
21. Herbert W. Armstrong, *Should We Listen to Others?* (Pasadena: Ambassador College reprint, 1960), p. 2.
22. *Ibid.*, pp. 2f.
23. *Ibid.*, p. 3.
24. Personal correspondence with the author, dated January 9, 1973.
25. Carl O'Beirn, unpublished material prepared "because a number have inquired as to the origin of The Church of God."
26. Personal correspondence with the author, dated December 11, 1972.
27. Russell Chandler, "The Armstrong Empire: Revolution and Revelations," *Christianity Today*, Mar. 15, 1974, p. 50.

27a. Personal correspondence with the author, reporting an "unquestionably reliable inside source," dated March 11, 1973. Cf. the full-page Worldwide Church of God advertisement in *Time*, July 31, 1972.

28. "Letters to the Editor," *Tomorrow's World*, July 1969, p. 35.
29. William H. Ellis, "Have You Found God's One True Church?", *The Plain Truth*, July 1965, p. 30.
30. *Ambassador College Correspondence Course*, Lesson 5 (1955, 1968), p. 12.
31. *Ibid.*, p. 13.
32. *Ibid.*
33. Leslie L. McCullough, "How To Use Your Second Tithe," *The Good News*, September-October 1971, p. 8.
34. *Ibid.*, p. 20.
35. *Ibid.*
36. Albert J. Portune, "The Tithe of the Tithe," *The Good News*, September-October 1971, p. 15.
37. Peter Geiger, *Akron Beacon Journal*, October 11, 1970, p. A6.
38. I. C. Peterson, *op. cit.*, pp. 20f.
39. Letter from Garner Ted Armstrong to "Dear Member of God's Church," August 15, 1972.
40. Herbert W. Armstrong, Letter to "Dear Brethren and Co-Heirs with Christ," May 5, 1969, p. 3.
41. *The Worldwide News*, March 18, 1974, p. 7.

41a. Theodore G. Phillips and William F. Dankenbring, "Success Thru Second Effort!", *The Good News*, January-April 1971, p. 25.

42. Roderick C. Meredith, "Tithing Pays Off—Here's the Proof!", *The Plain Truth*, February 1964, p. 41.
43. "Answers to Your Questions about the Foreign Work," *The Good News*, November-December 1972, p. 34.
44. *The Good News*, September-October 1970, p. 20.
45. Roderick C. Meredith, "Tithing Pays Off," *loc. cit.*, p. 27.

46. Leon Walker, "How Much Do You Hate Sin?", *The Good News*, January-April 1971, p. 12.
47. Herbert W. Armstrong, Letter to "Dear Brethren of God's Church," November 2, 1972, p. 4.
48. Russell Chandler and Bert Mann, "Six Ministers Resign from Armstrong Religious Sect," *The Los Angeles Times*, February 24, 1974, p. 18. *The Worldwide News*, Mar. 18, 1974, p. 7.
49. *Ibid.*
50. Alan Bestic, *Praise the Lord and Pass the Contribution*, p. 30.
51. Lester Kinsolving, "Sect Disclaims Bobby Member," *Pittsburgh Post-Gazette*, September 23, 1972, p. 5.
52. William F. Dankenbring, "Success Is More Than Money," *The Plain Truth*, Mar. 1974, pp. 11-13. "An Interview with H. Ross Perot." *Ibid.*, pp. 14-15.
52a. *Ambassador College Correspondence Course*, Lesson 50 (1968), p. 13.
53. Quoted by Noel Smith, *Herbert W. Armstrong and His World Tomorrow* (Springfield, Missouri: *Baptist Bible Tribune*, 1964), p. 38.
54. I. C. Peterson, *op. cit.*, pp. 8f.
55. *Ibid.*, p. 12.
56. *Ibid.*, p. 39.
57. Raymond F. McNair, "Needed—a World Super-Government," *The Plain Truth*, February 1964, pp. 11f.
58. Herman L. Hoeh, "Who Built the Great Pyramid?", *The Plain Truth*, May 1964, pp. 45ff.
59. Russell Chandler, "Defections Fewer Than Expected by Worldwide Church of God," *Los Angeles Times*, Mar. 16, 1974.
59a. *Ibid.*
59b. *The Worldwide News*, Mar. 4, 1974, p. 16.
60. "Garner Ted Armstrong 'Disciplined, Removed,' " *Pasadena Star-News*, April 25, 1972, p. 1.
61. Earl Hansen, "Where Are You, Garner Ted?", *Seattle Post-Intelligencer*, March 25, 1972, p. A8.
62. Carter Barber, "Vice-Chancellor Armstrong Said on Leave of Absence," *Pasadena Star News*, March 18, 1972, p. 2.
63. "Garner Ted Armstrong 'Disciplined, Removed,' " *loc. cit.*
64. "Garner Ted Armstrong, Where Are You?", *Time*, May 15, 1972, p. 87.
65. "Garner Ted Returns," *Time*, July 10, 1972, p. 71.
66. "Garner Ted: In Satan's Bonds?", *Christianity Today*, April 28, 1972, p. 42.
67. Earl Hansen, "Garner Ted Armstrong and His Church of God Spiral," *Seattle Post-Intelligencer*, April 22, 1972, p. A15.
68. Betty Medsger, "Father Shuts Off Son in Clash of Personalities in Church," *The Washington Post*, April 29, 1972, p. E10.
69. "Garner Ted Armstrong 'Disciplined, Removed,' "*loc. cit.*, p. 7.
70. *Herbert W. Armstrong's Holy Day Dilemma*, p. 1.
71. Lester Kinsolving, "Church of God Word Spreads," *Pittsburgh Post-Gazette*, March 11, 1972.
72. Herbert W. Armstrong, *The United States and British Commonwealth in Prophecy*, p. xii.

73. Herbert W. Armstrong, Letter to "Brethren of God's Church," May 31, 1972, p. 2 (emphasis added).
74. "The Autobiography of Herbert W. Armstrong," *The Plain Truth*, August 1965, p. 47.
75. Letter dated March 11, 1973.
76. *Christianity Today*, quoted in *Time*, July 10, 1972, p. 71.
77. "Radio Preacher Is Ousted by Father," *The New York Times*, May 7, 1972.
78. Lester Kinsolving, "Church of God Word Spreads," *Pittsburgh Post-Gazette*, March 11, 1972.
79. Personal correspondence with the author, dated March 11, 1973.
80. *New Orleans Times-Picayune*, February 4, 1973, p. TV3.
80a. Russell Chandler and Bert Mann, *op. cit.*, p. 18.
81. *Ibid.*, pp. 1ff.
82. Peter Geiger, *Akron Beacon Journal*, October 11, 1970, p. A6.

Chapter XII

1. "What Our Readers Say," *The Plain Truth*, January 1970, p. 2.
2. *Ibid.*, May 1963, p. 2.
3. "What Our Students Say," *Ambassador College Correspondence Course*, Lesson 5 (1971), p. 2.
4. *Ibid.*, Lesson 2 (1955, 1965), p. 2.
5. "What Our Readers Say," *The Plain Truth*, March 1973, p. 48.
6. "What Our Students Say," *Ambassador College Correspondence Course*, Lesson 2 (1955, 1965), p. 16.
7. "What Our Readers Say," *The Plain Truth*, February 1973, p. 49.
8. "What Our Students Say," *Ambassador College Correspondence Course*, Lesson 8 (1956, 1966), p. 2.
9. "Letters to the Editor," *The Plain Truth*, November-December 1970, p. 49.
10. "What Our Students Say," *Ambassador College Correspondence Course*, Lesson 31 (1963, 1967), p. 2.
11. "What Our Readers Say," *The Good News*, August 1969, p. 2.
12. "Letters to the Editor," *Tomorrow's World*, January 1970, p. 35.
13. Roger F. Campbell, "Herbert W. Armstrong: Does He Really Have the 'Plain Truth'?", *Moody Monthly*, October 1972, p. 55.
14. "Man Gets Sons After Saying Ex-Wife Believes in Witchcraft," *The Houston Post*, June 13, 1973.
15. *Ibid.*
16. Charles F. De Loach, *The Armstrong Error* (Plainfield, N.J.: Logos, 1971), p. 108.
17. Richard A. Marson, *The Marson Report* (Seattle: The Ashley-Calvin Press, 1970), p. 6.
18. *Ibid.*, p. 11.

19. Richard A. Marson, "The Armstrong Movement: A Former Member Speaks Out." Unpublished manuscript, 1971, pp. 68-71.
20. Wayne Leyendecker (as told to Roger F. Campbell), "We Escaped From Armstrongism," in *We Found Our Way Out* (Grand Rapids: Baker, 1964), p. 93.
21. *Ibid.*, p. 97.
22. Harry W. Lowe, *Radio Church of God*, p. 5.
23. *Ibid.*, p. 6.
24. *Ibid.*, p. 142.
25. Roger R. Chambers, *The Plain Truth About Armstrongism* (Grand Rapids: Baker, 1972), p. 7.
26. Walter R. Martin, *Herbert W. Armstrong and the Radio Church of God* (Minneapolis: Bethany Fellowship, 1968), p. 3 (taken from Walter R. Martin, *The Kingdom of the Cults*, published by Zondervan, 1965).
27. *Ibid.*, pp. 23f.
28. Roger F. Campbell, *Herbert W. Armstrong: Mr. Confusion* (Lincoln, Neb.: Back to the Bible Broadcast, 1971), p. 4.
29. Leslie K. Tarr, "Herbert W. Armstrong: Does He Really Have the 'Plain Truth'?", *Moody Monthly*, September 1972, p. 27.
30. Noel Smith, *Herbert W. Armstrong and His World Tomorrow* (Springfield, Missouri: Baptist Bible Tribune, 1964), p. 45.
31. *Ibid.*, p. 60.
32. "Herbert W. Armstrong: Let the Buyer Beware," *Eternity*, October 1972, p. 11.
33. William C. Martin, "The Plain Truth About the Armstrongs and the World Tomorrow," *Harper's*, July 1973, p. 74.
34. *Ibid.*, p. 82.
35. Bryan R. Wilson, "An Analysis of Sect Development," *American Sociological Review*, February 1959, p. 4. Used by permission.
36. *Ibid.*, p. 6.
37. *Ibid.*, p. 7.
38. *Ibid.*
39. *Ibid.*, p. 10.
40. Eric Hoffer, *The True Believer* (New York: Harper, 1951), p. 12.
41. Quotations from *The Good News* in William C. Martin, "The Plain Truth About the Armstrongs and The World Tomorrow," *Harper's*, July 1973, p. 80.
42. H. G. Wells, *The Outline of History* (New York: Macmillan, 1922), p. 719; quoted by Hoffer, *op. cit.*, p. 41.
43. *Ibid.*, p. 75.
44. Jan Karel Van Baalen, *The Chaos of Cults* (Grand Rapids: Eerdmans, 1960), p. 420.
45. *Ibid.*, p. 421.
46. Joseph Martin Hopkins, "Herbert W. Armstrong," *Christianity Today*, December 17, 1971, p. 7.
47. William C. Martin, "The God-Hucksters of Radio," *The Atlantic*, June 1970, p. 55.
48. Frederick Trautmann, "From Soap to Souls: The Armstrongs and 'The World Tomorrow,' " *Preaching Today*, March 1972, p. 10.
49. *Ibid.*, pp. 12-14.

Postscript

1. Cf. Herman L. Hoeh, "Does God Have a Headquarters Church for This Age?" *The Good News*, October 1953, pp. lf.
2. By Russell Chandler and Bert Mann; February 24, 1974, p. I–18.
3. "Why Did God Put You in His Church?" *The Good News*, May 1974, p. 31.
4. E.g., in the June 1967, March 1968, and September 1968 issues of *The Plain Truth.*
5. John H. Mitchell, Jr., and W. A. Sutton, "What Really Happened at Shreveport," *The Alternative*, January 1974, p. 2.
6. Cf. Floyce Korsak, "Armstrong Church Rift Reported," *Dallas Times Herald*, February 17, 1974, p. A–44; Jim Brigance, "Storm Rolls Over Church Sect," *Henderson* (Tex.) *Daily News*, February 28, 1974, p. 1.
7. "Garner Ted Ousts 15," *Houston Chronicle*, February 27, 1974.
8. Chandler and Mann, *loc. cit.*
9. *The Worldwide News*, March 18, 1974, p. 7.
10. On Rader's role in the Armstrong empire, cf. Russell Chandler, "Armstrong Aftermath: A New Church," *Christianity Today*, March 29, 1974, p. 44.
11. "Worldwide Church of God Controversies 'Boiling,' " *Dallas Times Herald*, March 10, 1974, p. A–35.
12. *The Worldwide News*, March 4, 1974, p. 16.
13. Russell Chandler, "Worldwide Church of God Is Split," *Louisville Courier-Journal*, March 3, 1974.
14. Garner Ted Armstrong, letter "To All Ministers and Deacons Worldwide," March 4, 1974.
15. Russell Chandler, "Armstrong Church: Split Decision," *Christianity Today*, Mary 24, 1974, p. 53.
16. *Ibid.*
17. "Ousted Ministers Form New Church," *Dallas Times Herald*, March 10, 1974.
18. "Did Christ Reorganize the Church?" *The Good News*, February 1939, p. 8.
19. Russell Chandler and Edward Plowman, "The Armstrong Empire: Revolution and Revelations," *Christianity Today*, March 15, 1974, p. 50.
20. *The Bulletin*, April 2, 1974, p. 50.
21. "A Personal Letter from Garner Ted Armstrong," *The Worldwide News*, March 4, 1974, p. 16.
22. "Worldwide Ministry Assembles," *The Worldwide News*, May 13, 1974, p. 1.
23. *The Worldwide News*, May 27, 1974, pp. 6, 8.
24. "Are We Ashamed of God's Truth?" *The Good News*, April-June 1973, p. 2.
25. *Ibid.*
26. "Beware the Day of the Sun!" *Ambassador College Bible Correspondence Course*, Lesson 30 (1963, 1967), pp. 9, 15.
27. "A Personal Letter from Garner Ted Armstrong," *The Worldwide News*, June 10, 1974, p. 7.

28. *The Bulletin*, April 2, 1974, p. 63.
29. David McKee, "Unhornswoggling Proves Fruitless for Head of Theology Research," *The Worldwide News*, April 29, 1974, p. 6.
30. "Church is Hit With Lawsuit," *Longview* (Tex.) *Morning Journal*, October 14, 1973, p. A–2.
31. Bert Mann, "Church Leader Named in Breach of Faith Suit," *Los Angeles Times*, February 9, 1974, p. I–28.

Bibliography

The listings below are limited to books, magazine articles, and pamphlets, published and unpublished about the Armstrong movement. Numerous newspaper articles, consulted in the process of research, are excluded. An inclusive file of Armstrong publications is held by Donald E. Kirsopp, 475 Wiley Drive, Baton Rouge, Louisiana 70808. St. Paul Publishers, 2698 Fessey Court, Nashville, Tennessee 37204, maintain a current bibliography of materials by and about the Armstrong organization.

"Alienated by Radio." *Time*, March 22, 1968, pp. 52f.

Anderson, Stanley E. *Armstrongism's 300 Errors Exposed by 1300 Bible Verses.* Nashville: Church Growth Publications, 1973. 215 pp.

_____. Exchange of Letters with Garner Ted Armstrong, Dec. 31, 1973–Jan. 26, 1974. 19 pp.

"Are You Keeping the New Moons Too?" *Messenger* (Syracuse, N.Y.: Book Fellowship), March 1973, p. 7.

"Armstrong Debacle." *Christian Vanguard*, June 1972, p. 8.

"Armstrong Debacle Confirmed." *Christian Vanguard*, Sept. 1972, p. 8.

"Armstrongism." *Baptist Challenge*, Feb. 1973, p. 5.

"Armstrong's Cult Suffers Suits and Splits." Eternity, May 1974, p. 8.

Benware, Paul N. *Ambassadors of Armstrongism: An Analysis of the History and Teachings of the Worldwide Church of God.* Philadelphia: Presbyterian and Reformed Publishing Company. 186 pp.

Bestic, Alan. *Praise the Lord and Pass the Contribution.* New York: Taplinger Publishing Co., 1971. 259 pp. Chapter 2, "God's Jet Set."

Bratt, John H. "Is the Armstrong Theology 'The Plain Truth'?" *The Banner*, Sept. 10, 17, 24, 1971.

Campbell, Roger F. "Herbert W. Armstrong: Does He Really Have the 'Plain Truth'?" *Moody Monthly*, Oct. 1972, pp. 36ff. Letters, Nov. 1972, p. 6.

———. *Herbert W. Armstrong: Mr. Confusion.* Lincoln: Back to the Bible Broadcast, 1970. 21 pp.

Carrozzo, Alfred E. "An Open Letter to My Brethren," Feb. 25, 1974. Box 642, Pasadena, Calif. 4 pp.

Cave, Marvin H. *Sabbath Day Confusion.* Annandale, Va.: The Printed Witness, 1971. 5 pp.

Chandler, Russell. "Armstrong Aftermath: A New Church." *Christianity Today*, March 29, 1974, p. 44.

———. "Armstrong Church: Split Decision." *Christianity Today*, May 24, 1974, p. 53.

———. "The Armstrong Empire: Revolution and Revelations" (ed. E. E. Plowman). *Christianity Today*, March 15, 1974, pp. 49f.

———. "Inside Armstrong's Empire." *Christianity Today*, March 15, 1974, p. 51.

Chambers, Roger R. *The Plain Truth About Armstrongism.* Grand Rapids: Baker Book House, 1972. 146 pp.

Chase, Barry. "Resume of Reasons for Resignation from Ministry of the Worldwide Church of God." Mesquite, Texas, Jan. 1974. 5 pp.

Churchill, Lorna. "The Worldwide Church of God: Some Observations." Davis, Calif., 1972. 6 pp.

Cress, Richard G. "Is Herbert W. Armstrong 'God's Prophet'?" *Facts of Our Faith* (Hawthorne, Calif.: Church of God Sabbatarian), Apr. 1972, pp. 5ff.

"Cult Evangelism: The Cunning of Armstrongism." *Soul Winner's Digest*, Fall 1967.

Dahlin, John E. "The Armstrong Movement in Serious Trouble." *The Discerner* (Minneapolis: Religious Analysis Service), Apr. 1972, pp. 2f.

———. "New Crisis in the Armstrong Organization." *The Discerner*, April-June 1974, pp. 12-14.

———. "The Status of the Cults in 1970." *The Discerner*, Jan. 1970, pp. 5ff.

"Dallas Federal Court Has a Suit Against Herbert and Ted Armstrong." *Sword of the Lord*, Feb. 22, 1974, p. 2.

Deck, Norman C. *The Wrong Teaching of Herbert W. Armstrong.* Halifax: People's Gospel Hour, n.d. 4 pp.

DeLoach, Charles F. *The Armstrong Error.* Plainfield, NJ: Logos International, 1971. 117 pp.

"Digging for Credit." *Time*, Sept. 3, 1973, p. 65.

Dugger, A. N., and C. O. Dodd. *A History of the True Religion.* Jerusalem: Mount Zion Reporter, 1968. 318 pp.

Ehrenstein, Herbert Henry. "The Truth About Herbert W. Armstrong." *Eternity*, July 1964, pp. 30ff.

"Eschatological Stirrings: Madman at the Mosque." *Christianity Today*, Feb. 22, 1970, p. 35.

"Garner Ted Armstrong, Where Are You?" *Time*, May 15, 1972, pp. 87f. Letters, June 19, 1972, p. 8.

"Garner Ted Has Come Home." *Christianity Today*, June 23, 1972, p. 42.

"Garner Ted: In Satan's Bonds?" *Christianity Today*, April 28, 1972, p. 42.

"Garner Ted Returns." *Time*, July 19, 1972, p. 71.

Geiger, Peter. "Underground Sect Training to Rule at Christ's Return." *Baptist Bible Tribune* (Springfield, Mo.), Oct. 16, 1970, p. 4. Reprinted from the Akron *Beacon-Journal*.

Grant, Robert G. *The Plain Truth About the Armstrong Cult*. Glendale, Calif.: United Community Church, 1969. 51 pp.

Gruss, Edmond C. "Herbert W. Armstrong and the Worldwide Church of God: A Survey." *Biblical Research Monthly*, Feb. 1973, pp. 3ff.

Haecker, Paul. *Ten Years in the Religion of Herbert W. Armstrong*. Houston, Texas, 1972. 18 pp.

Haines, Aubrey B. "Colleges Re-educate for Christ's Return." *The Christian Century*, Feb. 19, 1969, p. 264.

"Herbert W. Armstrong." *Baptist Bible Tribune*, Oct. 16, 1970.

"Herbert W. Armstrong." Bulletin for the Ministerial Association of Seventh-Day Adventist Ministers. Washington, D.C.: Review & Herald Publishing Association.

"Herbert W. Armstrong: Let the Buyer Beware." *Eternity*, Oct. 1972, p. 11.

"Herbert W. Armstrong Strips Son of Title, Duties." *Bible Advocate*, (Stanberry, Mo.), May 1972, p. 27.

Heydt, Henry J. "The Fallacy of British Israelism." *The Chosen People*, Apr.-May 1963.

Hofrenning, James. "Tomorrow's World?" *Lutheran Standard*, Oct. 15, 1968, p. 27.

Holly, Raymond G. "Anglo-Israelism—A Strong Delusion." *The Bible Standard and Herald of Christ's Kingdom* (Chester Springs, Pa.: Layman's Home Missionary Movement), June-Aug. 1973, pp. 42ff.

Hopkins, Joseph M. "Herbert W. Armstrong." *Christianity Today*, Dec. 17, 1971, pp. 6ff.

_____. "Mr. Jones, Meet Herbert W. Armstrong." *Eternity*, Oct. 1972, pp. 19ff.

Johnson, Maurice M. *Three Open Letters to Herbert W. Armstrong*. Orangeville, Calif.: n.d. 40 pp.

Judy, John C. "Letter to Herbert W. Armstrong and His Ministers." Glenmont, Ohio: Jan. 10, 1972. 7 pp.

Judy, Marie M. *The Voice of Freedom*. Unpublished manuscript, 1971. 30 pp.

Kenyon, Walter Wynn. *Herbert W. Armstrong and the Worldwide Church of God*. Unpublished manuscript, 1972. 45 pp.

Ketcham, R. T. "Herbert W. Armstrong and the World of Tomorrow—a Warning!" *Sword of the Lord*, Feb. 13, 1970, p. 3.

Kirban, Salem. *Armstrong's Church of God.* Chicago: Moody Press, 1970. 53 pp.

Kirsopp, Donald E. *Escape from Armstrong Slavery.* Unpublished manuscript, 1972. 30 pp.

Larsen, David L. "Cultic Distortion of the Holy Scriptures." *The Discerner*, Oct. 1970, pp. 5ff.

Larsen, Egon. *Strange Cults and Sects.* New York: Hart Publishing Co., 1972. 245 pp.

Lauriault, Erwin H. *Commentary on Armstrong Doctrines.* Unpublished manuscript, n.d. 132 pp.

Leyendecker, Ruth and Wayne, with Roger F. Campbell. "We Escaped from Armstrongism." In James R. Adair and Ted Miller, eds., *We Found Our Way Out.* Grand Rapids: Baker Book House, 1965. Chapter 12.

Lowe, Harry W. *Radio Church of God.* Mountain View, Calif.: Pacific Press, 1970. 143 pp.

_____. *The True Israel of God: The Anglo-American-Israel Theory Examined.* Mountain View, Calif.: Pacific Press, 1963. 12 pp.

Lutz, Martin W. "Looking at the Religious World—Armstrongism: The Plain Truth or Plain Falsehood?" *Northwestern Lutheran* (Milwaukee), March 16, 1969, pp. 94f.

McCormick, W. J. McK. *Armstrongism—Solid Rock or Shifting Sand?* Lisburn, Northern Ireland: Evangelical Tape Outreach, n.d. 8 pp.

_____. *Do Herbert W. Armstrong and Garner Ted Armstrong Speak the Plain Truth?* Belfast: Raven Publishing, 1968. 12 pp.

Mann, Bert. "The Plain Truth About the Worldwide Church of God." *Christian Herald*, Part I: June 1974, pp. 20ff., Part II: July 1974.

Marrs, Roy; Wilbur Dornberger, and Paul Heavilin. "1972—Herbert W. Armstrong's 'Year of Judgment.' " *Facts of Our Faith*, Apr. 1972, pp. 7ff.

Marson, Richard A. *The Marson Report Concerning Herbert W. Armstrong.* Seattle, 1970. 175 pp.

_____. *The Worldwide Church of God: A Former Member Speaks Out.* Unpublished manuscript, 1972. 185 pp.

Martin, Walter R. *Herbert W. Armstrong and the Radio Church of God in the Light of the Bible.* Minneapolis: Bethany Fellowship, 1968. 32 pp. Reprinted from *The Kingdom of the Cults* (Bethany, 1968), ch. 15.

_____. "Herbert W. Armstrong—Cultist." *Living Today*, Sept. 1971, pp. 16ff.

Martin, William C. "The God-Hucksters of Radio: 'Keep Those Cards and Letters Coming In.' " *Atlantic Monthly*, June 1970, pp. 51ff.

——. "The Plain Truth About the Armstrongs and the World Tomorrow." *Harper's Magazine*, July 1973, pp. 74ff.

Mead, Frank S. *Handbook of Denominations in the United States.* Nashville, Abingdon, 1970. "Worldwide Church of God," pp. 76f.

Mitchell, John H., Jr., and W. A. (Bill) Sutton. *The Alternative.* Shreveport, La.: Church of God—Shreveport Conference, Jan. 1974. 8 pp.

Monroe, Charles. "A Synoptic History of the Churches of God in the Latter Days." *Facts of Our Faith*, Jan. 1969, pp. 12ff.

Morris, James. *The Preachers.* New York: St. Martin's Press, 1973. 418 pp. Chapter VIII, "The Armstrongs," pp. 319ff.

Moyer, Lloyd. "The Armstrong Cult." *The Sower* (Church of Christ, Little Rock, Arkansas), Jan. 1970.

Murch, James DeF. "Forerunner of the Millennium?" *Christian Standard*, April 19, 1969, pp. 7f.

Neitsch, Mrs. Robert. "Letter to Dr. Herman L. Hoeh of Ambassador College." Pasadena, Oct. 1, 1970. 50 pp.

"Oddball Religion." *The Prairie Overcomer*, Nov. 1972, p. 506.

Odom, Robert L. "Herbert W. Armstrong and His 'Radio Church of God.' " *Hour of Prophecy*, Dec. 1972, pp. 1ff.; Jan. 1973, pp. 5ff.

Okoniewski, Dorothy C. *The Worldwide Church of God: A Study in Fundamentalism.* Unpublished manuscript, 1971. 55 pp.

Petersen, William J. *Those Curious New Cults.* New Canaan, Conn.: Keats Publishing, 1973. Chapter 10, "Herbert W. Armstrong and His Plain Truth," pp. 109ff.

Peterson, I. C. *Reflections from a Head of the Dragon Point of View.* Edited transcript of tape by Conrad J. Comeau, former jet pilot to the Armstrongs. 1971. 39 pp.

"A Pseudo-Biblical Appeal." *Moody Monthly*, Sept. 1972, p. 16.

Religion Analysis Service. *The Delusions of Herbert W. Armstrong*, n.d. 16 pp.

"Report on Ambassador College, Pasadena, Calif." Archdiocese of Los Angeles, 1969. 1 p.

"Résumé of Michael Denis Rohan." Jerusalem: Israeli Foreign Ministry, 1969, Distributed by St. Paul Publishers, Nashville.

Rice, John R. "Are Anglo-Saxon People the Lost Ten Tribes?" *Sword of the Lord*, Sept. 7, 1962.

Rohrer, Norman B. "Mr. Confusion Aggrandizes." *Wesleyan Advocate*, Jan. 26, 1970, p. 3.

Schwartz, George M. *The Armstrong Empire.* Unpublished manuscript, 1970. 300 pp.

Smith, Noel. *Herbert W. Armstrong and His World Tomorrow.* Springfield, Mo.: *Baptist Bible Tribune*, 1964. 65 pp.

——. "Why Everything's Free." *Baptist Bible Tribune*, Oct. 16, 1970, p. 5.

Smith, Paul B. *Other Gospels.* Denver: Gospel Advance Press, 1970. 160 pp. Chapter 9, "The Armstrong Polycult."

Starkes, M. Thomas. *Confronting Popular Cults.* Nashville: Broadman, 1972. Chapter III, "Anglo-Israelism and the Armstrongs," pp. 44ff.

——. *The World Tomorrow?* Atlanta: Home Mission Board of the Southern Baptist Convention, 1972. 12 pp.

Strauss, James D. "The World Tomorrow: Voice of Anglo-Israelism." *Christian Standard,* Nov. 14, 1971, pp. 11f.

Stump, Al. "Hanky-Panky and Revolt in the Worldwide Church of God." *True,* July 1974, pp. 30ff.

Sumner, Robert L. *Herbert W. Armstrong, A False Prophet.* Murfreesboro, Tenn.: Sword of the Lord Publishers, 1961. 24 pp.

Tarr, Leslie K. "Herbert W. Armstrong: Does He Really Have the 'Plain Truth?' " *Moody Monthly,* Sept. 1972, pp. 24ff.

"Temporary Silence for Prophet of Doom." *Catholic Herald* (London), Sept. 1, 1967, p. 3.

Tinkcom, Donald M. *Church of Brotherly What?* Shelton, Wash., 1972. Unpublished manuscript. 7 pp.

Trautmann, Fredrick. "From Soap to Souls. The Armstrongs and 'The World Tomorrow.' " *Preaching Today,* March 1972, pp. 10ff.

——. "How the Truth Is Made Plain: The Armstrongs and The World Tomorrow." *Today's Speech,* Nov. 1969, pp. 40ff.

Trefry, Robert A. *The Theology of Herbert W. and Garner Ted Armstrong.* Unpublished master's thesis, Dallas Theological Seminary, 1968.

"Trouble in the Empire," *Time,* March 4, 1974, p. 50.

Twisselmann, Hans-Jürgen. *Bringt Die Welt Von Morgen Die Reine Wahrheit?* Bodenborn, Germany: Bundes-Verlag, 1970. 32 pp.

Unger, Walter. "The Plain Truth About Herbert W. Armstrong." *Mennonite Brethren Herald,* July 14, 1972, pp. 2f.

"The Vice President is Missing." *Christianity Today,* Apr. 14, 1972, p. 39.

A Well Used Quote. Anonymous tract by two former members. Nashville: St. Paul Publishers, 1971. 11 pp.

Whalen, William J. "The Fastest Growing Church in America—The Worldwide Church of God." *U.S. Catholic,* Nov. 1972, pp. 19ff.

Who is Qualified to Be Your Minister? Pasadena: 20th Century Church of God, 1974. 18 pp.

"Will Garner Ted Armstrong Repent?" *The Messenger,* June-July 1972, pp. 1f.

Wilson, Paul. *The Armstrong Heresy.* Denver: Wilson Foundation, n.d. 23 pp.

Wright, J. Stafford. "Herbert Armstrong and the World Tomorrow." *The Evangelical Christian,* Nov. 1967, pp. 19f.

General Index

Scriptural Index